MW00335799

SRA

Open Court Reading

Grade 3 • Book 2

Themes

- Animals and Their Habitats
- Government at Work
- Art on the Move

Acknowledgments

Grateful acknowledgment is given to the following publishers and copyright owners for permissions granted to reprint selections from their publications. All possible care has been taken to trace ownership and secure permission for each selection included. In case of any errors or omissions, the Publisher will be pleased to make suitable acknowledgments in future editions.

Animals and Their Habitats

Sonoran Night by Shirley Anne Ramaley and art by Anne Reas; from Ladybug Magazine, February 2011. Copyright © by Carus Publishing Company. Reproduced with permission. All Cricket Media material is copyrighted by Carus Publishing Company, d/b/a Cricket Media, and/or various authors and illustrators. Any commercial use or distribution of material without permission is strictly prohibited. Please visit http://www.cricketmedia.com/info/licensing2 for licensing and http://www.cricketmedia.com for subscriptions.

Einstein Anderson: The Mighty Ants and Other Cases by Seymour Simon Copyright 2014 ©by Seymour Simon. Used by permission of StarWalk Kids Media.

Is This Panama? A Migration Story by Jan Thornhill. Adapted from *Is this Panama*? by Jan Thornhill, illustrated by Soyeon Kim. Used with permission of Owlkids Books Inc.

Government at Work

The United States Capitol by Holly Karapetkova. Rourke Educational Media, Vero Beach, FL 32964

Marching with Aunt Susan by Claire Rudolf Murphy. First published in the United States under the title MARCHING WITH AUNT SUSAN: Susan B. Anthony and the Fight for Women's Suffrage by Claire Rudolf Murphy, illustrated by Stacey Schuett. Text Copyright© 2011 by Claire Rudolf Murphy. Illustrations Copyright© 2011 by Stacey Schuett. Published by arrangement with Peachtree Publishers. All rights reserved.

So You Want to Be President? by Judith St. George. Text copyright ©2000 by Judith St. George, Illustrations copyright ©2000 by David Small. All rights reserved. Published by Philomel Books, a division of Penguin Putnam Books for Young Readers.

Art on the Move

LITTLE MELBA AND HER BIG TROMBONE by Katheryn Russell-Brown, illustrated by Frank Morrison. Text Copyright ©2014 by Katheryn Russell-Brown. Illustrations Copyright ©2014 by Frank Morrison. Permission arranged with LEE & LOW BOOKS, Inc., New York, NY 10016. All rights not specifically granted herein are reserved.

Ah, Music! by Aliki. Used by permission of HarperCollins Publishers.

MHEonline.com

Send all inquiries to:
McGraw-Hill Education
8787 Orion Place
Columbus, OH 43240

ISBN: 978-0-07-669178-4
MHID: 0-07-669178-0

Printed in the United States of America

2 3 4 5 6 7 8 9 LWI 21 20 19 18 17

Program Authors

Carl Bereiter, Ph.D.
Professor Emeritus at the Ontario Institute for Studies in Education, University of Toronto

Andrew Biemiller, Ph.D.
Professor Emeritus at the Institute of Child Study, University of Toronto

Joe Campione, Ph.D.
Professor Emeritus in the Graduate School of Education at the University of California, Berkeley

Doug Fuchs, Ph.D.
Nicholas Hobbs Professor of Special Education and Human Development at Vanderbilt University

Lynn Fuchs, Ph.D.
Nicholas Hobbs Professor of Special Education and Human Development at Vanderbilt University

Steve Graham, Ph.D.
Mary Emily Warner Professor in the Mary Lou Fulton Teachers College at Arizona State University

Karen Harris, Ph.D.
Mary Emily Warner Professor in the Mary Lou Fulton Teachers College at Arizona State University

Jan Hirshberg, Ed.D.
Reading and writing consultant in Alexandria, Virginia

Anne McKeough, Ph.D.
Professor Emeritus in the Division of Applied Psychology at the University of Calgary

Marsha Roit, Ed.D.
Reading curricula expert and professional development consultant

Marlene Scardamalia, Ph.D.
Presidents' Chair in Education and Knowledge Technologies at the University of Toronto

Marcy Stein, Ph.D.
Professor and founding member of the Education Program at the University of Washington, Tacoma

Gerald H. Treadway Jr, Ph.D.
Professor Emeritus, School of Education at San Diego State University

UNIT 4

Animals and Their Habitats

UNIT 5

Government at Work

UNIT 6

Art on the Move

UNIT 4

Animals and Their Habitats

BIG Idea

How do animals interact with their environments?

Theme Connections

How do animals survive in different habitats?

Background Builder Video

connected.mcgraw-hill.com

Genre Fable

Essential Questions

What kinds of animals live in the country? What kinds live in the city? Why do you think animals are better suited for one place over another?

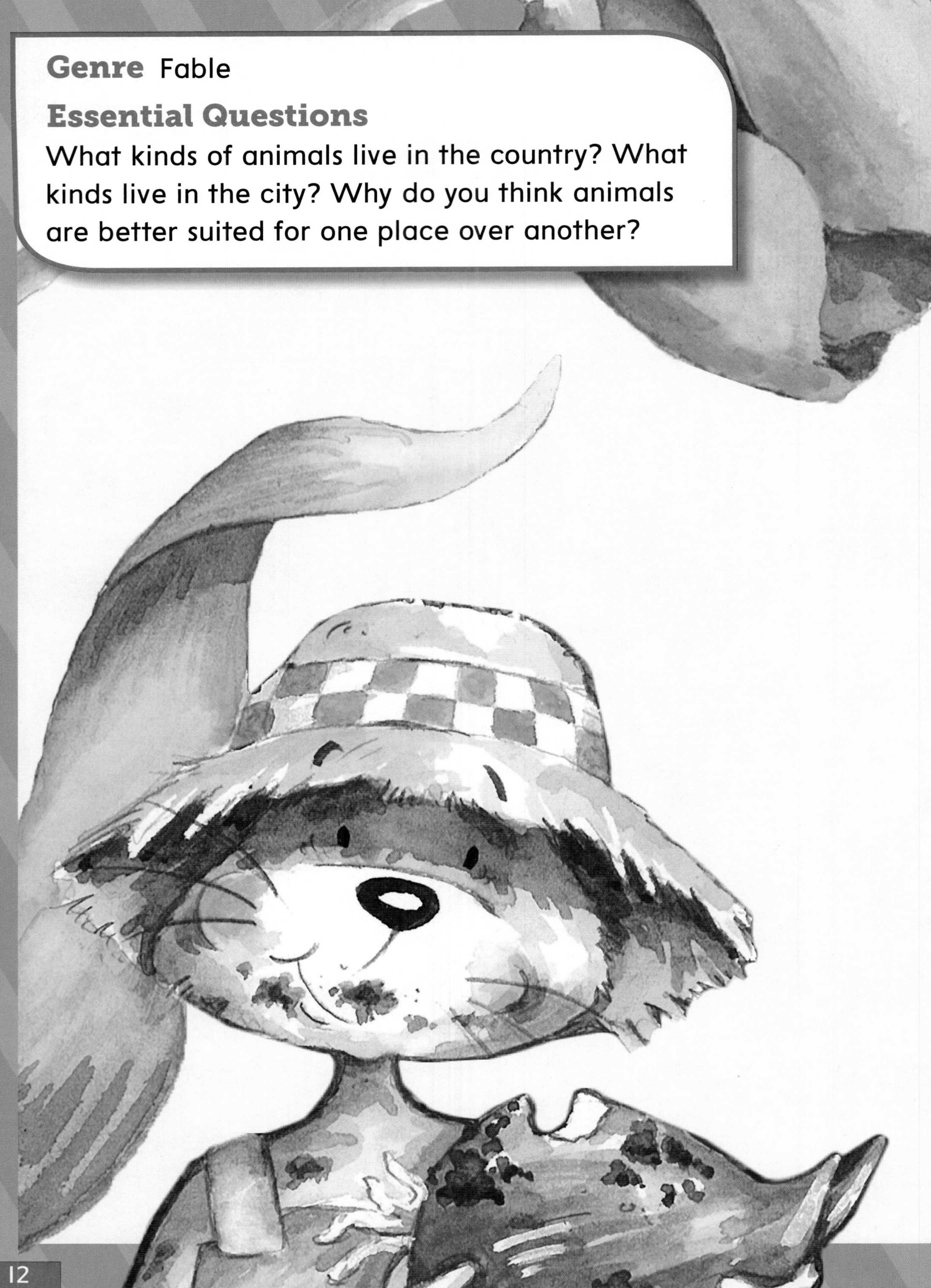

The Country Mouse and the City Mouse

by Vidas Barzdukas
illustrated by Nicole Rutten

One day, Country Mouse called City Mouse on the telephone. They were cousins, but they had not seen each other in a long time.

"Come visit me at the farm," Country Mouse suggested. "There is plenty of extra space in the hay loft. We can picnic in the meadow during the day and look up at the stars at night."

"What a fabulous idea!" City Mouse said excitedly. "I've always wondered what it is like out in the country."

City Mouse packed a suitcase and arrived at the farm that evening.

“Welcome!” Country Mouse called from the rafter of the barn. She scampered down and hugged City Mouse affectionately. ”Let’s get your suitcase put away, and then I can show you around.”

Country Mouse gave her cousin a tour of the farm. They visited green pastures and a pond surrounded by purple and yellow lilacs. City Mouse sat down on a rock and smiled contentedly.

“It sure is quiet and peaceful here,” City Mouse remarked. “What do you do for excitement?”

“I do lots of things!” Country Mouse answered. “I watch the clouds and listen to the birds sing. I count the number of croaks from the bullfrogs in the pond. Sometimes I collect colorful leaves all day long!”

“That doesn’t sound too exciting to me,” City Mouse mumbled to herself.

“Where are my manners?” Country Mouse said, hopping off the rock. “You have had a long trip, and you must be hungry. Let’s see if I can find you a snack.”

City Mouse followed Country Mouse back into the barn. Country Mouse searched underneath the hay for food. With a smile, she pulled up a half-eaten carrot.

“Here we are!” Country Mouse exclaimed happily. “One carrot, good as new . . . well, kind of.”

“Are those teeth marks?” City Mouse asked.

Country Mouse sniffed at the carrot. “These teeth marks are from Daisy. She’s a horse. The carrot must have fallen out of her mouth while she was eating.”

“Great,” City Mouse muttered. “But, do you have anything not covered in horse saliva?”

“Let’s go into the yard and see if we can find more food,” Country Mouse said.

In the yard, Country Mouse started sniffing for food. She sniffed under craggy rocks and thorny flowers. She sniffed around muddy puddles and decaying tree stumps. She even sniffed under a pile of steaming compost. City Mouse tried sniffing too, though she did not know what she was sniffing for. And what she did sniff did not smell very appealing.

Country Mouse hunted all over the farmyard for food. Eventually, City Mouse got tired and just stood by the fence, watching.

“Here we go!” Country Mouse finally said. She proudly pointed at the food she had gathered. She had collected five seeds, a rotting tulip bulb, and some musty kernels of corn.

City Mouse could not keep her feelings inside any longer.

"Seeds, bulbs, and corn?" City Mouse asked. "My dear, how can you eat such inadequate food as this? How long did it take you to find all this food?"

Country Mouse thought for a minute. "Four hours," she declared.

"You spent four hours looking for food and this is all you came up with?" City Mouse said. "That is not a lot of food."

Country Mouse blushed. She thought it was plenty, and had enjoyed finding it.

"Don't feel embarrassed," City Mouse said. "Come back with me to the city."

"I live in luxury," she boasted. "The finest foods are at my fingertips. Do you want nice cheese? It is there. How about some fresh fruit? We can get it. Would you like some scrumptious nuts? Come with me to the city and see for yourself. I will gladly share all of this with you, my friend."

"Well, I've never been to the city," Country Mouse said. "But if you like it, I am sure I will too."

Country Mouse and City Mouse traveled to the city. On the way, they were caught in a heavy rainstorm and both mice were drenched. Being used to living out in the elements, Country Mouse barely noticed, but City Mouse was even more eager to get home.

When they arrived at her home though, it was clear that City Mouse had not exaggerated. On the table sat half-eaten salads, sandwiches, and some kind of tasty stew. Country Mouse had never seen so much food. Her mouth opened in awe.

"You get to eat all this food?" Country Mouse asked in amazement.

"I could never eat all of it," City Mouse explained. "Thankfully, I do not need to eat it all. There is food on the table all the time."

Suddenly, City Mouse's large ears twitched.

"Do you hear that growling?" City Mouse asked.

"That's my stomach growling for all this food," Country Mouse said.

"That sounds like Thunder," City Mouse whispered.

"That's because it's raining outside," Country Mouse said.

"No, Thunder is the family dog!" City Mouse cried.

The two mice turned around slowly. Looming menacingly over the table was Thunder, the largest dog Country Mouse had ever seen. He scrutinized the two mice and licked his lips.

"Run!" City Mouse yelled. She grabbed Country Mouse and ran for the edge of the table. Country Mouse could barely keep up. Together they jumped off the table. The dog's teeth snapped shut inches from them as they dove through a hole in the wall.

The mice huddled together inside the hole. Outside, the dog tore apart the table setting trying to find them.

Country Mouse shuddered. "That was close!" she groaned.

"It sure was!" City Mouse answered. "And a lot of fun! We almost didn't get away this time. . . ."

"This time?" Country Mouse asked, horrified. "This has happened before?"

"That dog chases me all the time," City Mouse said. "But I usually hear him coming a mile away and I am way too fast for him."

"Well that's the fastest I have ever moved in my life, and I still almost got caught," Country Mouse admitted.

When Thunder finally turned away, City Mouse and Country Mouse scurried outside.

"I think we can sneak back in and try again, if you feel like having some fun," City Mouse said with a hopeful tone.

"I don't know if I can handle any more of your kind of fun," Country Mouse said. "Thank you for inviting me, but I think I should head home. City life does not agree with me. My ears are not big enough to listen for dogs all the time and I am not fast enough to keep running away. I want peace and tranquility. You are welcome to come with me and live safely in the country."

"Thank you, but I think it is best that I stay here," City Mouse responded. "Country life does not agree with me. My nose isn't strong enough to sniff out hidden food and I do not have the patience to be searching for food all day. I want the abundance and excitement of the city."

The two mice hugged and promised to visit each other more often. However, they went back to their spaces realizing they were best suited to live in their own homes.

You will answer the comprehension questions on these pages as a class.

Text Connections

1. How does the text describe Country Mouse's habitat? How does the text describe City Mouse's habitat?
2. Country Mouse prefers a tranquil habitat, and City Mouse prefers a luxurious habitat. Which mouse are you more like? Why?
3. Country Mouse and City Mouse have different habitats. However, each habitat provides basic things the mice need in order to survive. What are those things? Are these things that people need, too?
4. The fable "The Country Mouse and the City Mouse" shows that one kind of animal (a mouse) can survive in more than one kind of habitat. However, each animal must develop skills unique to its habitat. What special skill does Country Mouse have? What special skill does City Mouse have?

Did You Know?

Mice need to eat all the time! Some eat up to 20 meals a day.

Look Closer

Keys to Comprehension

1. In Country Mouse's habitat, finding food is difficult. In City Mouse's habitat, finding food is dangerous. How does each mouse feel about these challenges?
2. What is the moral of this fable? What details help convey this message to the reader?

Writer's Craft

3. Some writers use a figure of speech called *hyperbole.* A hyperbole is an exaggeration used to emphasize a point. Reread page 22. What is the hyperbole on this page? What fact does this hyperbole exaggerate?
4. What point of view does each mouse have about the other's habitat? How does your point of view differ?

Concept Development

5. Look at the illustration on page 16. How does it help you understand how City Mouse feels in this part of the story?

Write

Think of some things you need to survive, as well as some everyday things that make you happy. Then describe your perfect habitat.

Read the story. Then discuss it with your class.

Vocabulary Words

- **abundance**
- **compost**
- **craggy**
- **elements**
- **inadequate**
- **luxury**
- **musty**
- **saliva**
- **scrumptious**
- **scrutinized**
- **tone**
- **tranquility**

Nothing "Tops" a Personal Pizza

Last night my friend Rich's mom let us make our own personal-sized pizzas. It was the best thing ever! It felt luxurious to be able to make a pizza with only the toppings I like. It also felt lucky, when I learned about Rich's taste in pizza.

All I wanted on my pizza was mozzarella, tomatoes, and basil. Rich, on the other hand, wanted to experiment. While scrutinizing recipes on the Internet, he got super-excited when he found one with bleu cheese. "*Bleck* cheese would be a better name for it!" I exclaimed. Rich said he didn't like my tone, but I was just being honest. The stuff is craggy and crumbly and, well, *blue.* And it smells musty, like used socks. *Yuck!*

After choosing our recipes, Rich and I went out into the elements to get vegetables from his mom's garden. From the abundant selection, I chose tomatoes and basil, and Rich chose spinach and chives. Then we brought them inside for his mom to chop.

Next, we topped our pizzas and Rich's mom popped them in the oven. While the pizzas baked, we cleaned up the kitchen. Then we put the vegetable scraps in a can so they could be composted later. As we worked, my salivary glands kicked into overdrive. The smells from the oven were really amazing!

When the pizzas were done, we settled back in tranquility to enjoy our creations. Words inadequately describe the experience. In my opinion, there is nothing more scrumptious than a pizza prepared by yours truly!

Concept Vocabulary

Think about the word *habitat.* Can a very cold place be a habitat? Can a very dry place be a habitat? Why or why not?

Extend Vocabulary

Think of four foods that you would describe as *scrumptious.* Write them in your Writer's Notebook. Then write a sentence about each food that tells what you like about it.

Read this Science Connection. You will answer the questions as a class.

Text Feature

Charts let people see information in an organized way.

The Life Cycle

"The Country Mouse and the City Mouse" is a fable, but it teaches a good lesson about animals and their habitats. For each animal, there are habitats they will survive well in, survive less well in, or not be able to survive in at all.

Think about all the kinds of plants, animals, and other organisms (living things) you know about. Then consider how different they are. Their shapes, colors, and sizes vary wildly. Also, their ways of eating, thinking, and growing also differ vastly. However, all organisms experience this life cycle: birth, growth, reproduction, and death.

Birth is the time in life when an organism is born. After it is born, the organism experiences growth—it grows until it reaches maturity, or adulthood. Then the organism reproduces, or makes more organisms like it. Finally, the organism passes away. New organisms take its place in the cycle of life.

Look at the chart on the next page. It provides information about the life cycle of a few common organisms. What other organisms do you know about? What information could you add to the chart?

Life Spans

Organism	At Birth	As an Adult	Average Length of Growth Cycle after Birth	Average Length of Life
Mouse			5 to 7 weeks	about 3 months in the wild (longer in captivity)
Bull Frog			2 to 3 years	up to 9 years in the wild
Bean Plant			about 6 weeks	one growing season (60 to 100 days)

1. How is the chart helpful? What plant or animal would you like to add to this chart?
2. According to the chart, what are some things that all the organisms have in common?
3. What differences are shown by the chart?

Go Digital

What are some other plants and animals that interest you? What can you learn about their life cycles?

Genre Folktale

Essential Questions

How do plants and animals depend on each other? How can environmental changes impact animals and their habitats?

A Saguaro's Story

by Lindsay Evans
illustrated by Matt Loveridge

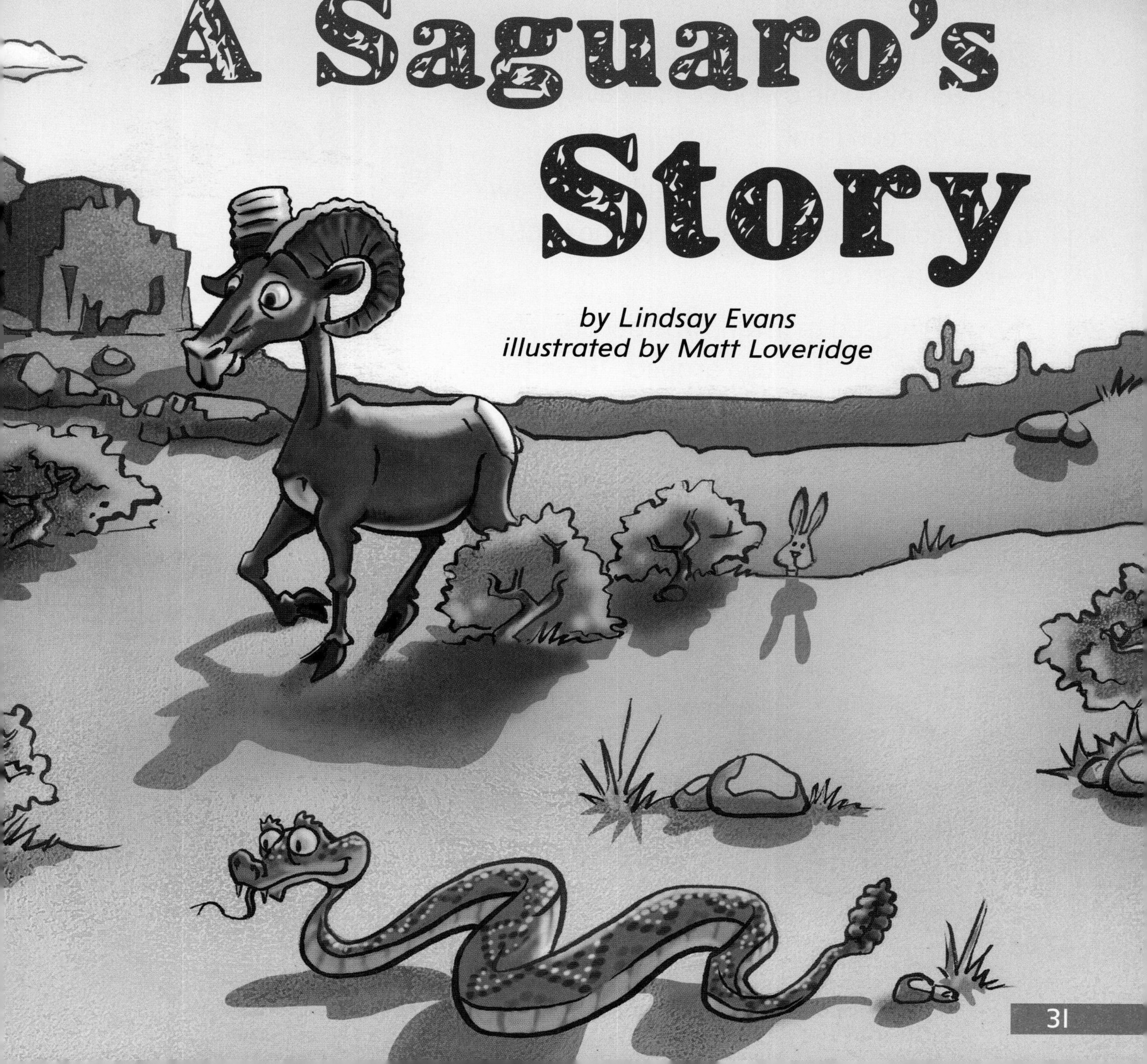

The majestic saguaro cactus baked in the midday sun.

Two months had passed without rain and the drought was a miserable time. The cactus was shrinking, and the pleats on its sides were deepening. The water within it was drying up.

The cactus could not continue to support its various guests. Before long, it might not even have the water it required to survive.

"This is an extraordinary crisis!" screeched the screech owl. The owl lived in a cavity in the cactus. "We need rain!"

"Calm yourself," advised the red-tailed hawk, who resided in a nest on an arm of the cactus. "We are going to survive."

The owl refused to listen. "The desert animals are upset," the owl argued. "Soon they will start chewing on our cactus!"

The hawk lived happily in her stick nest. The cactus was tall, and it was a good spot from which to hunt.

Other birds, such as the screech owl, lived inside the saguaro. A gila woodpecker and a gilded flicker had dug out "rooms" in the trunk of the cactus. A purple martin, an elf owl, and a sparrow lived in the other holes. Other birds had left the holes behind. The holes made cool, shaded shelters. High above the desert floor, the holes had also kept birds safe from predators—the animals who hunted them.

In the drought, safety from predators was becoming more important every day. Thirsty pack rats, mule deer, jackrabbits, and bighorn sheep were coming to the saguaro. They wanted to eat the juicy, water-rich flesh of the cactus.

The cactus had sharp spines, but the animals would not wait much longer. Soon they would attack. They would eat around the spines.

Wishing for happier times, the saguaro began to dream about the past...

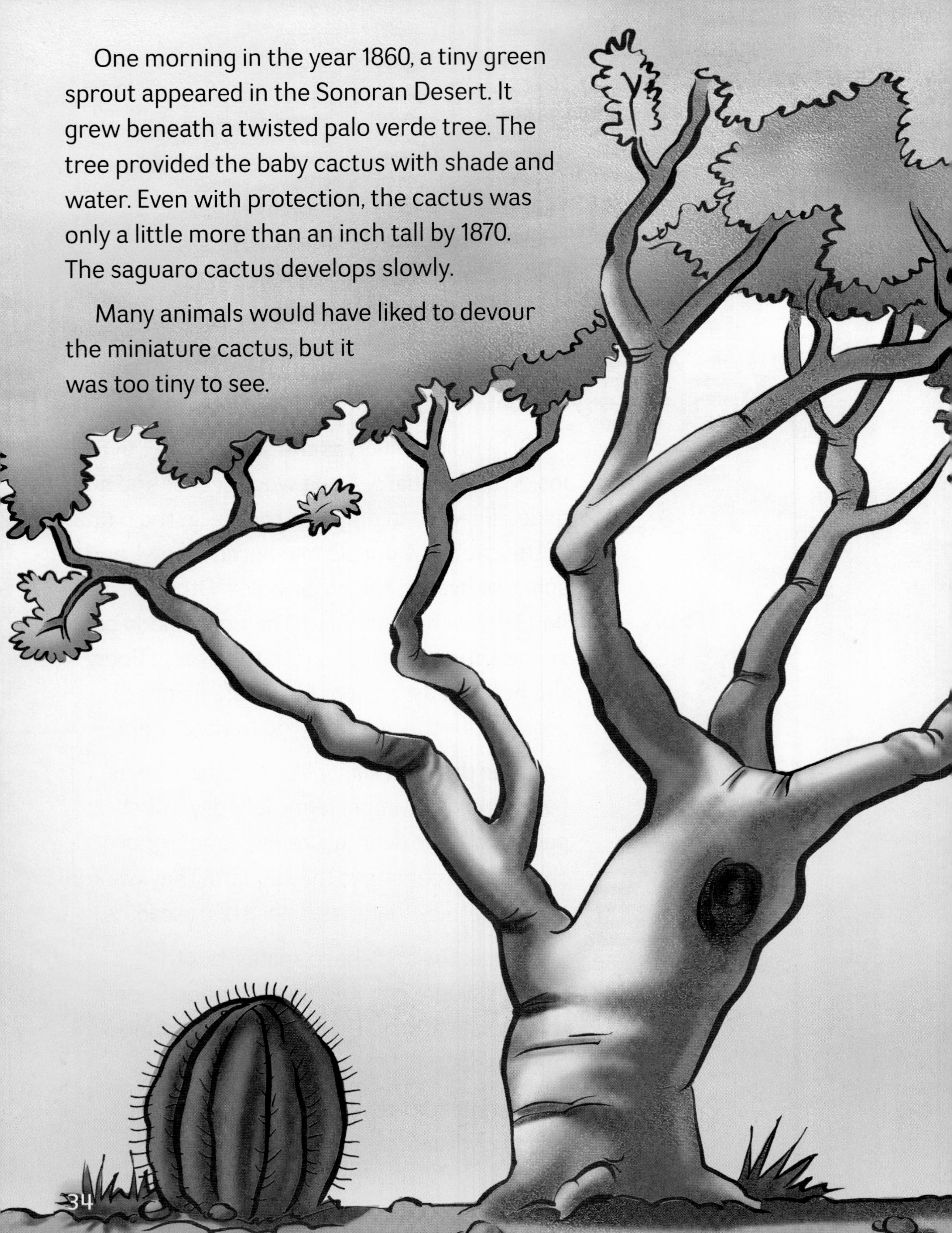

One morning in the year 1860, a tiny green sprout appeared in the Sonoran Desert. It grew beneath a twisted palo verde tree. The tree provided the baby cactus with shade and water. Even with protection, the cactus was only a little more than an inch tall by 1870. The saguaro cactus develops slowly.

Many animals would have liked to devour the miniature cactus, but it was too tiny to see.

Now it was 1895. Thirty-five years had passed. A new stage in the life of the cactus had arrived.

The saguaro began to develop flowers. They sprouted first at the top of its trunk. The saguaro flaunted its flowers proudly. Now it was really attracting attention! Birds and insects came daily, drawn by the nectar in the flowers.

Several feet high now, the cactus cast a lengthy shadow. It was pleased with itself. To grow, the cactus drew more water from the parched desert soil. As a result, the palo verde tree died. *Good bye, my provider,* the cactus thought. *This is the way of the desert, but I am grateful to you.*

When the saguaro was fifty years old, it started to grow arms – not just one or two, but five!

Now I am the provider, the saguaro thought happily, *for I can care for my desert friends.* Its arms extended in welcome.

Birds came first. They desired the nectar of the saguaro's flowers, so they built homes. Some homes were in the saguaro's huge arms, but others were in holes in its sides. *I have become a kind of hotel,* the cactus realized dreamily.

The cactus also produced fruit. Its juicy, sweet fruit fed many desert animals.

Suddenly the saguaro awakened from its dream of the past, but an idea remained. How could it overcome its enemies? Feed them, of course! Nourish them with fruit—the fruit that clung to its flowered limbs.

However, the cactus could not release the fruit on its own. Could the birds offer any assistance? All they seemed concerned about was saving themselves. Their chattering clearly showed their rising panic.

It was a difficult time for the cactus. Throughout the day, the birds' argument—and the drought—went on.

Two days later, something happened in the saguaro's world. It changed everything.

It was nearly sunset, and the desert was cooling off. The red-tailed hawk always hunted then.

As the hawk flew off, she left her greatest possession unprotected: her home. The stick nest was high up in the saguaro, so it was safe from enemies on the desert floor. However, it was no safer from other birds than if it sat on the ground, in the open – especially if a powerful bird decided to capture it.

This is exactly what happened. A great horned owl swooped down out of the early evening haze and quickly took over the hawk's nest.

No other bird wanted to risk its life to defend the hawk's nest. After all, this newcomer was quite large, and it was too powerful for any other bird to challenge. Alone, no bird would stand a chance against the great horned owl.

Naturally the red-tailed hawk viewed matters differently. When the hawk returned home from her hunt to find the owl settled in her nest, she became frantic.

"Where will I raise my family?" she sobbed. She glanced at the nearby birds as if to beg, *Please help me!*

"*Ho-ho-hoo-hoo-hoo*," the great horned owl mocked. Then she glared at the hawk. *Find yourself a new home*, her look said. *This is my dwelling now.*

The red-tailed hawk fluttered down among the smaller birds. "Listen," she said, "you must understand some things about this newcomer. If she gets hungry enough, she will attack other birds. So we are all in danger."

"But what can *we* do?" screeched the screech owl.

"This part is simple," announced the purple martin, who secretly had been hoping for an opportunity to show his leadership. "We just have to cooperate. Now here is my idea..."

The birds listened carefully. The saguaro listened too, but with sadness. It could only observe silently. *There is a more critical problem*, it wanted to say.

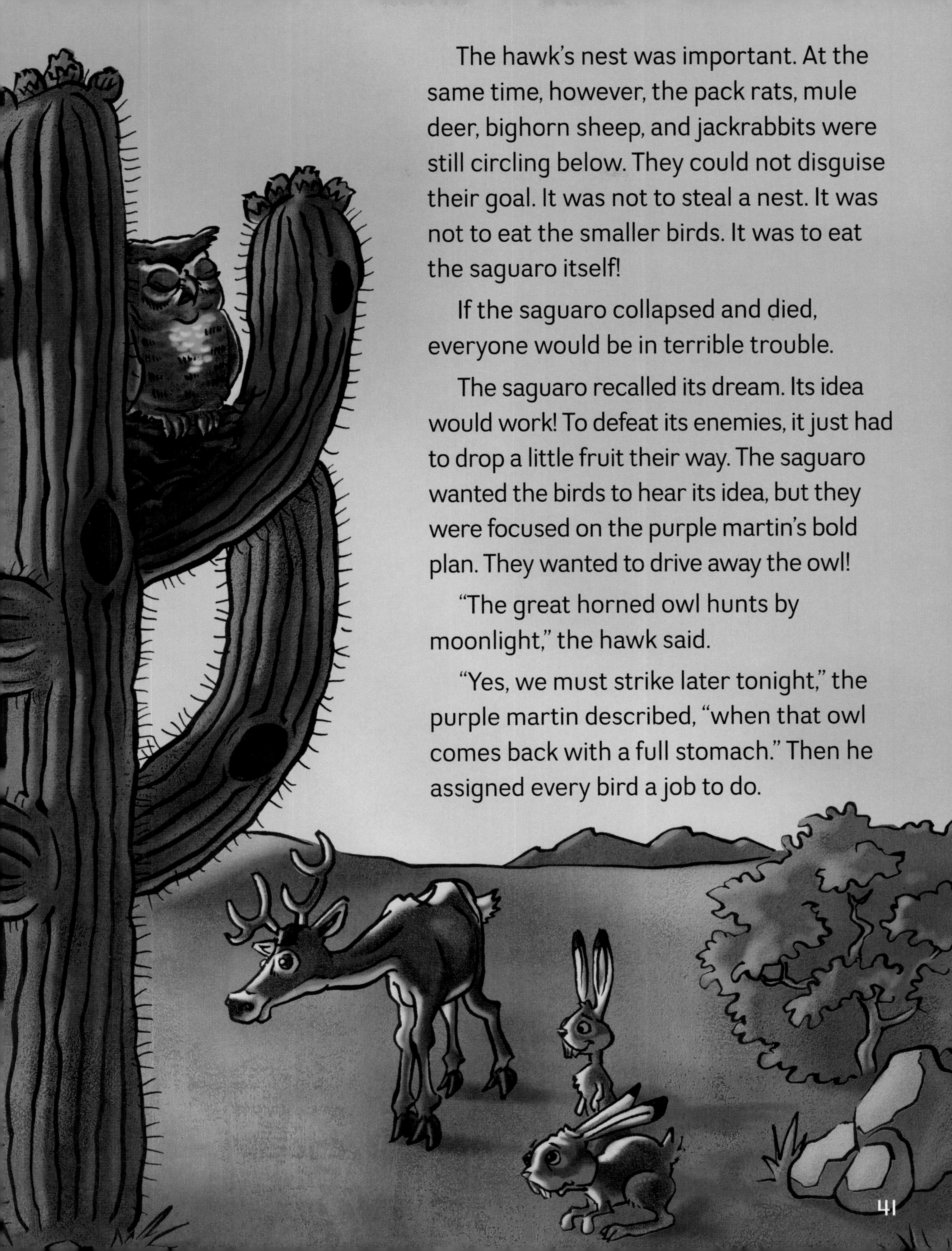

The hawk's nest was important. At the same time, however, the pack rats, mule deer, bighorn sheep, and jackrabbits were still circling below. They could not disguise their goal. It was not to steal a nest. It was not to eat the smaller birds. It was to eat the saguaro itself!

If the saguaro collapsed and died, everyone would be in terrible trouble.

The saguaro recalled its dream. Its idea would work! To defeat its enemies, it just had to drop a little fruit their way. The saguaro wanted the birds to hear its idea, but they were focused on the purple martin's bold plan. They wanted to drive away the owl!

"The great horned owl hunts by moonlight," the hawk said.

"Yes, we must strike later tonight," the purple martin described, "when that owl comes back with a full stomach." Then he assigned every bird a job to do.

At moonrise the giant owl left the cactus, as the hawk had said. The other birds watched and waited.

An hour later they heard a terrifying "*Ho-ho-hoo-hoo-hoo*!" The shadow of the giant horned owl swept over the saguaro's tenants. The birds froze, but just for a moment.

Suddenly the screech owl rose up and stunned the great horned owl with his screech. The gila woodpecker pecked the newcomer's head. The gilded flicker and the sparrow fluttered about to confuse her.

Now the red-tailed hawk leaped into battle against the great horned owl. The hawk fought mightily. After all, she was fighting for her home!

The hawk's courage inspired the others. They pounced upon the owl, attacking from all sides.

Just as the owl flapped away, the cactus started to shake. The birds glanced down. What they saw was far worse than the great horned owl.

Down below were the jackrabbits, pack rats, bighorn sheep, and mule deer. They were chewing holes in the saguaro!

"Listen to me, everyone!" the purple martin shouted. "We have to support our saguaro!"

Then he gave the birds new orders.

Yes, please, thought the saguaro. *Help me*!

The birds responded to the martin's commands. They landed atop the cactus and flapped as powerfully as they could. The top of the cactus and its branches trembled with the birds' flapping and jerking. Sure enough, it happened. One by one, the saguaro's fruit plopped to the desert floor.

The animals below stopped chewing the cactus and ate the fruit instead. Then they left, satisfied with their delicious meal.

With their precious home saved, the birds relaxed once again. The red-tailed hawk settled into her nest. The screech owl and the elf owl sighed. The martin was relieved his plan had worked.

Two days later, the first summer rain drifted in. *It is the way of the desert,* the saguaro thought—this time, happily.

Sonoran Night

by Shirley Anne Ramaley
illustrated by Anne Reas

Breeze stills,
Moonlight blankets the desert floor.
Rabbit rests beneath a palo verde tree.

Coyote yips,
Tortoise crawls into a burrow,
Woodpecker darts into her saguaro nest.

Rattler coils behind a rock,
Antelope graze with wary eyes,
Horned owl perches on a cottonwood branch.

Midnight arrives,
But the desert is awake.
The hunters and hunted are watchful.

Essential Questions

What animals come out at night?
Why?

You will answer the comprehension questions on these pages as a class.

Text Connections

1. In the story, which animals use the saguaro cactus as a home? What makes the saguaro cactus a good home for them?
2. Which animals use the saguaro cactus for food and water?
3. Recall the mice from "The Country Mouse and the City Mouse." Do you think either of them could survive in the saguaro cactus's habitat? Why or why not?
4. Think about what you have learned so far about animal habitats. Is there really such a thing as a perfect home? Explain your answer.

Did You Know?

The saguaro cactus can weigh up to 4,800 pounds. More than 80 percent of its weight is from water.

Look Closer

Keys to Comprehension

1. Think about the birds in this story. How do they compete with each other? How do they cooperate?
2. In what way does the saguaro cactus depend on the birds?

Writer's Craft

3. The author of this selection uses a figure of speech called *personification.* In personification, nonhuman things, such as plants, animals, and objects, have human characteristics. Reread page 37. In what ways does the cactus act like a human?
4. When the *palo verde* tree dies, the saguaro cactus says it is "the way of the desert." Then the cactus says this again when the rain finally comes. What do you think this phrase means?

Concept Development

5. Look at the illustration on pages 40–41. What is the mood of the birds and the other desert animals? How does the illustration help you understand this part of the story?

Write

Describe how other animals work together to survive.

Read the story. Then discuss it with your class.

Vocabulary Words

- bold
- challenge
- collapsed
- cooperate
- crisis
- devour
- frantic
- nourish
- resided
- simple
- stage
- support

Running the Distance

I am not really an athlete, but I can run pretty fast. So, this year I decided to put my skills to the test. I boldly signed up for my school's sprinting race—at least, that is what I thought I did. As it turns out, I accidently signed up for the long-distance race instead!

There is a big difference between sprinting and distance running. Sprints are short races run very quickly, while long-distance races require lots of endurance. I was completely unprepared for this challenge! When I realized my mistake, I frantically called my friend, Stacy.

Stacy resides in another town, but she is always supportive, even from far away. She is great at talking me through crises and helping me form plans for getting past them. This time, she suggested a training schedule. She said I should run every day and gradually increase my distance in stages.

I got to work right away! I ran before dinner every day. Every few days I made my route a little longer. Also, Mom happily cooperated in my training! She made me nourishing smoothies and well-balanced meals that I devoured after each run.

By the day before the race, I was about to collapse from all that running! Still, I was worried I had not trained enough. I called Stacy again, and she told me simply to have fun.

So, that is what I did. I ran in the race and did not place first, but I did not place last, either. And I did have fun! I'm going to keep on training so that I can run the race even better next year.

Concept Vocabulary

Think about the word *dependence.* Where do you see examples of dependence at school and in your community?

Extend Vocabulary

Copy the word web into your Writer's Notebook. Fill it in with words related to *bold.* That could include antonyms, synonyms, or related words.

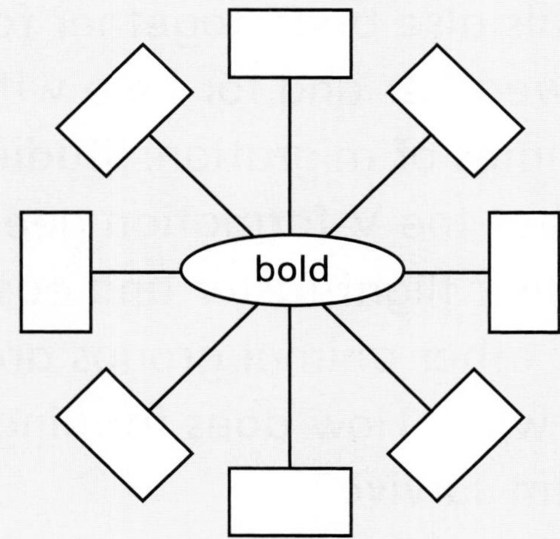

Read this Science Connection. You will answer the questions as a class.

Text Feature

Charts let readers see information in an organized way.

Group Survival

Have you ever noticed the way that some animals like to be in groups? In "A Saguaro's Story," a group of birds worked together to save their habitat. While the events of that story would not happen in real life, it is true that animals often group together. Being together helps the animals survive.

Different groups have different ways of helping each other survive. For example, wolves hunt in packs in order to catch larger prey. If they worked alone, they could not hunt large animals.

Some species protect each other from predators and help families raise their young. A full grown elephant does not have many natural predators, but calves can be vulnerable to lions or hyenas. In order to protect their young, elephants will group together.

Animals also band together for warmth in cold weather and for help with travel during times of migration. Studies have shown that the V-formation geese fly in makes their flight faster and easier.

What other animal groups are you familiar with? How does forming a group help them survive?

Here are some ways that birds benefit from being in groups.

	Cause	Effect
	Penguins huddle together during a storm.	The penguins share body heat and stay warm.
	Smaller birds band together when a large bird competes for food or nesting areas.	Together, the smaller birds can drive off the big bird. This removes the threat to the smaller birds' food sources and nesting grounds.
	Geese fly in a V-formation when they have to travel long distances.	The V-shape acts like a wedge. It slices through air currents, making the birds' flight faster and easier.

1. How is the information in this chart categorized?
2. What are some reasons for birds flocking together?
3. How are the images in this chart helpful?

Go Digital

What are the benefits of being in a herd of horses or a wolf pack? What are ways that other animals help each other survive?

Genre Realistic Fiction

Essential Questions

How do people use animals? What are some special features of animals you are familiar with? How can special animal features be useful for people?

Einstein Anderson and the MIGHTY ANTS

by Seymour Simon
illustrated by Valerio Fabretti

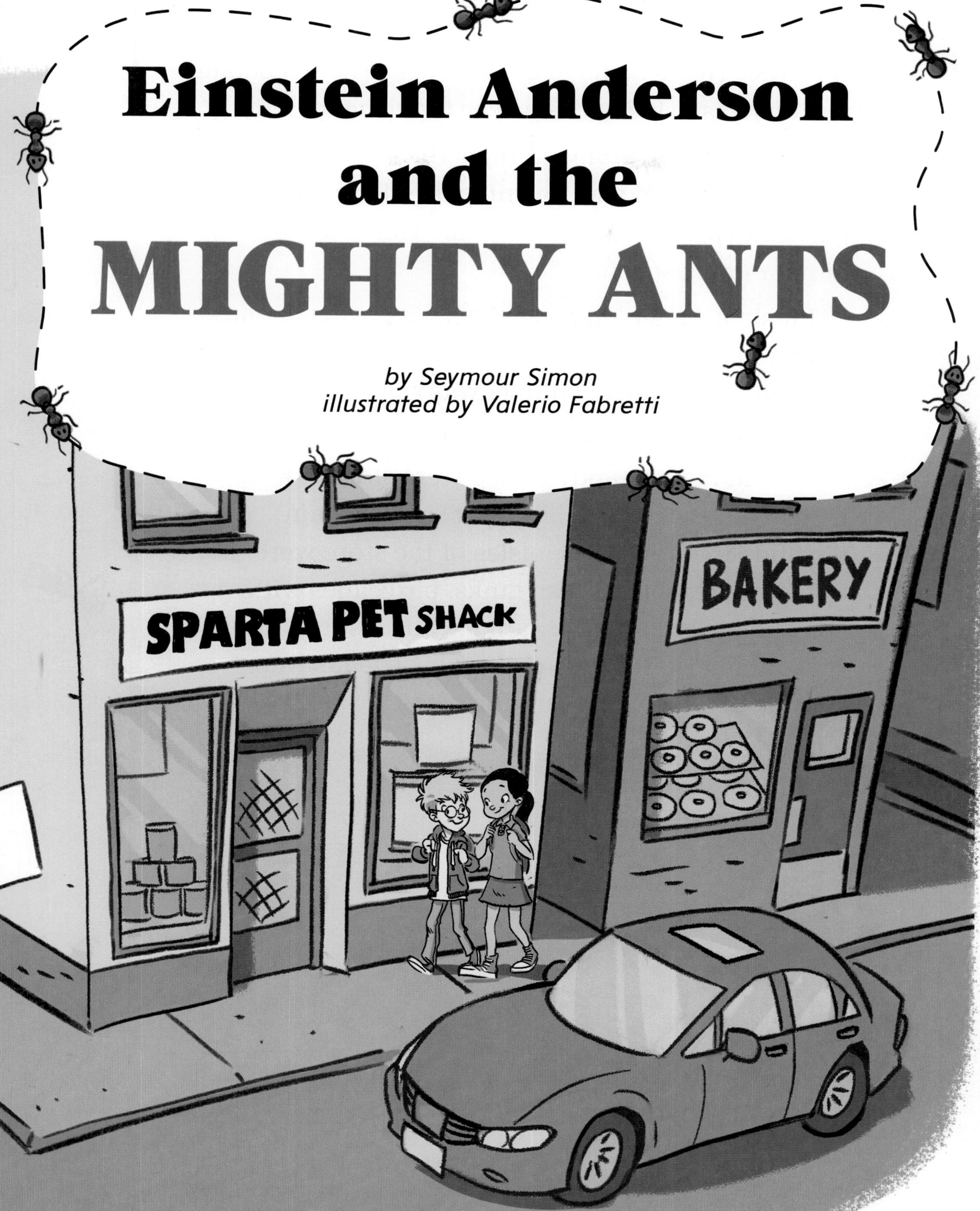

“This is more than just a pet, *Einstein*,” said Stanley Roberts. “This is going to create a whole new economy and StanTastic Industries will be the center of it!”

“Oh, come on, Stanley,” replied Paloma, shaking her head and frowning. Her long, black ponytail swayed back and forth. “This is another of your crazy schemes.”

Einstein Anderson pushed his glasses back onto the bridge of his nose and looked from Paloma to Stanley, then sighed. Paloma was right, this did seem like another crazy scheme.

He and Paloma and Stanley were standing in Sparta Pet Shack, a large pet store right in the middle of town. The aisles of the store were lined with brightly lit fish tanks, bird cages with colorful birds, and more tanks with all sorts of small animals. But Einstein and his friends were looking at a display of ant farm kits.

"I don't care what you say, *Einstein*," Stanley said, mockingly. "You think you're such a genius, but this time, you're wrong."

Stanley was in Einstein and Paloma's class at Sparta Middle School. He thought he knew a lot about science, too. Unfortunately, he never bothered to read much about science or even watch a science show on television. Stanley's big dream was to invent some new kind of technology and become a billionaire like Mark Zuckerberg or Steve Jobs. He'd even thought up his own corporation, StanTastic Industries.

Usually Stanley dressed the way he imagined the CEO of a big corporation would dress, in a suit jacket, a white shirt, and red and blue striped tie. But today, to visit the pet store, he was dressed like Einstein, in blue jeans, T-shirt, and sneakers.

"Come on, Stanley," Paloma protested. "This is just like the time you bought a baby Loch Ness Monster. Remember that?"

Stanley looked a little embarrassed. It was true. Einstein and Paloma had proved that his baby "Loch Ness Monster" was really just a salamander.

"I knew it wasn't a Loch Ness Monster," he said, "I was just joking around. Anyway, this time is different."

Paloma frowned. "Yeah, right!" she muttered.

Paloma was almost always right, but sometimes Einstein thought she was a little too quick to tell people they were wrong. Like now.

"Stanley, what are you going to do with all these ants?" she said, sounding annoyed. "Train them to do tricks?"

"Do you think I'm nuts?" Stanley quipped. Then, before Paloma could reply, he added dramatically. "I'm going to create a breed of giant ants. We'll be able to harness them to do work. Think of all the energy we'll save! And all the money I'll make."

Paloma turned to Stanley. "What are you talking about?" she asked. "What will you do with giant ants?"

"An ant can carry many times its own weight. It can climb straight up a wall. It can fall from a tall building and not get hurt," Stanley recited this like he'd practiced it many times.

He took out his phone. "Look," he said excitedly, and held up the screen. On it was a photo of a very large ant. "This is the bulldog ant from Australia. It grows to be an inch and a half long. Just think if it was the size of a real bulldog! Why, it would be super strong."

"Like a super hero," Paloma said, giggling.

"Hey, that reminds me," Einstein said. Paloma and Stanley both turned to him at the same time. They knew that Einstein had the habit of making up puns and silly jokes.

“Not now, Einstein,” they said, together.

“Well, at least I got you two to agree on something,” he said. “But what I was going to say was, Stanley could call his giant ants eleph-ants!”

“Hey, that’s not a bad idea!” Stanley said. “Uh, do you mind if I use it?”

“This *is* nuts,” Paloma objected. “How are you going to train ants to get together and carry heavy objects?”

“Well, ants already work together,” Einstein pointed out. “They do it naturally.”

“See?” Stanley said. “They do it naturally!”

“And it *is* true that ants are very strong for their size,” Einstein added. “They can carry maybe twenty times their weight, or more. An Olympic weightlifter can only lift about five or six times his own weight. Of course an ant weighs almost nothing, a tiny fraction of an ounce—just a few milligrams—so carrying twenty times its weight isn’t that much.”

"Yeah," Stanley nodded. "But twenty times their weight. Think about it."

"I don't have to think about it!" Paloma replied impatiently. "I know all about ants. Like they don't have bones like us. Their shells are their skeletons—exoskeletons. Their muscles are *inside* their skeletons. Plus, they have very thick muscles compared to their size."

"Yeah, that's what I said," Stanley told them. "But the main thing is how strong they are. Imagine how much stronger they will be if they are the size of a dog. Or a horse! If an ant was a hundred pounds, it could carry two thousand pounds or more."

"Well, okay. Forget about the strength for a minute," Paloma said impatiently. "How are you going to breed the ants and make them bigger?"

"The instructions come with the kit," Stanley said, pointing to the ant farms. "I'll start with small ants and then pick the biggest queens. It will take a while, but at the end I'll be famous—and rich!"

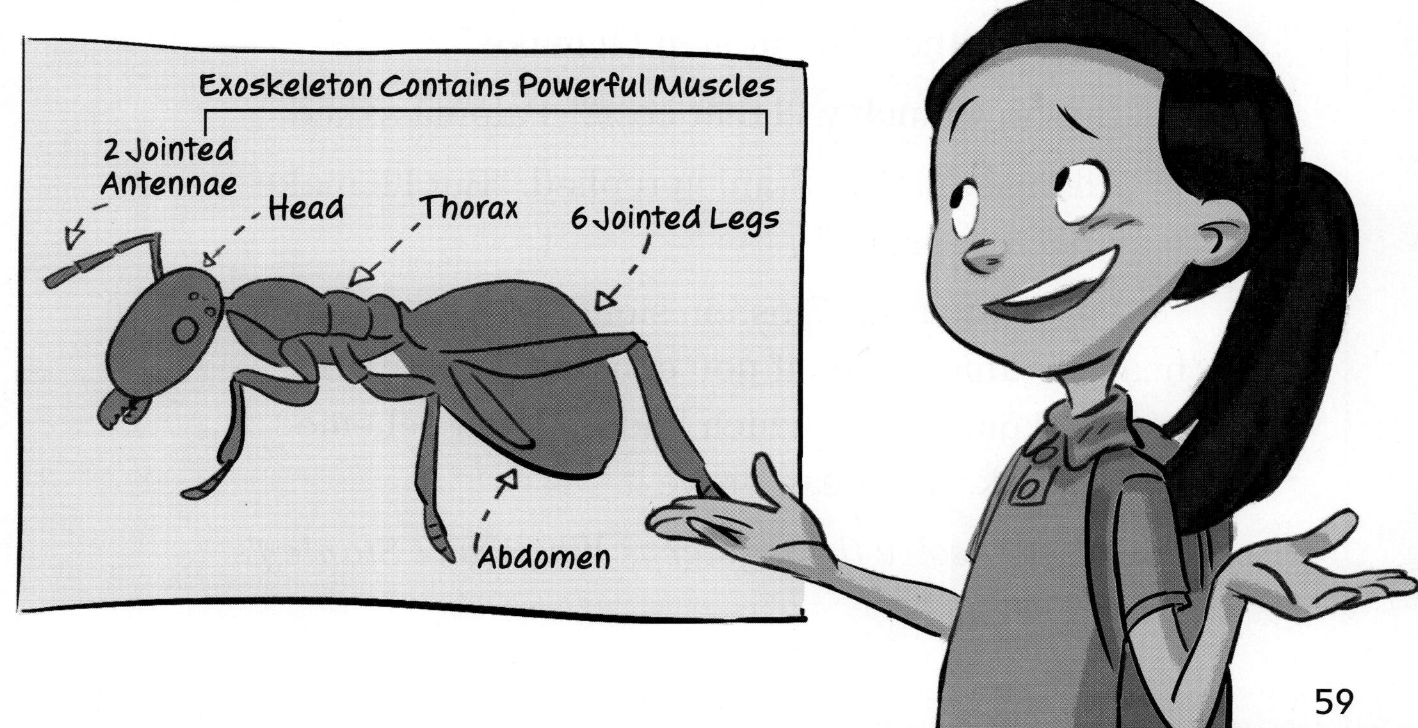

Just then, the clerk near the front of the store called out. He was a tall, thin high-school kid, who wore a plaid flannel shirt and dirty tan pants. His long brown hair was held back by a bandana.

"Hey, kid!" the clerk said. "Are you going to order those ant farms or not?"

"Ant *farms*?" Paloma repeated. "How many are you going to buy?"

"Two dozen," Stanley said calmly. "The more ants I raise, the more money I'll make."

"But how much will that cost?" Paloma asked.

"All my savings," Stanley replied. "But I'll make it all back in profit."

"I'm afraid not." Einstein sighed and shook his head. "Stanley, even if you could figure out how to breed giant ants, which I doubt, your scheme won't work. And I can prove it."

Can you solve the mystery? Why won't Stanley's scheme work?

"Oh, you're just jealous," Stanley huffed. "Because I thought of it and you didn't."

"Maybe you thought of it," Einstein told him, "but you didn't think of one important thing. An ant's muscles are relatively larger than bigger animals' muscles."

Stanley looked confused. "Relatively larger?" he said.

"That's what I've been trying to tell you," Einstein explained. "It has more muscle for its weight than bigger animals. Compared to the whole ant, ant muscle is very thick. So it's not hard for an ant to lift many times its weight. But an ant is very, very tiny."

"But if you made the ant bigger…" Stanley began.

"Its muscles would get bigger," Einstein said.

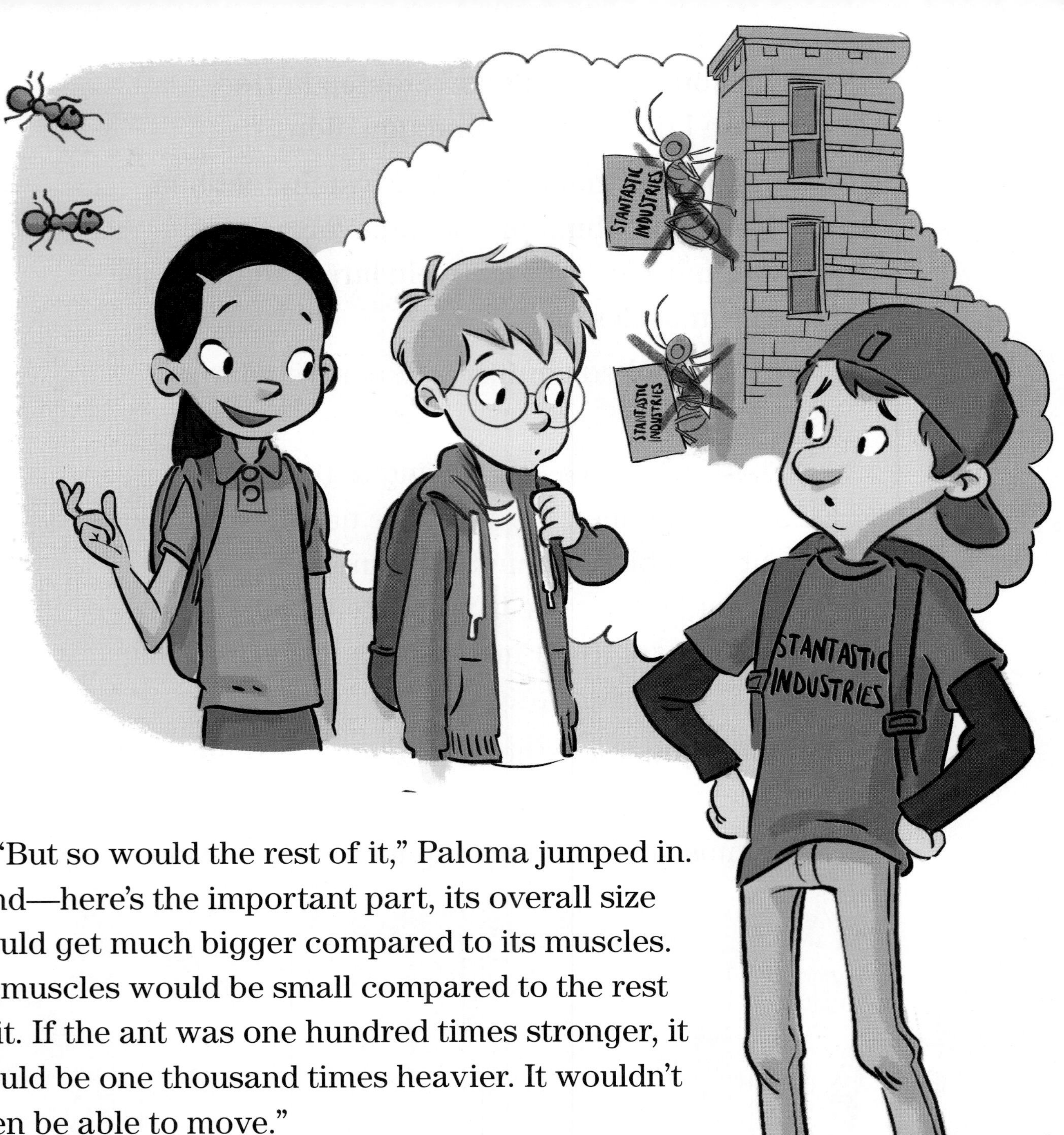

"But so would the rest of it," Paloma jumped in. "And—here's the important part, its overall size would get much bigger compared to its muscles. Its muscles would be small compared to the rest of it. If the ant was one hundred times stronger, it would be one thousand times heavier. It wouldn't even be able to move."

"That means it wouldn't be able to carry anything," said a disappointed Stanley.

"It wouldn't even be able to carry itself," Einstein said. "A gigantic ant would collapse under its own weight."

"Giant ants are just something you see in movies," Paloma told him. "They can't really exist."

"Hey, kid!" the clerk called out again. "What about it?"

Stanley shook his head. "Uh, no thanks," he said. "I just realized my calculations were incorrect." The clerk shrugged and went back to texting on his phone.

"Don't feel bad, Stanley," Einstein said, as the three of them left the store. "I have a better idea for you."

"You do?" Stanley said, brightening up.

"Sure," Einstein said with a serious look. "You could breed ants that had frog legs."

"Ants with frog legs," Stanley replied, his eyes widening. "Is it possible?"

"Sure," Einstein told him. Then he started to laugh. "Haven't you ever heard of ant-phibeans?"

Essential Question

How do animals work together to shape their habitat?

Busy Buzzy Bees

by Tanya Anderson

One busy buzzy bee
finds a field of fragrant flowers
and—quick as can be—
flies back to the hive.

She dances round and round,
sharing the secret spot,
signaling detailed directions
to the rest of her worker sisters.

They take off toward the target,
then land on the pretty petals,
nibble at the nectar,
and gather pollen on their furry legs.

Then, one by one, they return
to the hive, the queen awaiting,
to build the community comb,
to turn the nectar into honey,
these busy buzzy bees.

You will answer the comprehension questions on these pages as a class.

Text Connections

1. What details does the story include about ways in which ants can show their strength?
2. Why does Stanley think it will be easy to get his giant ants to do work for him?
3. Stanley does not say much about how he plans to raise ants the size of bulldogs. What do you think ants of that size would need in order to survive?
4. Einstein says that ants work together naturally. What is another story you have read in this unit about animals that work together? What are the animals, and how do they work together?

Did You Know?

Ants come from the same order of insects as wasps and bees.

Look Closer

Keys to Comprehension

1. According to Stanley, how would giant ants be a major benefit to our society?
2. What does Stanley hope to become someday? How would raising giant ants help him reach his goal?

Writer's Craft

3. Sometimes writers use similes to help readers understand something in a new way. A simile uses the word *like* or *as* to compare two things. Reread page 57 to find a simile about Stanley's giant ants. To what are the ants compared?

Concept Development

4. Look at the illustration on page 59. What technical term from the text does it help to explain?
5. Compare and contrast the setting of this story with the setting of "Einstein Anderson and the Hurricane Hoax." How are the themes, settings, and plots different or alike?

Write

Describe a new type of animal that you would like to breed. What would it look like? What skills would it have?

Read the story. Then discuss it with your class.

Vocabulary Words

- corporation
- economy
- exoskeletons
- harness
- schemes
- technology

Comic Ideas

Anyone who knows me knows I am a big fan of comic books. I have always enjoyed the exciting stories and amazing art. Now I have decided to write my own superhero comic book. I am not yet sure about how I want the story to go, but I have sketched a picture of the main character that is inspiring some ideas.

In the sketch, my superhero looks like an ordinary girl. However, she wears a shiny, gray jumpsuit. When she puts on her jumpsuit, it is like donning an exoskeleton. The suit is impenetrable, and it enables the girl to do amazing things!

The key to the jumpsuit's power is its technologically advanced fabric. The fabric has silicon threads in it that collect the sun's rays like a solar panel. Each thread harnesses enough energy to power a car. Imagine what a whole suit of those threads can do!

Like most superheroes, I imagine mine will fight a scheming villain. I have not thought of a name for him yet. But like many villains, I think mine will be motivated by greed. He will try to steal from major corporations, and he will threaten to overturn the global economy. But he will not be a match for my superhero! And he will never see her coming. After all, who would expect to be foiled by a girl in a shiny, gray jumpsuit?

Concept Vocabulary

Think about the word *biology*. What kinds of things would you learn about in a book or class about biology?

Extend Vocabulary

Copy the word web into your Writer's Notebook. Fill it in with words related to *harness*. That could include antonyms, synonyms, or related words.

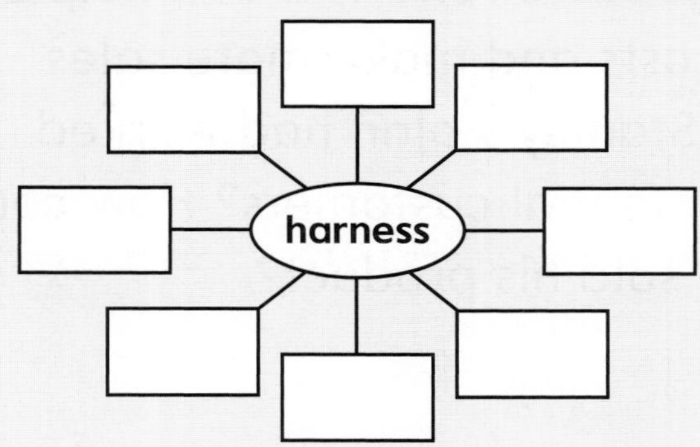

Read this Social Studies Connection. You will answer the questions as a class.

Text Feature

A **bar graph** is helpful for making number comparisons.

Economy and Technology

In "Einstein Anderson and the Mighty Ants," Stanley dreamed of becoming rich by selling his powerful worker ants. His plan was not based on scientific facts, so it did not work out. Had the science worked though, Stanley would have still been faced with marketing and selling his ants.

In an economy, people buy and sell goods. These goods are produced and distributed by businesses. Some businesses make goods to sell, while others acquire and package the goods.

People who own businesses are always interested in finding better, faster, and less costly ways to produce and distribute their goods. Customers want to buy high-quality goods at low prices.

This is where technology comes in. Technology can make goods easier to produce, and it can improve the quality of the goods. In short, it can help businesses cut costs and make more sales.

If Stanley's plan had worked, who were his potential customers? How could he have sold his product?

15
12
9
6
3
0

- Without the Mixer
- With the Mixer

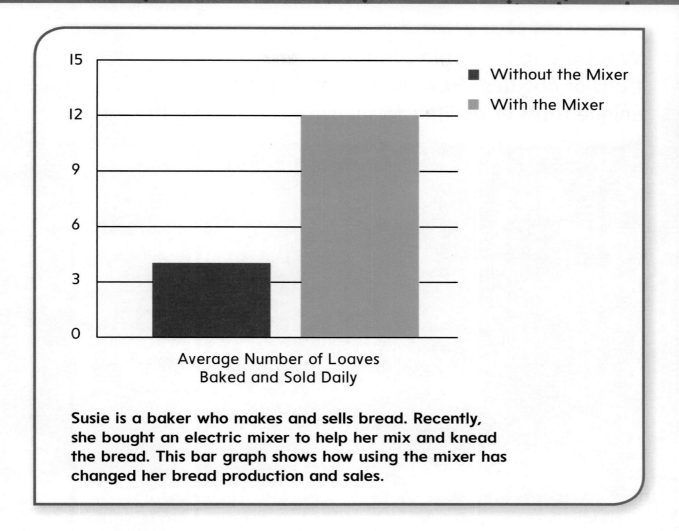

Average Number of Loaves Baked and Sold Daily

Susie is a baker who makes and sells bread. Recently, she bought an electric mixer to help her mix and knead the bread. This bar graph shows how using the mixer has changed her bread production and sales.

1. How is the bar graph helpful?
2. Has using an electric mixer helped or hurt Susie's bread sales? How do you know?
3. An electric mixer is a piece of technology. What has technology changed about Susie's bread-making process?

Go Digital

What are some other examples of technology that helps businesses produce and sell goods?

Genre Informational Text

Essential Questions

What are some animals that have unique traits or abilities? How do animals use their unique traits or abilities to survive?

Amazing ANIMALS

by Karen E. Martin

What unique traits does this animal have?

Unique Abilities

People have different traits that help them succeed in life. People who are tall, fast, or strong may become athletes. Someone with musical talent could become a popular singer. A person who is good with language might become a writer. Each person uses his or her own special traits to get along in the world.

Animals have special traits, too. Some animals have special coloring that helps them hide from predators. Other animals are amazingly strong or fast. They can work hard or run away from danger. Many animals have special traits that help them survive in difficult habitats. They may be able to tolerate very cold weather or even go without water for a long time. Each animal's unique traits and abilities help it survive—and thrive—in the natural world.

Safety in Numbers

The zebra is one animal that has special coloring: black and white stripes all over its body. These stripes can confuse predators such as lions or hyenas. When a herd of zebras runs, the stripes make the animals blur together, making it difficult to tell one animal from another. Predators then have a harder time trying to catch them.

The stripes may help ward off insects too. Insects seem to avoid the zebra's stripes for some reason. Why is this important? Because some insects in the zebra's habitat carry deadly diseases. When insects bite animals, the animals can become sick and die. Fewer bites mean fewer sick zebras.

Many other animals use special coloration to hide in plain sight. Can you see the animals in these photos? (Check your answers on page 81!)

Underwater Adaptations

To deal with both predators and prey, the octopus uses its many unique traits. One is its ability to change color. An octopus can instantly change color to blend in with the terrain. Because an octopus has no bones, its soft, flexible body can squeeze into tiny spaces. This allows it to hide from predators.

An octopus has arms that are pure muscle. The arms can move in any direction to help the octopus walk, swim, hunt, and eat. The arms have suckers that can grasp prey, too.

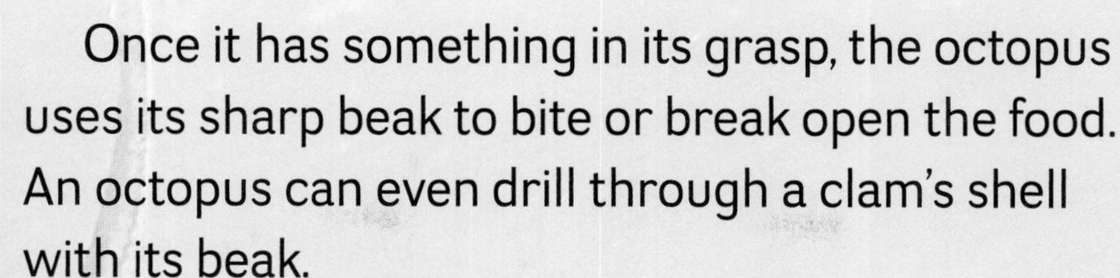

Once it has something in its grasp, the octopus uses its sharp beak to bite or break open the food. An octopus can even drill through a clam's shell with its beak.

The octopus has some unusual defenses, too. When it is in trouble, it can squirt a dark cloud of ink to confuse predators. Then it uses its siphon to swim away—fast! A siphon is like a tube. The octopus jets water through it at speeds of up to 25 miles per hour!

And in a real emergency, an octopus can break off its own arm to escape. The arm will then grow back.

Another sea creature possessing a very unusual trait is the anglerfish. It lives in the deepest, darkest part of the ocean. Food is hard to find there. Luckily, the anglerfish has a light on the top of its head. It uses the light to lure prey into its waiting jaws. *Munch!*

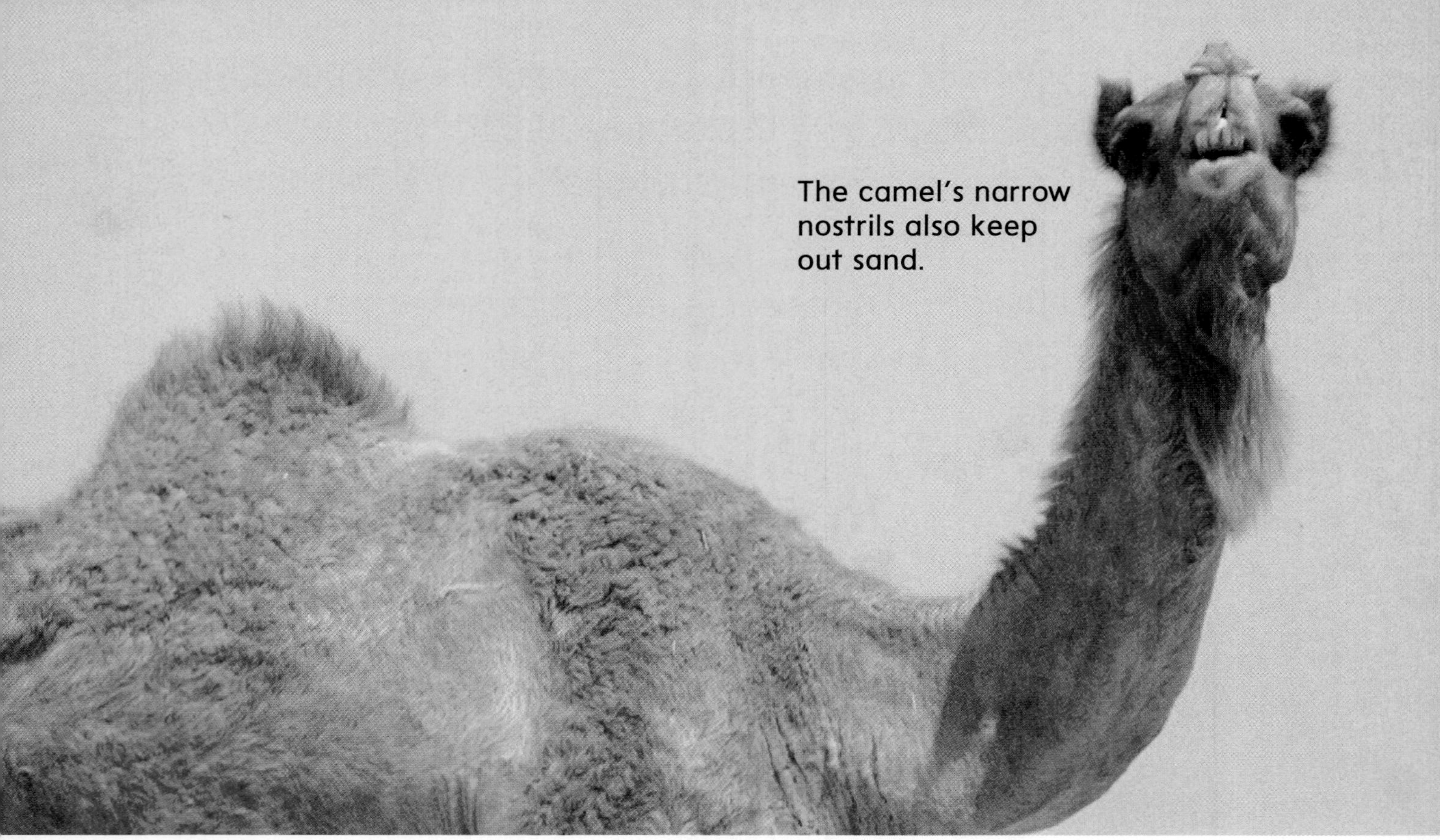

The camel's narrow nostrils also keep out sand.

Dunes Dweller

A camel has many traits that help it survive in the desert—a place where few other animals can live. Wide feet keep a camel from sinking into the sand. Hairy eyelashes keep sand out of its eyes. Thick fur keeps it warm at night. This fur also protects the camel from sun and heat during the day.

A camel's most famous trait is its hump. Its hump is made of fat—up to 80 pounds of it! The camel's body can break down this fat into energy and water. This creates a big advantage in the desert, where it is often hard to find food and water. A camel can go for weeks without eating or drinking. When it does find water, it can drink 30 gallons in just 13 minutes! That's as much water as one person drinks in two months.

Small but Powerful

Ants are some of the strongest creatures on Earth. They can carry up to 50 times their own body weight, which is about the same as a person lifting a truck! This strength allows ants to do massive amounts of work. They find and carry food. They dig dirt, build nests, and keep things clean. They care for the queen ants and their young.

Ants fight off enemies, too. Some ants have super-fast jaws that snap shut like a trap. These jaws can spring shut at up to 145 miles per hour! They can bite off the head of another insect.

Fire ants have another incredible trait: they work together to form "rafts" during a flood. The ants use their legs to hold onto each other. Then they float on top of the water. Fire ants can survive like this for months.

Frozen Frogs?

You probably know that bears hibernate in the winter. They store fat and then go to sleep for many months while winter passes.

But have you heard about the wood frog? It doesn't just hibernate for the winter—it freezes! As soon as a wood frog touches ice, it begins to freeze. Its heart stops. Its breathing stops. Its brain activity stops. Ice fills the space between its vital organs. The wood frog can remain this way for days, weeks, or even months.

How does this happen? Before winter arrives, the frog stores up sugar. When cold weather comes, the sugar floods the frog's cells. The sugar acts like antifreeze in a car: it lowers the freezing point of the cells. Some of the water from the cells freezes, but not all of it. That allows the cells to survive—so the frog survives as well.

Amazing Animals

Animals use many different traits to stay alive. These traits help them survive in places that other animals could not. They help the animals avoid predators. They also help the animals catch prey. What special animal trait do you think is the most amazing?

Did you find the animals in the photos from page 75?

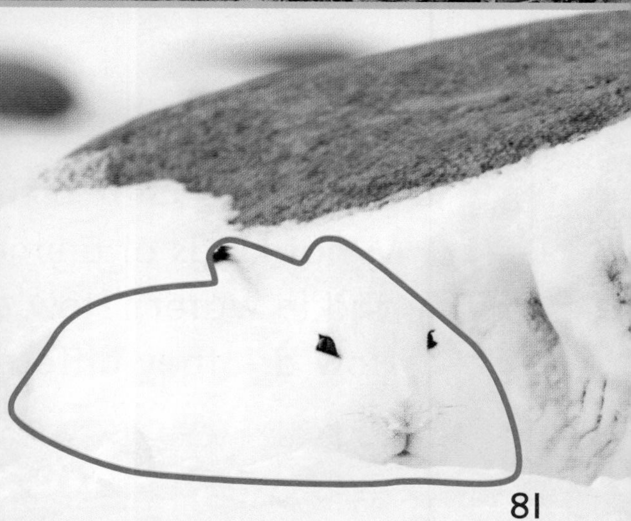

The Platypus

by Sharon Konkus

Essential Questions
What kinds of animals can live on land and in water? How are they similar? How are they different?

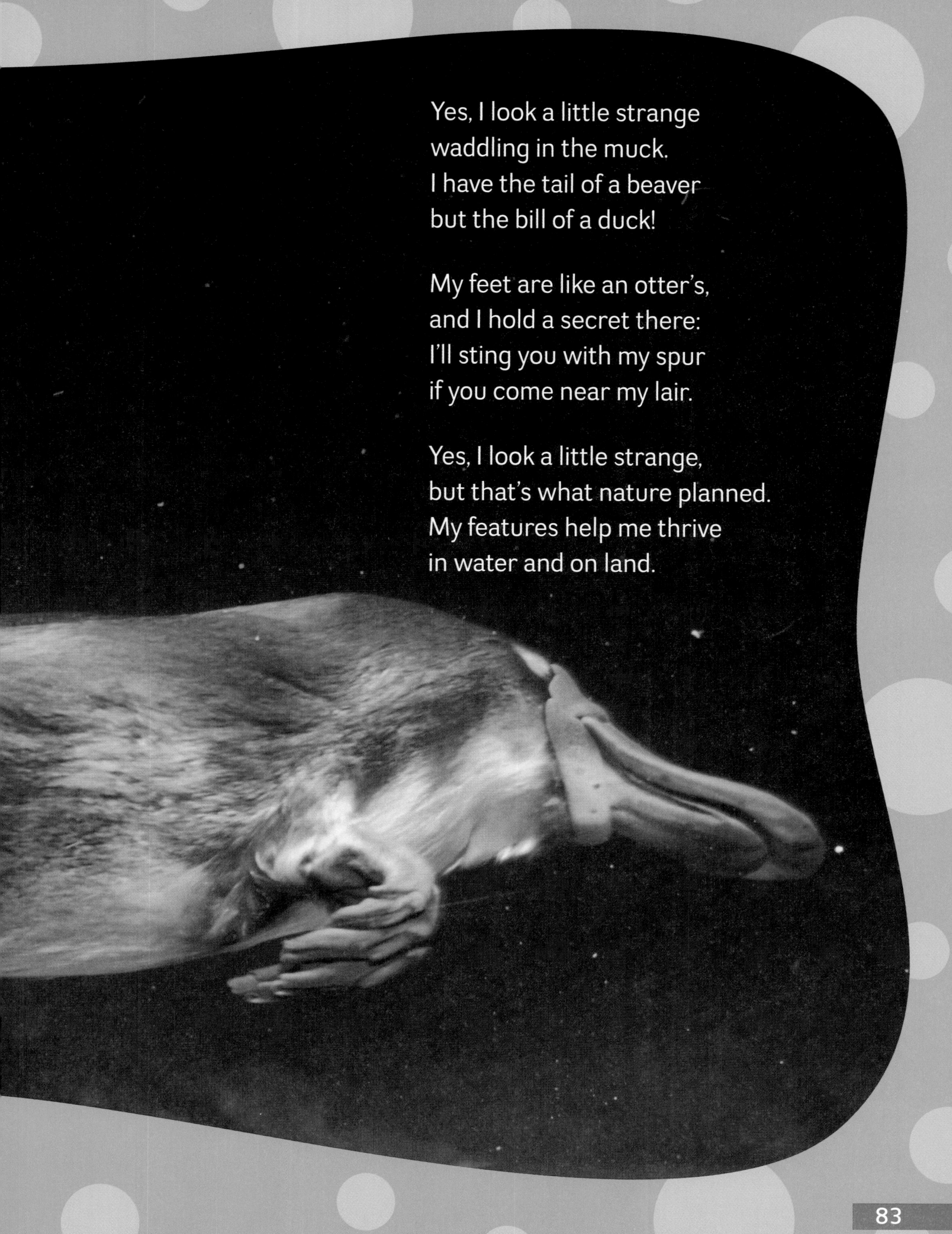

Yes, I look a little strange
waddling in the muck.
I have the tail of a beaver
but the bill of a duck!

My feet are like an otter's,
and I hold a secret there:
I'll sting you with my spur
if you come near my lair.

Yes, I look a little strange,
but that's what nature planned.
My features help me thrive
in water and on land.

You will answer the comprehension questions on these pages as a class.

Text Connections

1. Think about the unique animal traits described in this selection. What are some general ways in which these traits help animals survive?
2. Look at the photo of a giraffe in its habitat on page 81. What do you think the giraffe's color and markings have to do with its survival? Explain your answer.
3. In "Einstein Anderson and the Mighty Ants," Einstein says that ants naturally work together and are very strong for their size. How do these traits help an ant survive?
4. New technologies are often inspired by the ways that animals adapt to their environments. Can you think of a human invention that mimics one or more of the animal traits described in this selection? What is the invention, and how does it make use of the animal's trait?

Did You Know?

Skunks can spray smelly oil to defend themselves, but they only do so when it is absolutely necessary. This is because it takes skunks up to 10 days to replenish their oil.

Look Closer

Keys to Comprehension

1. Reread the second paragraph on page 74. What sentence tells the main idea for the whole selection?
2. Reread page 80. What do the details in the third paragraph help explain?

Writer's Craft

3. Find the word *predators* on page 75. What do you think this word means? What context clues help you understand the word's meaning?
4. What text features does this text contain? How do they help readers understand and locate information within the text?

Concept Development

5. Writers often use words such as *because, so,* and *therefore* to signal causes and effects. Reread the last paragraph on page 80. What signal word for cause and effect is used in this paragraph? What cause does it signal? What effect does it signal?

Write

Observe a wild animal from your neighborhood. Then describe one or two traits that help it survive.

Read the story. Then discuss it with your class.

Vocabulary Words

- **advantage**
- **defenses**
- **lure**
- **terrain**
- **tolerate**
- **ward off**

Trip Report

"So, how was it?" Dad asked Will and Ryan. The two cousins had just returned from a backpacking trip to Lake Michigan's sand dunes. Ryan was an experienced hiker, but this had been Will's first time to go backpacking.

"Absolutely horrendous!" responded Will, half-jokingly.

Ryan laughed. "Aw, it wasn't so bad, was it?" he asked. Will rolled his eyes.

"Will is just a little out of shape, that's all," Ryan said, winking at Dad.

"Hey, I'm in fantastic shape! I'm just not used to trekking millions of miles across three terrains!" said Will defensively. "We weren't just on flat land; we had to climb hills and slog through sand to reach our camping spot."

"Also, you don't have much tolerance for the heat," ribbed Ryan.

"We are in agreement on that point," said Will. "And do you know what else I cannot tolerate? Mosquitos!"

"Yeah, the mosquitos were pretty unbearable," said Ryan. "They swarmed us from every direction."

"And that citronella bug repellent that supposedly wards them off barely helped," Will continued. "All it did was make us smell like furniture polish!" Ryan guffawed at this remark.

"Still, you have to admit that our campsite had its advantages," said Ryan.

"Yes, it did," agreed Will. "It was easy to walk to the beach from our site."

"I bet you were lured to the beach often, to escape the heat and mosquitos," Dad chimed in.

"You've got that right!" said Will.

"So, do you think I will ever convince you to go backpacking again?" Ryan asked Will.

"Perhaps," replied Will, "but only if I can choose our destination!"

Concept Vocabulary

Think about the word *adaptation*. What are some adaptations that affect the way animals look? What are some adaptations that affect the way an animal behaves?

Extend Vocabulary

Copy the web below into your Writer's Notebook. Then fill it in with different examples of *terrain*.

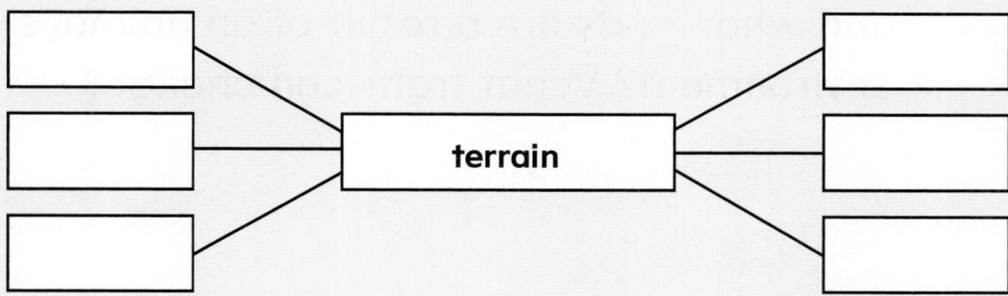

Read this Science Connection. You will answer the questions as a class.

Text Feature

A **line graph** can show how something changes over time.

Animal Traits

In "Amazing Animals," you read about some animals that have unique traits that help them survive. An animal's traits include its physical characteristics as well as its skills and behaviors. Animals are born with many of their traits. They inherit these traits from their parents, who inherited them from their parents, and so on. A zebra's stripes or a giraffe's long neck are examples of inherited traits.

However, animals are also able to develop new traits. For example, an animal can learn a skill. Or, the animal can develop physical features that its parents did not have. The animal may do this to survive changes to its habitat. These changes may include a new predator or a sudden difference in climate. Or these traits could be forced upon the animal. These changes may come from a scarcity of food or a loss of habitat.

What are some examples of animal traits? What kinds of traits are inherited, and what kinds are a result of an animal's environment? What traits can change?

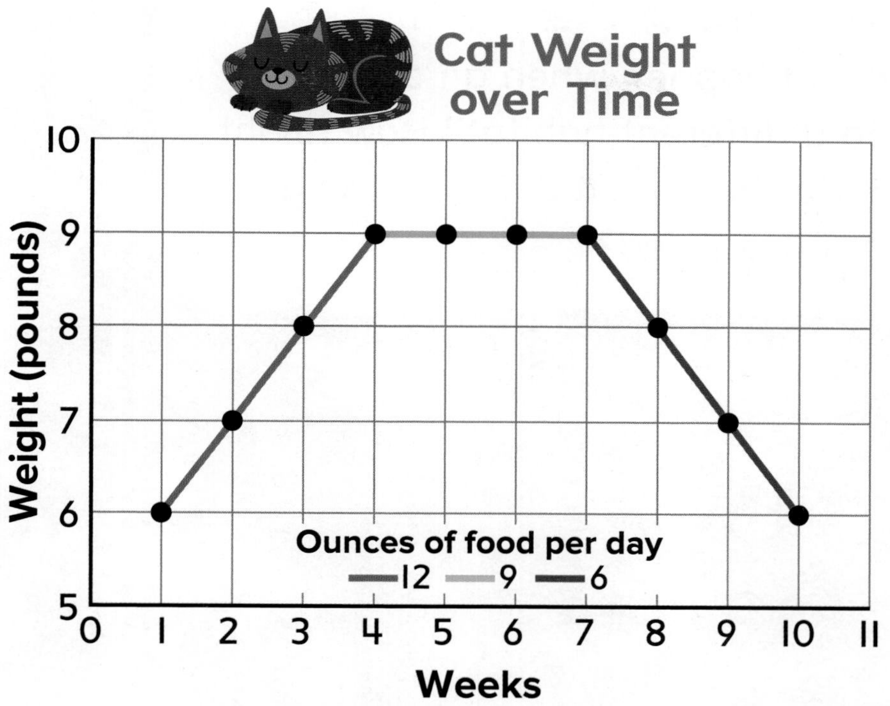

1. Amos's cat had become overweight, so his vet recommended that he decrease the amount of food he fed the cat. How does the line graph show the decrease in food?
2. What happened to the cat's weight when Amos first decreased the amount of food?
3. What happened to the cat's weight when Amos further decreased the amount of food given?

Go Digital

Do you think an animal's weight is the only physical characteristic that changes with its environment? What other physical characteristics can change?

Genre Informational Text

Essential Questions

What could happen when an animal moves to a different habitat? How might your habitat be affected if something new was introduced?

Ecosystem Invaders

by Nancy Morris

Upsetting the Balance

Picture a peaceful stream. Some plants grow on the land along its edges, while others grow right in the water. Frogs hop from rock to rock. Some fish lay eggs, and reptiles doze in the mud. Bears splash in the stream as deer nibble at flowers on the shore. A hawk swoops down from the sky to grab a mouse.

The stream you are picturing is a healthy ecosystem. It has a balance of living and nonliving things. The flowing waters have many healthy food chains.

Now picture an animal from a different ecosystem moving to this stream. You may not be able to tell where the animal comes from, but you know it does not belong there! This new animal has no competition for food. Because of this, it causes many problems.

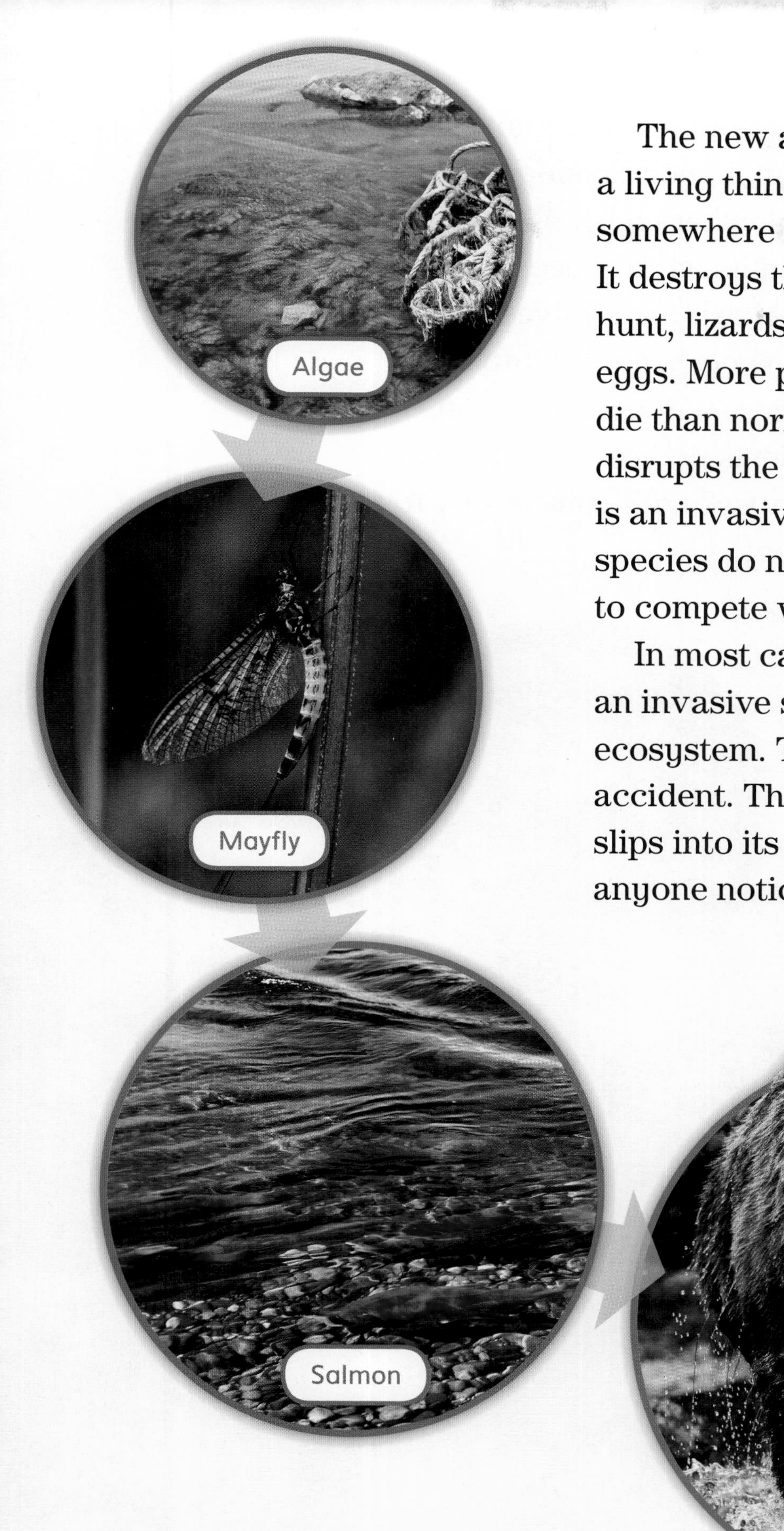

The new animal is an invader, a living thing that has moved somewhere it may not belong. It destroys the places where frogs hunt, lizards sleep, and fish lay eggs. More plants and animals die than normal. The new animal disrupts the food chain because it is an invasive species. The native species do not have adaptations to compete with it or fight it.

In most cases, people bring an invasive species to a new ecosystem. This is often by accident. The invasive species slips into its new home without anyone noticing.

Sometimes people do not know the harm a species is capable of causing. They decide to bring it somewhere new. After all, a plant or an animal in its natural ecosystem does not hurt the place where it lives. The trouble starts when a species moves into an ecosystem where it does not belong.

What problems do you think invasive species can cause? Let's learn about four of them to find out.

Zebra Mussels Flex Their Muscles

The zebra mussel is a freshwater animal. It gets its name from the dark and light stripes on its shell, which remind some people of a zebra. Zebra mussels are very small. In fact, most are about the size of the nail on your finger. Do not let the size fool you, though. This little mussel can cause big trouble!

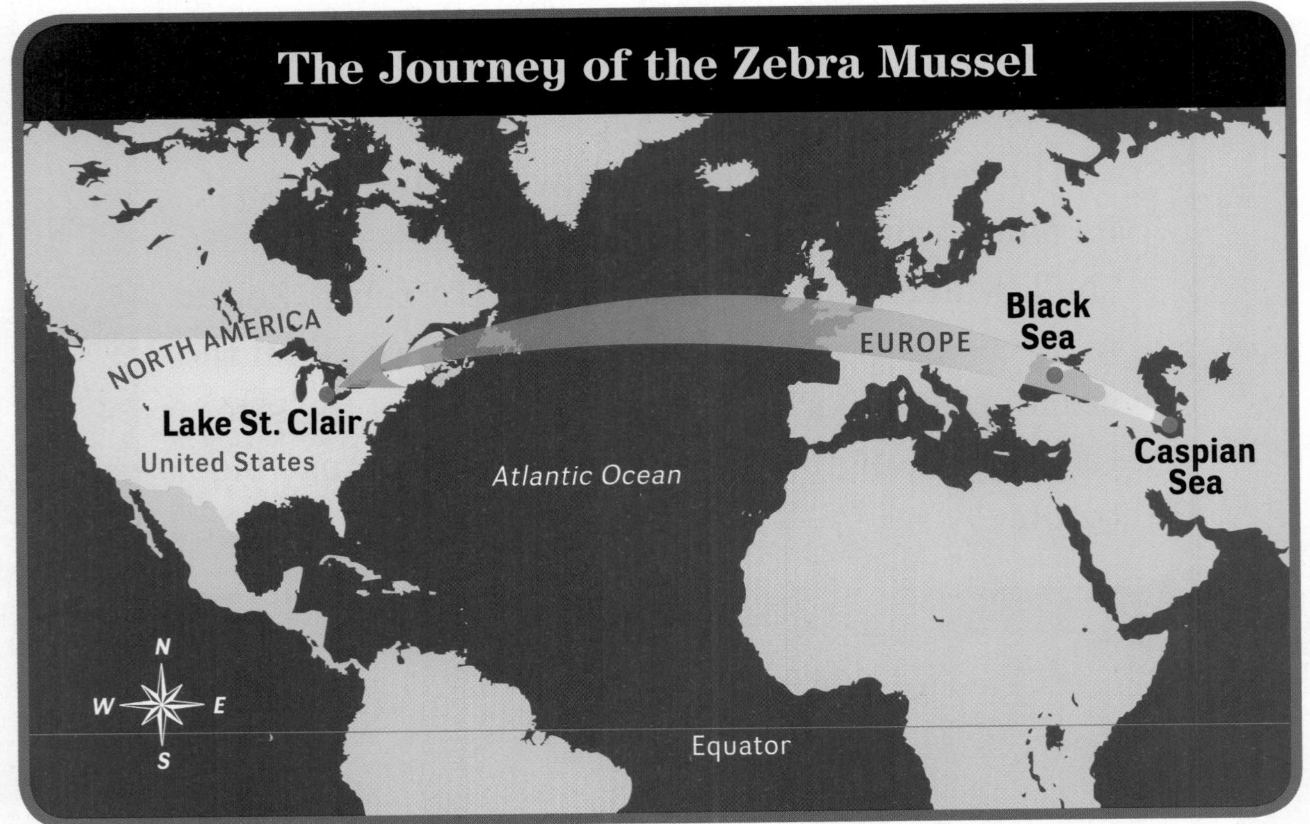

Zebra mussels first lived only in the Caspian and Black Seas in Europe and Asia. In 1988, scientists were confused when they found zebra mussels in Lake Saint Clair in the United States. Nobody had ever seen zebra mussels there before.

Scientists learned that ships had brought the striped invaders to the lake. The zebra mussels had been living on the ships. When some of this water spilled into the lake, the zebra mussels were released and soon spread to other places.

How did these tiny invaders spread so quickly? A female zebra mussel makes millions of eggs. The eggs hatch quickly, and then the young drift in the water. Once they hit something solid, they stick to it and do not let go. Other mollusks, turtles, and crayfish cling to boats. The mussels move with these things and spread quickly.

Zebra mussels damage an ecosystem because they eat so much. They eat tiny water organisms called plankton. Native species also eat plankton. The native species can starve when the zebra mussels eat so much of their food source.

Zebra mussels also cling to native mussels and clams. What happens then? The native animals cannot open their shells. They cannot eat or breathe. These native animals die and then other animals no longer have food.

So how can the invaders be stopped? People who use boats can help stop zebra mussels from spreading. They can clean their boats carefully before they move them to a new lake or stream.

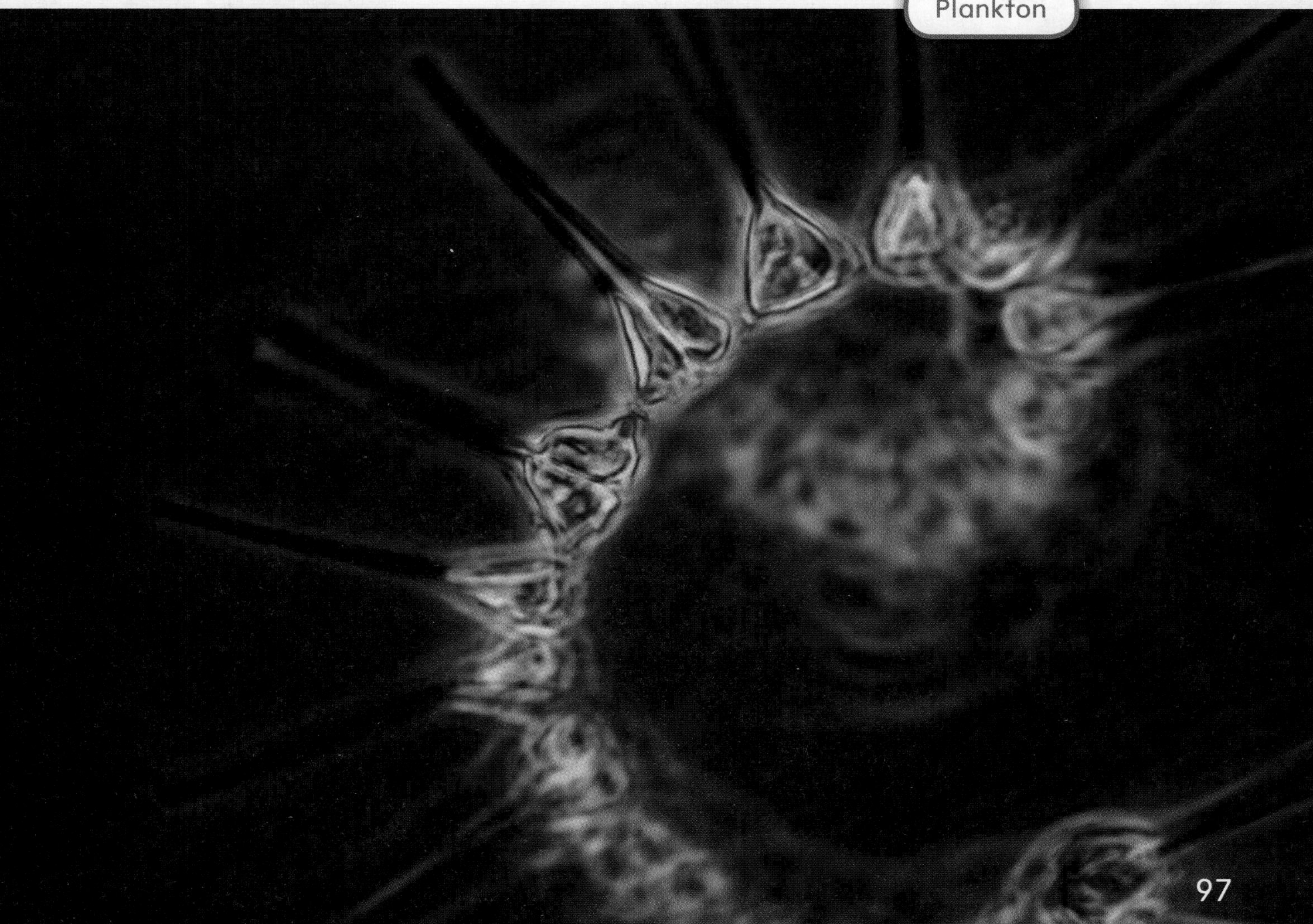

Plankton

Good Pigs Gone Bad

Another invader brought by boat is the feral pig, but unlike zebra mussels, feral pigs were brought to the U.S. on purpose.

The feral, or wild, pig is not like the tame animals you can find on farms. Spanish explorer Hernando de Soto first brought pigs to North America in 1539. Many farmers let their pigs run free over the years. As a result, some of the pigs ran away to live in the wild.

Much later, hunters brought a pig called the Eurasian wild boar to North America. The people who brought these pigs thought it might be fun to let them go free, and then hunt them.

Feral pigs in the wild.

Today, feral pigs in the United States are a mix of de Soto's animals and the Eurasian wild boars. They are an invasive species in more than twenty states.

It should be no surprise to you that feral pigs behave like…pigs! They love to eat and dig. When they root around for food, they destroy plants. They ruin streams and ponds. Feral pigs gobble eggs and small animals. They disrupt ecosystems at every level.

Native species are helpless against the feral pig. Feral pigs destroy their ecosystems and eat up almost everything in their path. Plants and animals cannot grow back fast enough.

Many feral pigs also carry diseases. These diseases can spread to other animals and even people. Feral pigs can also make life hard for farmers. How do you think they harm farmers? The pigs destroy crops and kill farm animals.

The feral pig has few natural predators except people. Hunting or trapping them is the only way to get rid of these wild animals. But it's nearly impossible to get them all, so the invaders are here to stay.

Dogs are often used to hunt feral pigs.

Sneaky Snakes

The brown tree snake first lived only in Australia and some of its surrounding islands, where there is little food. The shortage of food keeps the population of snakes under control. That helps keep them from doing harm to their home ecosystems.

In the late 1940s, the brown tree snake came to Guam, and it caused a lot of trouble. This small island in the Pacific Ocean is about six thousand miles west of San Francisco.

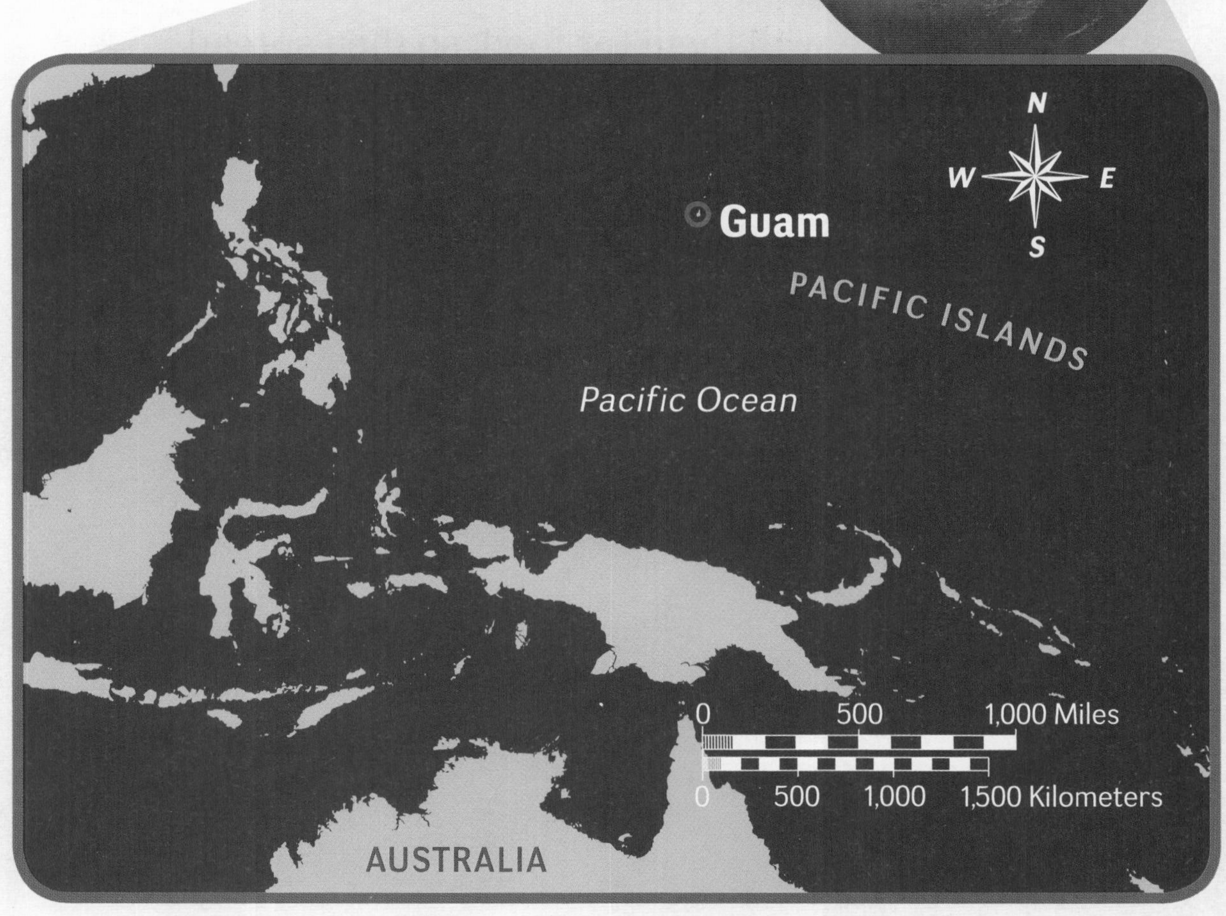

Brown tree snakes live in trees and other places, such as logs and caves. They can go a long time without food. This is why the snakes could live through the journey to Guam.

People did not know they were bringing brown tree snakes to Guam. The snakes hid like stowaways in many different ships. Once the snakes invaded the island, they started eating birds and other small animals.

Guam had no tree snakes before the brown tree snakes arrived, so the native species were not able to protect themselves. Nature had not given these species anything they could use to fight off the new hunters. To make matters even worse, the snakes had no predators. No other animals could compete with them for food, so they spread very quickly.

Brown tree snake

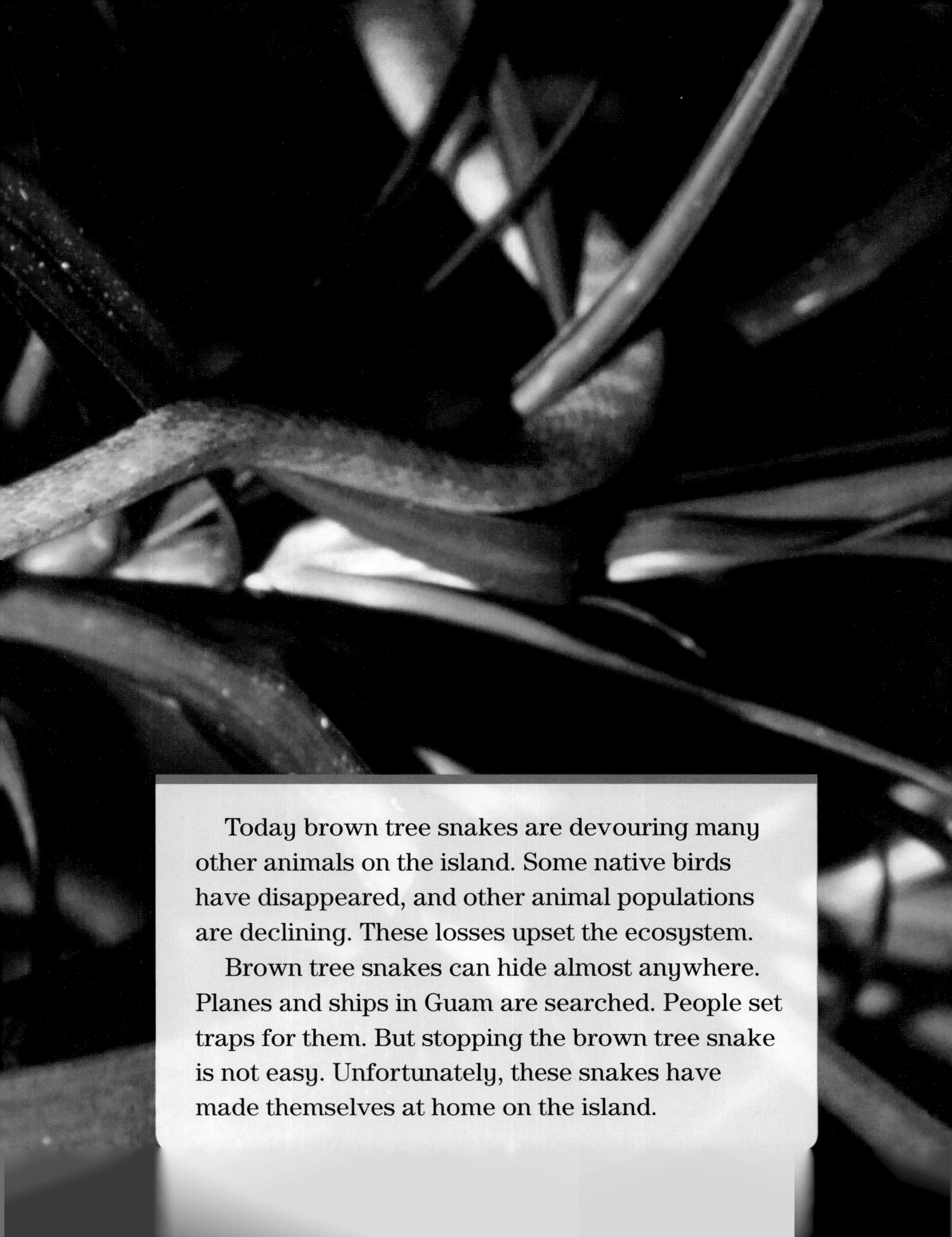

Today brown tree snakes are devouring many other animals on the island. Some native birds have disappeared, and other animal populations are declining. These losses upset the ecosystem.

Brown tree snakes can hide almost anywhere. Planes and ships in Guam are searched. People set traps for them. But stopping the brown tree snake is not easy. Unfortunately, these snakes have made themselves at home on the island.

A Japanese garden

A Beautiful Invader

Believe it or not, some pretty plants can also be invasive species!

In 1876, the United States turned one hundred years old, and Americans decided to hold a big party in Philadelphia. Many countries built fancy exhibits for this huge party.

The Japanese made a garden filled with lots of interesting plants. A beautiful vine called kudzu was in the garden. American gardeners saw this plant and wanted to grow it in their gardens.

Its large leaves were shaped like hearts, and its fragrant purple flowers smelled great. Soon after the exhibit, Americans began to plant this ornamental vine in their gardens.

Farmers grew kudzu and sold it. Other people planted the vine on hills and near water. They used kudzu to keep soil from washing away.

It's too bad no one guessed that this plant would be so hard to control!

Kudzu

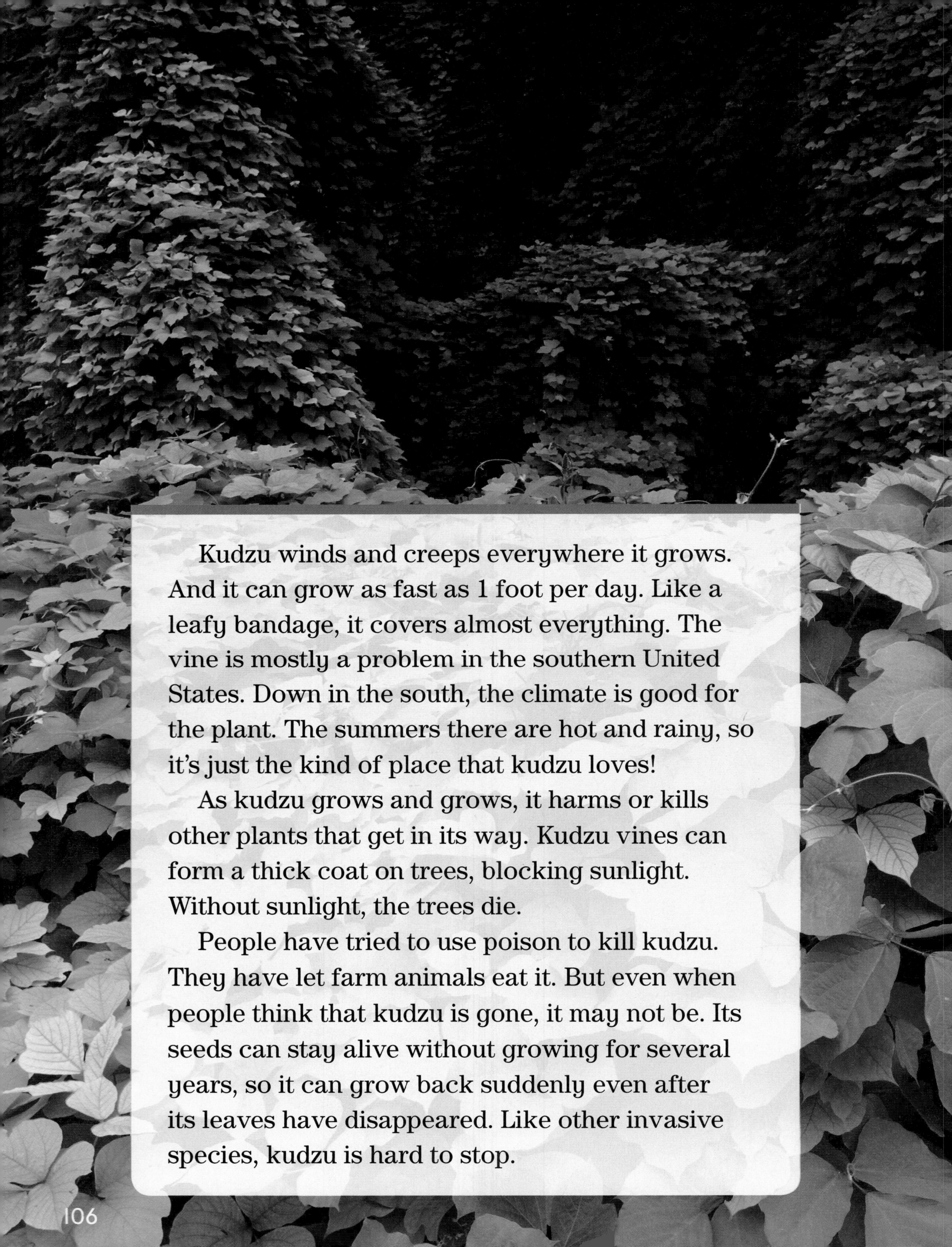

Kudzu winds and creeps everywhere it grows. And it can grow as fast as 1 foot per day. Like a leafy bandage, it covers almost everything. The vine is mostly a problem in the southern United States. Down in the south, the climate is good for the plant. The summers there are hot and rainy, so it's just the kind of place that kudzu loves!

As kudzu grows and grows, it harms or kills other plants that get in its way. Kudzu vines can form a thick coat on trees, blocking sunlight. Without sunlight, the trees die.

People have tried to use poison to kill kudzu. They have let farm animals eat it. But even when people think that kudzu is gone, it may not be. Its seeds can stay alive without growing for several years, so it can grow back suddenly even after its leaves have disappeared. Like other invasive species, kudzu is hard to stop.

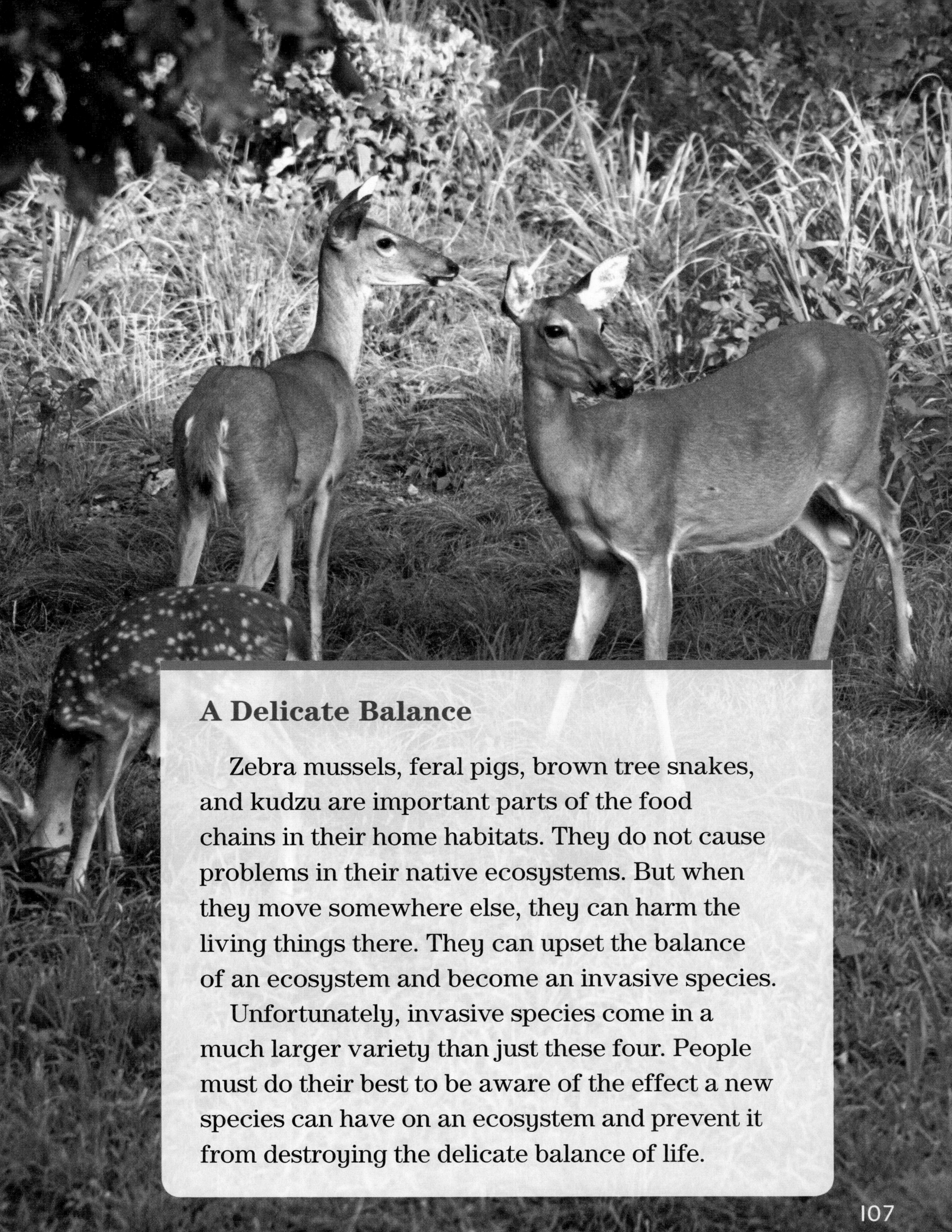

A Delicate Balance

Zebra mussels, feral pigs, brown tree snakes, and kudzu are important parts of the food chains in their home habitats. They do not cause problems in their native ecosystems. But when they move somewhere else, they can harm the living things there. They can upset the balance of an ecosystem and become an invasive species.

Unfortunately, invasive species come in a much larger variety than just these four. People must do their best to be aware of the effect a new species can have on an ecosystem and prevent it from destroying the delicate balance of life.

You will answer the comprehension questions on these pages as a class.

Text Connections

1. How is an invasive species dangerous to its new habitat?
2. According to this selection, plants and animals can do great harm in areas where they do not belong. In the beginning the invasive species thrive. However, do you think they could ever become dangerous even to themselves? Explain your answer.
3. Think about "Einstein Anderson and the Mighty Ants." Stanley had a plan to create giant ants. If he had succeeded, could the ants have become an invasive species? Explain your answer.
4. Governments often have strict rules about the kinds of plants and animals allowed into their country. Why is it a good idea to have these kinds of rules in place?

Did You Know?

Pet dogs can also be considered an invasive animal species.

Look Closer

Keys to Comprehension

1. Look at the food chain diagram on page 93. What sequence of actions does it show?
2. How do humans cause the spread of invasive species?
3. Reread the text on page 107. The main idea of this section is that life has a delicate balance. What details support the main idea?

Writer's Craft

4. An author's point of view is the author's opinion on a subject. What opinion does the author state in the last paragraph on page 107? Do you share this opinion? Explain why or why not.

Concept Development

5. Look at the photograph on page 106. How does it help you understand the facts about kudzu provided in the text?

Write

Think about your favorite animal. Describe the environment where it might be considered an invasive species.

Read the story. Then discuss it with your class.

Vocabulary Words

- **belong**
- **carry**
- **cling**
- **effect**
- **Eurasian**
- **flex**
- **fragrant**
- **level**
- **mussel**
- **ornamental**
- **root**
- **tame**

A Swanky Thank You

It was Aunt Gloria's final day in town, after staying with Mom and me for a whole month.

"Tonight, I am treating us all to an evening of fine dining!" she announced.

Mom and I squirmed—we feel a greater sense of belonging at the local Burger Shack than at a fancy restaurant. However, Aunt Gloria insisted.

"This is my way of thanking you for your hospitality," she said. Apparently, this was an effective argument. The next thing I knew, all three of us were at a ritzy restaurant downtown.

Aunt Gloria's expertise at fine dining is several levels above Mom's and mine, so we let her order for the table. She decided to tame our hunger with an appetizer of steamed mussels. A waiter carried our order to the kitchen and then returned with a plateful of shelled seafood.

An enticing buttery scent wafted fragrantly across the table. But I could not bring myself to try the mussels. I kept visualizing the way a live mussel clings to its shell and flexes its muscle to hold it closed. I resigned myself to rooting through the fridge for something to eat at home.

But then the next dishes came, and they turned out to be wonderful! We had salad decorated with flowers. "They are not ornamental—they are edible!" declared Aunt Gloria. Next we enjoyed a savory Eurasian chicken dish. Aunt Gloria explained that it combined flavors from European and Asian cuisines.

We all feasted, and even I left the restaurant quite satisfied. Thanks to Aunt Gloria, this fine dining experience was a delicious one!

Concept Vocabulary

Think about the word *indigenous*. What are some plants and animals that are indigenous to the area where you live?

Extend Vocabulary

Copy the word web into your Writer's Notebook. Fill it in with words related to *fragrant*. That could include antonyms, synonyms, or related words.

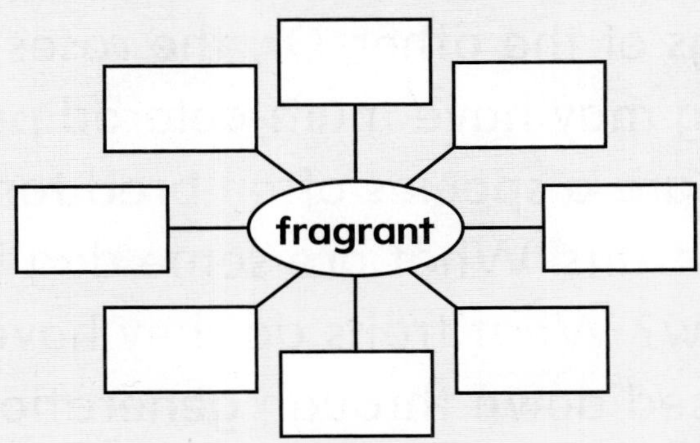

Read this Science Connection.
You will answer the questions as a class.

Text Feature

Charts let readers see information in an organized way.

Variations of Traits

Plant and animal families pass down two kinds of traits to their offspring: physical and behavioral. Physical traits include the color, size, and shape of body parts. Behavioral traits include things like temperament, skills, and instincts.

Plants and animals usually mate only within their own species. For example, pigs mate with other pigs, and roses mate with other roses. For this reason, all offspring within a species will share certain traits. Pigs always have snouts, and roses always have flowers.

However, there are often different breeds within one species. For example, some pigs are Eurasian wild boars, and others are domesticated pigs. Also, some roses are white, and others are pink.

When two different breeds mate, their offspring gets a mixture of traits. For example, the pigs' offspring might have the head size of one parent and the markings of the other. Or, the roses' plant offspring may have multi-colored petals.

Dogs are a species often bred for specific traits. What are some dog breeds you know? What traits do they have that are passed down through generations?

Labrador Retriever parent

+

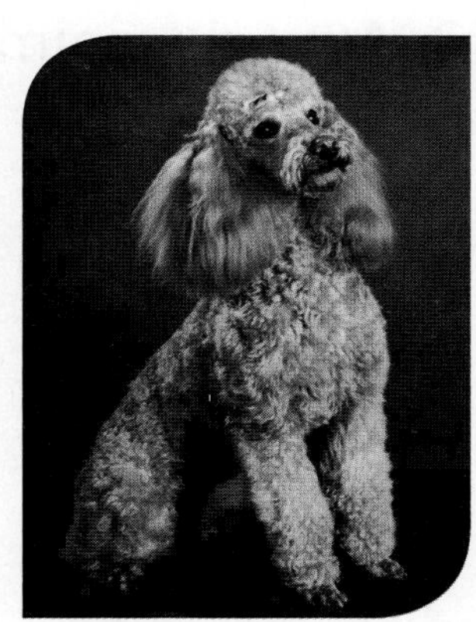

Standard Poodle parent

=

Labradoodle offspring

The Labradoodle is a popular breed of dog. The parents of a Labradoodle are a Labrador retriever and a Poodle.

1. How is this chart helpful?
2. What physical traits do all of the dogs share?
3. How does the Labradoodle take after each of its parents?

Go Digital

Other than dogs, what are some examples of animals that humans breed?

Genre Fantasy

Essential Questions

How do different animals deal with weather changes in their habitat? Why do animals prefer particular habitats?

Is This Panama?

A Migration Story

by Jan Thornhill
illustrated by Soyeon Kim

When Sammy, the young Wilson's warbler, woke up, his toes were colder than they'd ever been before. Even though it was still August, frost twinkled and sparkled on every leaf of his home near the Arctic Circle. Sammy shivered, partly because he was cold and partly because he was excited. If it was *this* cold, it must be time for him to make his first migration south to Panama.

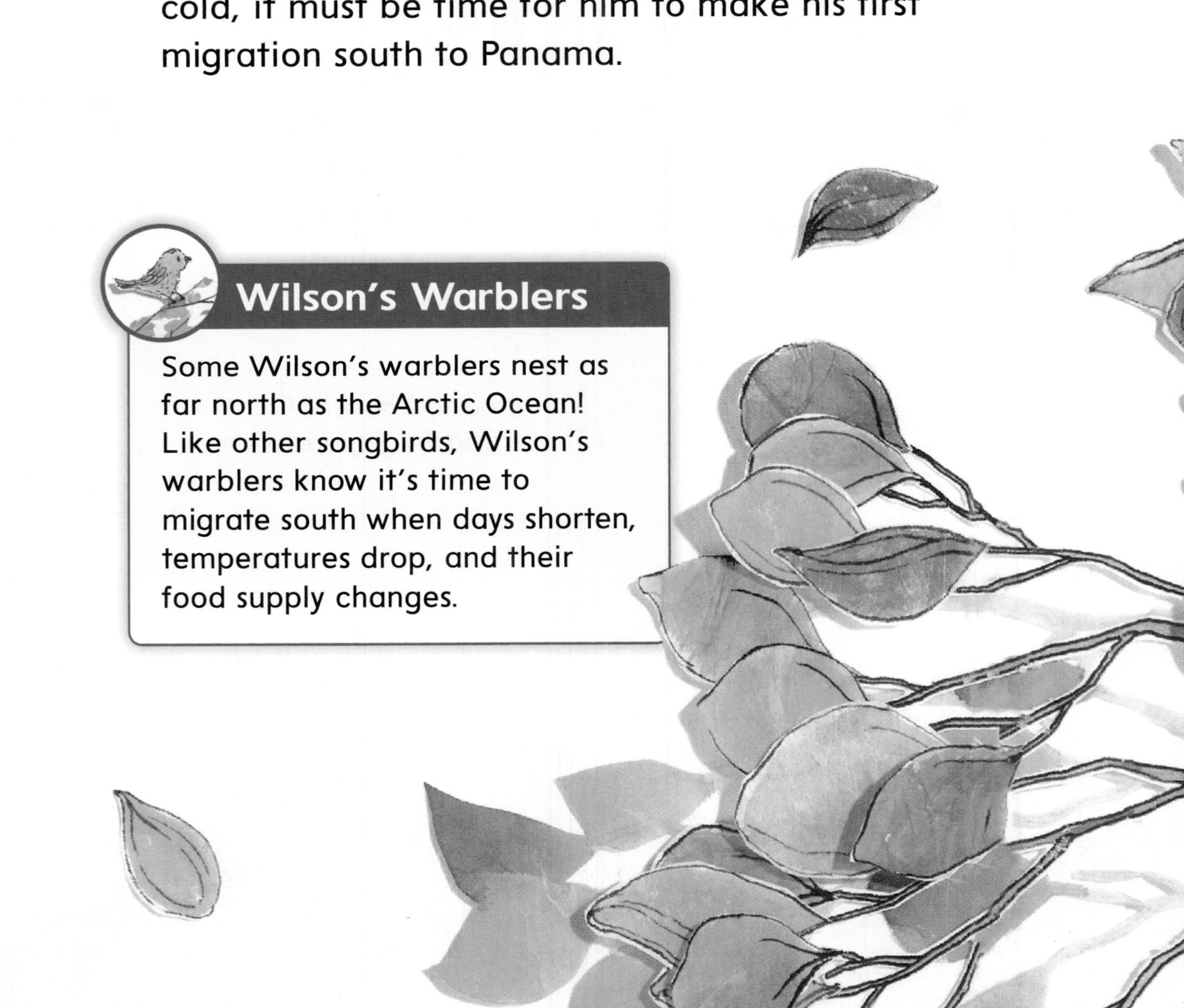

Wilson's Warblers

Some Wilson's warblers nest as far north as the Arctic Ocean! Like other songbirds, Wilson's warblers know it's time to migrate south when days shorten, temperatures drop, and their food supply changes.

Sammy had heard about Panama from older Wilson's warblers. They said that Panama was warm all year long—even at night. Sammy had also heard that some insects in Panama were as big as warblers. He wasn't sure if he believed that, though.

But where *were* all the other warblers? Usually there was somebody foraging for food nearby. Sammy hopped up to the top of the tallest dwarf birch expecting to see someone he knew, but there was no one. Sammy was worried. He didn't know how to get to Panama by himself.

Sammy spotted a ptarmigan. All summer the ptarmigans had been hard to see because their brown feathers blended in so well with the landscape. Lately, though, their brown feathers were being replaced by white ones.

"Have you seen any warblers?" Sammy trilled.

"Nope," clucked the ptarmigan. "I bet they've flown south. Warblers always fly south."

"Is that what you do?" asked Sammy.

"Don't have to," said the ptarmigan. "There's lots of food for me here. And I grow special feathers for winter. Soon I'll be almost completely white."

"Everybody will be able to see you!" said Sammy. "Won't that be dangerous?"

"Silly Sammy," chuckled the ptarmigan. "I'll be almost invisible once the snow comes. But you, Sammy, you'd better start flying south."

Ptarmigans

Ptarmigans are some of the only birds that can live year-round in the far north. Along with their white winter camouflage, they grow a thick undercoat of down and "boots" of feathers to keep their toes cozy. To stay warm at night and during snowstorms, they dig "snow caves" for shelter.

Sammy flew higher and longer than he'd ever flown before. He flew for a whole hour, and he was getting tired. A caribou was grazing below. Sammy dipped down close.

"Is this Panama?" he asked. "I'm supposed to migrate south to Panama."

"I'm going south," the caribou snorted loudly—because caribou always snort loudly. "But I've never heard of Panama. I'm heading to my winter forest."

"Why don't you just stay here?"

"It's very windy out in the open. The snow gets hard and crusty. In the forest the snow is softer, so it's easier for me to use my hooves to scoop it off the lichens I like to eat."

"I don't like lichens," said Sammy. "I like insects."

"Then you'd better keep going. I haven't seen any insects at all today."

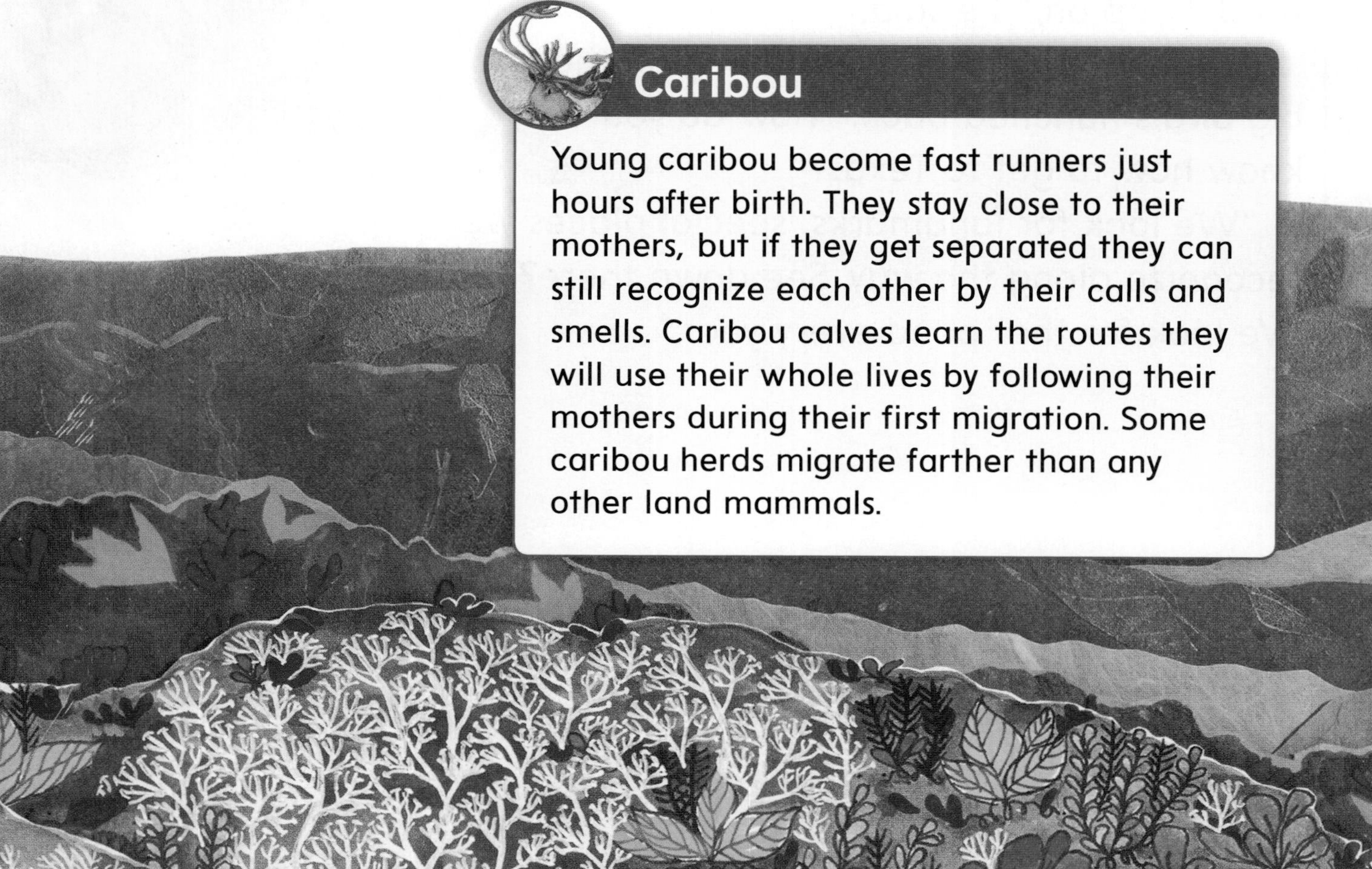

Caribou

Young caribou become fast runners just hours after birth. They stay close to their mothers, but if they get separated they can still recognize each other by their calls and smells. Caribou calves learn the routes they will use their whole lives by following their mothers during their first migration. Some caribou herds migrate farther than any other land mammals.

Sammy had been flying for several hours when he heard a strange trumpeting noise. A flock of sandhill cranes was passing high above him. The birds were fast, and Sammy had to flap his wings like crazy to catch up.

"Are you going to Panama?" he asked breathlessly.

"Never heard of it," drawled one of the cranes. "We're migrating south to Texas."

Another crane noticed that Sammy was tired. "Hop on," he said.

"Thanks," said Sammy, landing on the big bird's hunched back. "How do you know how to get to Texas?"

"We look for landmarks, special places we recognize along the way. See down there? We look for that pond every year."

For the next few days, Sammy hitched rides with the cranes and spent the nights with them in marshes, where the gangly birds used their long beaks to probe the mud for roots and worms. But Sammy couldn't see well enough in the dark to find insects to eat. So he said good-bye and continued on his own.

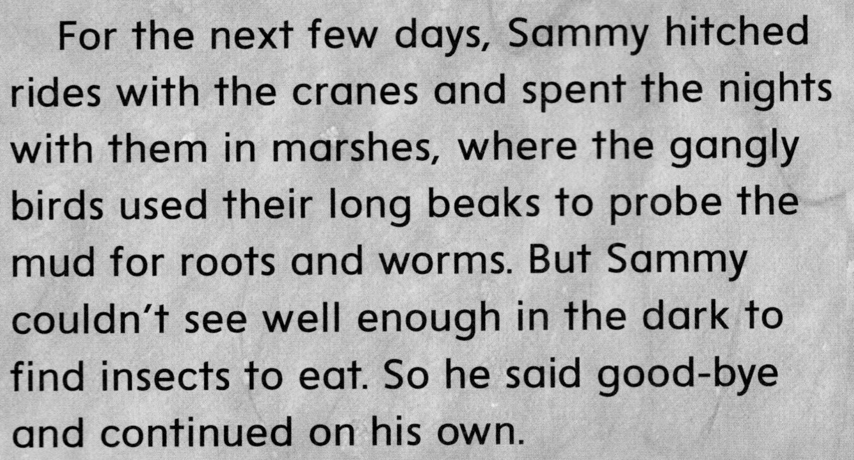

Sandhill Cranes

Because sandhill cranes travel in family groups, the young are shown the way to migrate by their parents. Following the adults, the young learn to recognize landmarks along their migration routes as well as the best places to rest and feed.

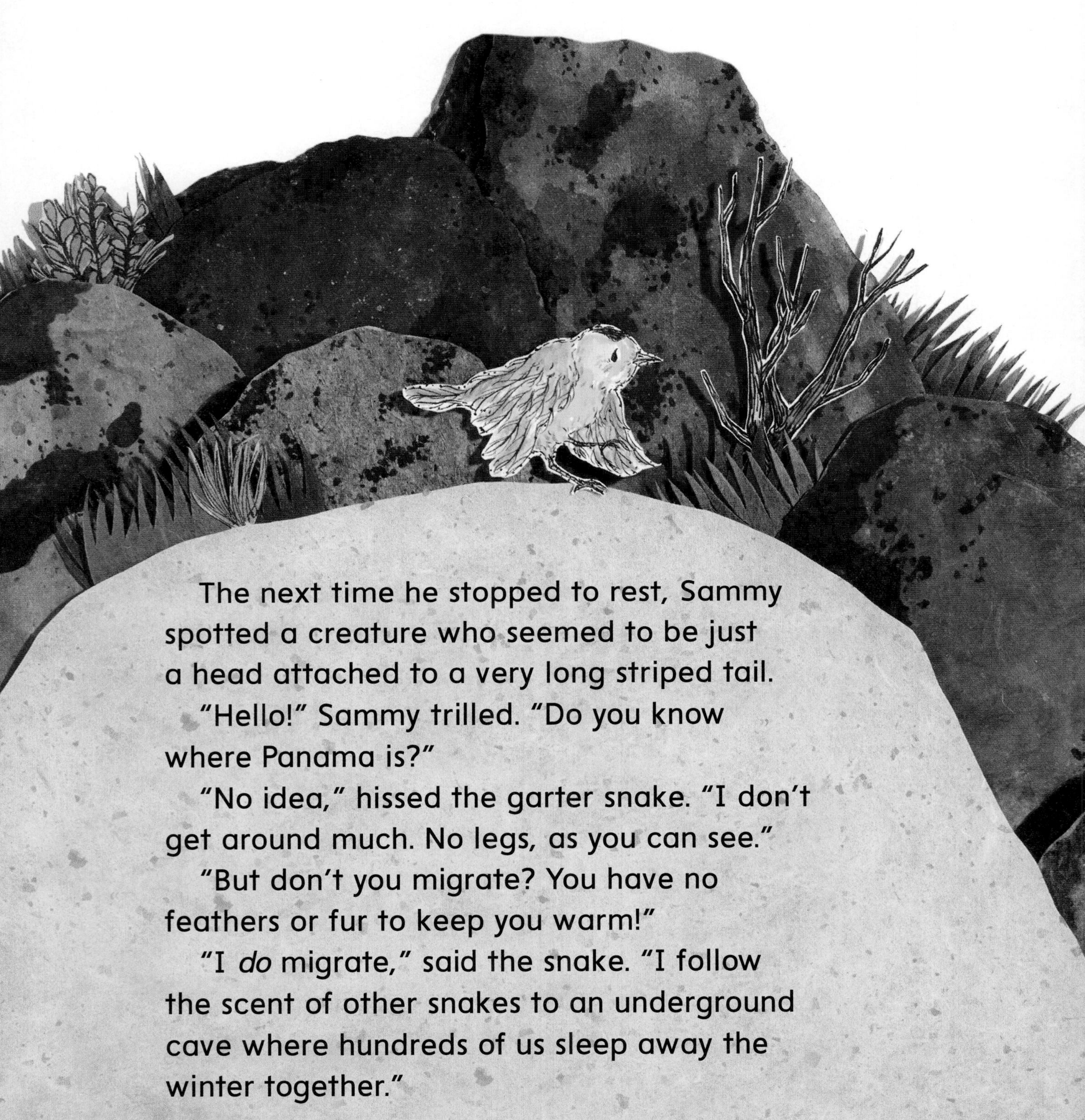

The next time he stopped to rest, Sammy spotted a creature who seemed to be just a head attached to a very long striped tail.

"Hello!" Sammy trilled. "Do you know where Panama is?"

"No idea," hissed the garter snake. "I don't get around much. No legs, as you can see."

"But don't you migrate? You have no feathers or fur to keep you warm!"

"I *do* migrate," said the snake. "I follow the scent of other snakes to an underground cave where hundreds of us sleep away the winter together."

"There are no snakes where I come from," said Sammy.

"Too cold, probably," hissed the snake. "We like places that have hot summers and lots of frogs and earthworms and..."

"You eat frogs and earthworms?" asked Sammy.

"Oh, yes. And guess what else I sometimes eat?"

Sammy had an idea what the answer might be, so he flew off quickly, wondering if he could smell his way to Panama.

Garter Snakes

Garter snakes are cold-blooded reptiles, so the ones that live in the north have to hibernate in underground caves so they won't freeze. Some of these caves, or hibernacula, can shelter up to ten thousand snakes! Snakes use their flicking tongues, not their noses, to capture scents. These scents, or chemical signals, are then "read" by the Jacobson's organ on the roofs of their mouths.

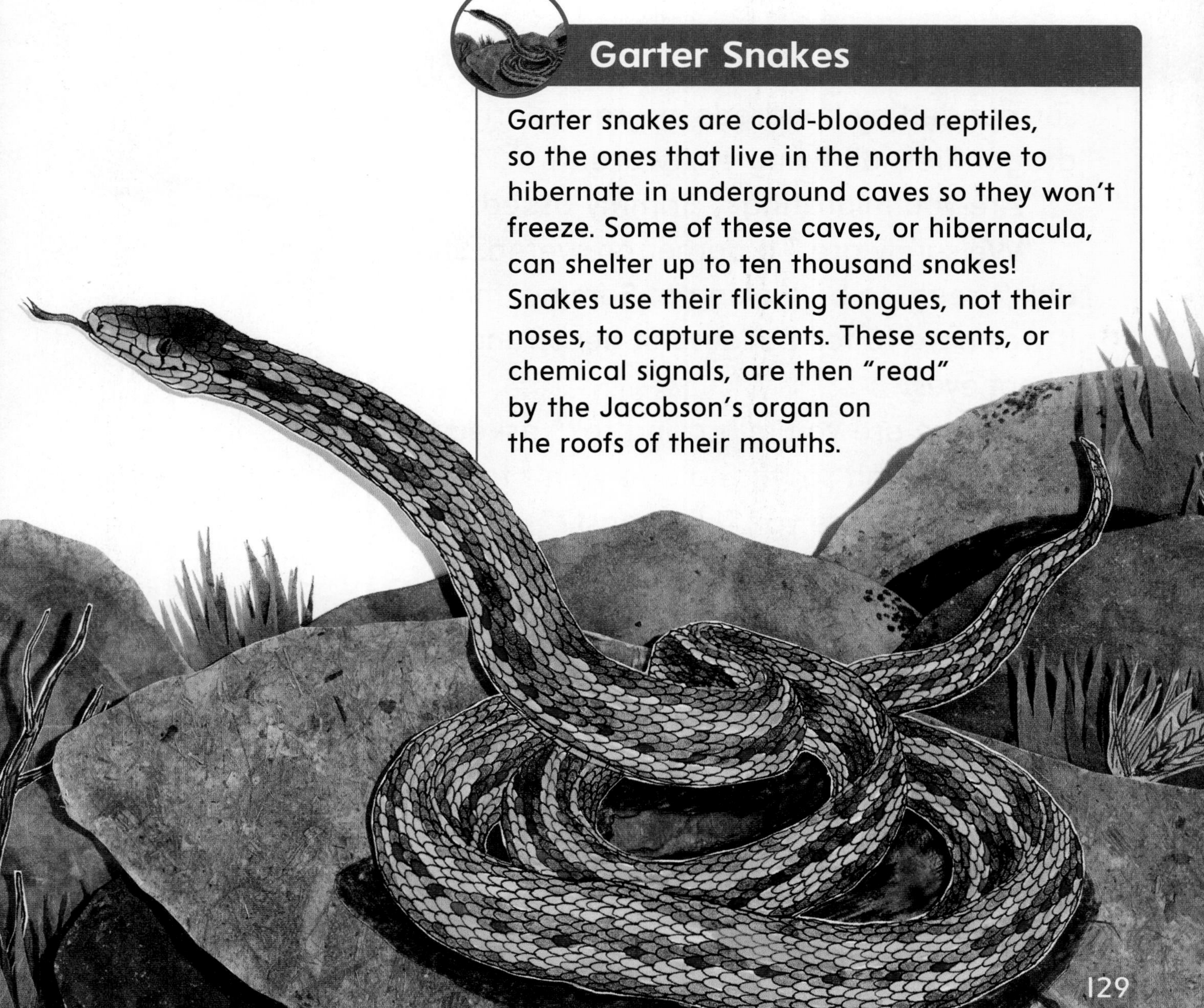

Near a huge lake, Sammy was suddenly surrounded by hundreds of green darner dragonflies, all flying eastward.

"Are you migrating?" Sammy asked.

"We surely are," a darner answered. She didn't seem to be looking at Sammy, though it was hard to tell because of her strange insect eyes.

"Where are you migrating to?" asked Sammy.

"Far enough south that we won't freeze."

"Then why are you flying east?"

"We're following the shoreline. It can be dangerously windy over the open water."

Sammy could fly faster than the dragonflies, so off he went ahead of them.

Green Darner Dragonflies

Though we don't know why some green darners migrate, we do know they only migrate during daylight hours. Since they often follow shorelines or long hilly ridges, they might look for unique landforms to figure out which way to go.

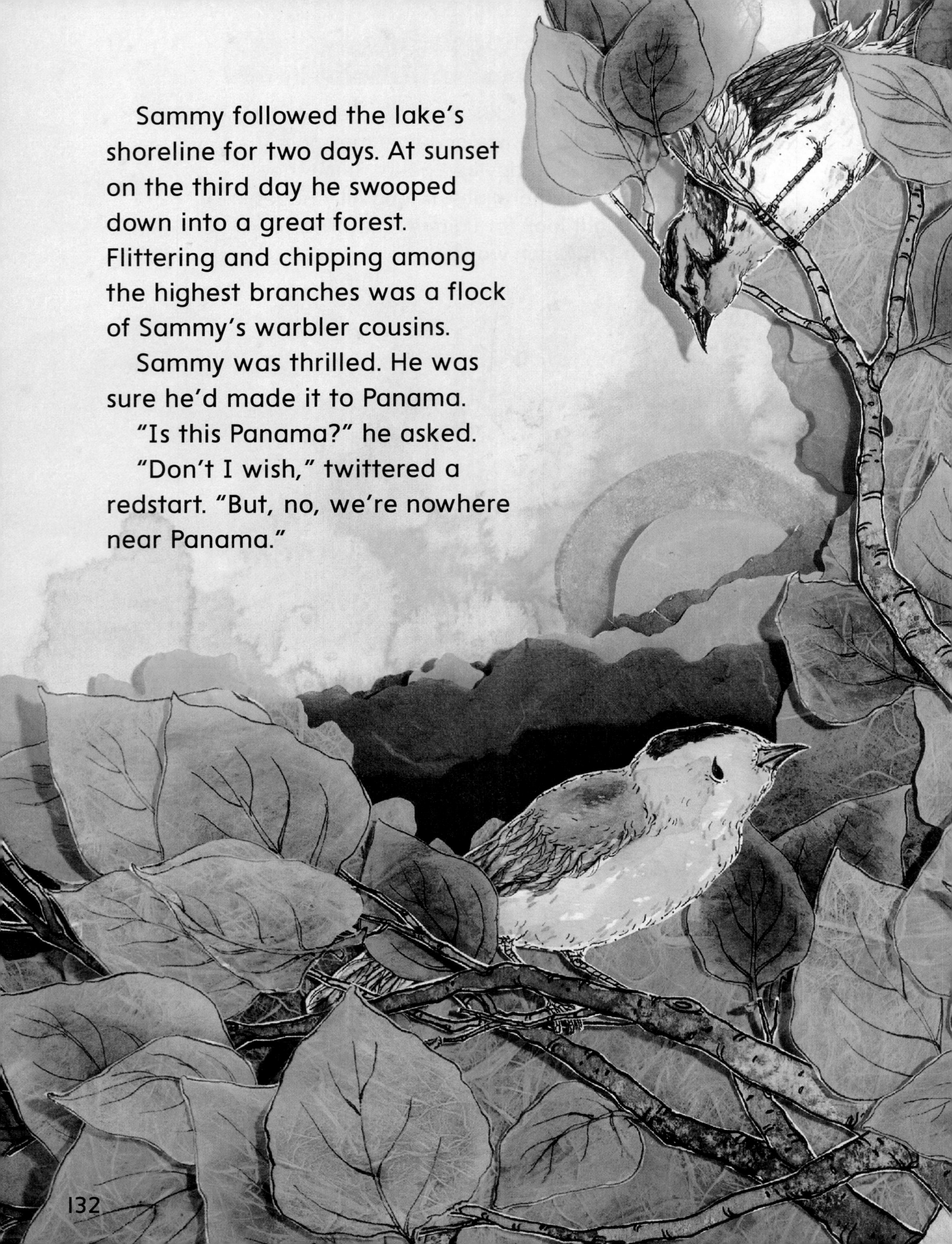

Sammy followed the lake's shoreline for two days. At sunset on the third day he swooped down into a great forest. Flittering and chipping among the highest branches was a flock of Sammy's warbler cousins.

Sammy was thrilled. He was sure he'd made it to Panama.

"Is this Panama?" he asked.

"Don't I wish," twittered a redstart. "But, no, we're nowhere near Panama."

Sammy was disappointed, but then he brightened. "Can you show me the way?"

"Sure! We're about to take off."

"But it's almost dark!" cried Sammy.

"Warblers *do* migrate at night, you know," said a Blackburnian warbler. "We follow the stars."

"The stars?!" said Sammy, astonished.

"Of course! We look for patterns that match the 'star maps' we have in our heads. When it feels just right, we fly."

Sammy stared up at the darkening sky. One group of twinkling stars made him feel all quivery inside.

"I think I feel it!" he sang, and off he flew with the other warblers.

Warblers

All fifty species of North American warblers are migratory. They often migrate in mixed flocks, which makes them a favorite of birdwatchers since many are very colorful. Each species has its own preferences of habitats for nesting in the summer and for wintering. Some fly all the way to Chile in South America for the winter, while others, like Sammy, only go as far as Panama.

A couple of nights later, Sammy was surprised to see stars glittering below him.

"Those aren't real stars," a black-throated green warned. "Just try to ignore them."

But a few minutes later, stars were absolutely everywhere. Sammy didn't know which way to fly. He was so confused he became separated from the flock.

Sammy was becoming frantic when he saw another Wilson's warbler. Maybe it was someone who could help him! They were almost close enough to touch beaks when—*BONK!*—Sammy smacked into something hard and flat and invisible. Stunned, he twirled down to the ground.

Sammy was lucky. He wasn't badly hurt when he hit the window and was able to fly away from the buildings to a meadow. Exhausted, he fell asleep.

Sammy woke up surrounded by hundreds of fluttering orange-and-black wings.

"Is this a butterfly party?" he asked.

"Oh no," one of the monarchs answered. "We just stopped to rest on our way south to Mexico."

"Is Mexico close to Panama?" Sammy asked.

"Pretty close," said the butterfly, "but I think Panama's farther."

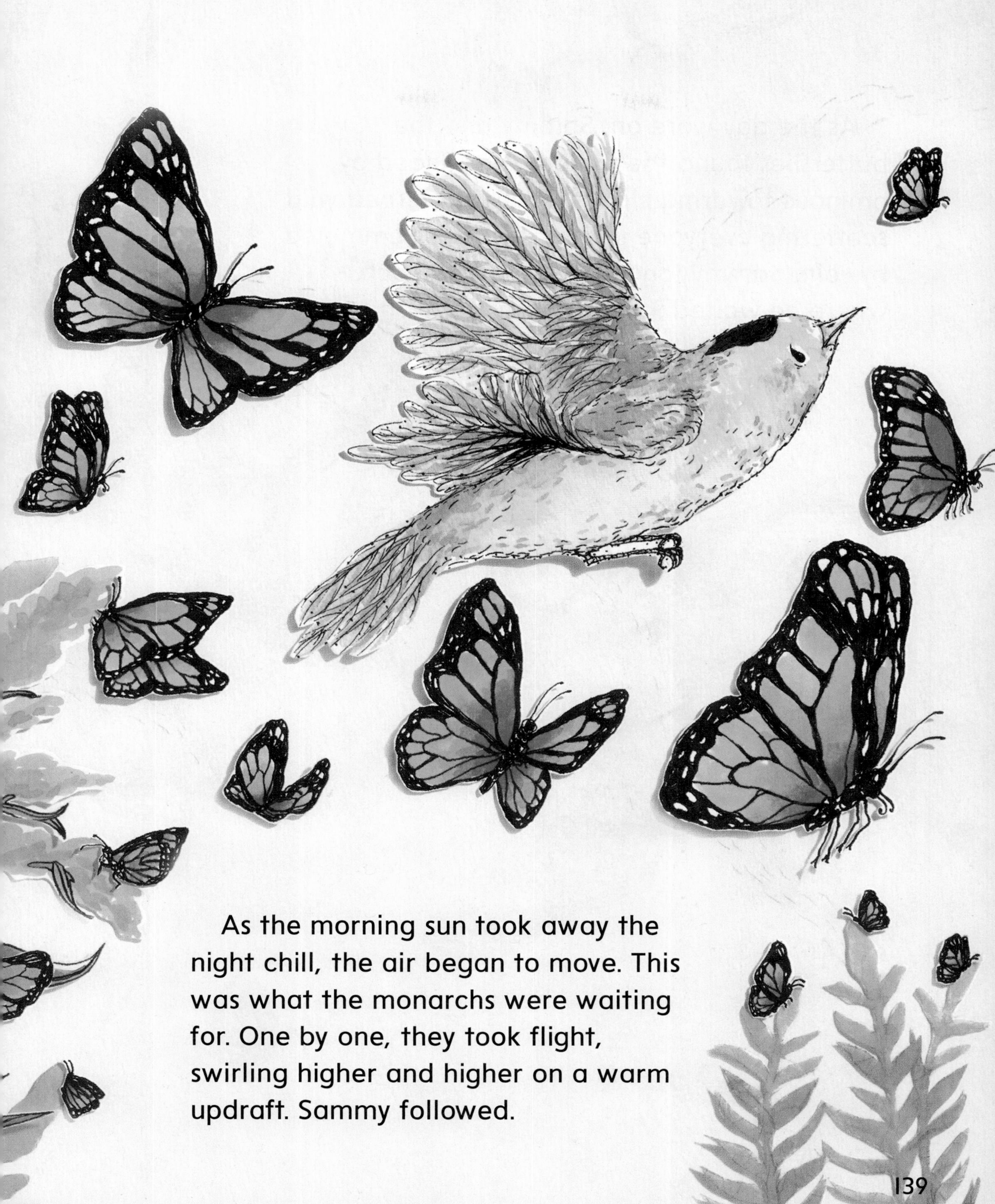

As the morning sun took away the night chill, the air began to move. This was what the monarchs were waiting for. One by one, they took flight, swirling higher and higher on a warm updraft. Sammy followed.

As the day wore on, Sammy and the butterflies found themselves surrounded by ominous towering clouds. The wind turned wild, scattering everyone in all directions. Pummeled by rain, Sammy landed alone on a beach, where he waited for the storm to end.

Monarchs

Like many other butterflies, most monarchs have short lives; they grow, reproduce, and then die. But some monarchs are special. These ones—the last generation of the season—migrate. Millions fly all the way to Mexico, where they spend the winter hibernating in mountain forests. Sometimes there are so many roosting monarchs in the trees that branches break from the weight.

At the water's edge, a long-legged bird was rearranging his wet feathers with his long beak.

"Pah!" he muttered. "Grounded! Me! Unbelievable!"

"I was grounded, too," Sammy piped in.

"No kidding," grumbled the bird. "But everybody knows Hudsonian godwits like me fly all the way to Patagonia in one go! No stopovers!"

"Is Patagonia near Panama?" asked Sammy.

"Just twice as far is all." The godwit stretched out his wings.

Sammy followed the bigger bird out over open water. Soon there was only a vast expanse of ocean far below. For two days and two nights Sammy struggled to keep up. His wings had never been so sore, and he was out of breath.

"Got...to...rest..." he panted.

"Not me," said the godwit. "No more stopovers! But there's a tiny island way down there."

"Whew!" said Sammy, and down he went.

Hudsonian Godwits

Godwits have the longest nonstop migration of any bird in the world and can fly almost ten thousand kilometers (six thousand miles) in one go. They don't have to stop to eat because they eat so much before migration that their weight doubles before they take off!

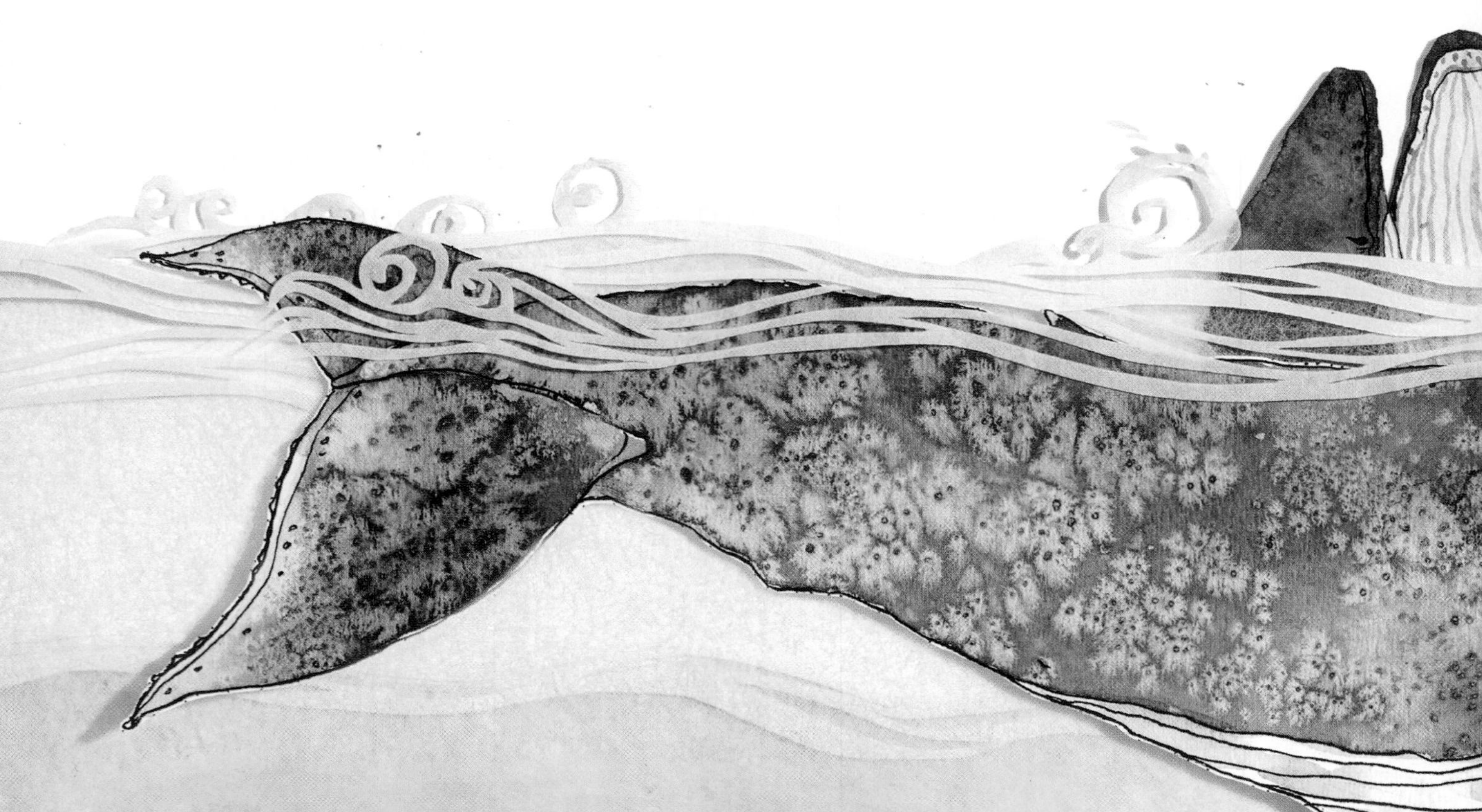

Just as Sammy landed, a geyser of water blew out of a gaping hole in the middle of the island. The water came down like rain, drenching Sammy. Then the island started to move! Sammy ran uphill as fast as he could so he wouldn't fall into the ocean. And then he saw the eye. The eye was almost as big as Sammy.

The island introduced herself as a humpback whale. She was migrating south to warmer waters to calve.

"But what are you doing way out here?" the whale asked. Her voice was much deeper and slower than Sammy's, so she was a little hard to understand.

"I'm migrating to Panama!"

"You're a tad off course," said the whale, trying to be kind. "But I could get you a bit closer."

Humpbacks can swim very fast when they want to, but Sammy's new friend was so busy chatting with other migrating whales that in a whole day they barely got anywhere.

Sammy wanted to move faster. And he was hungry. The whales pointed him in the right direction, and off he flew.

Humpback Whales

Humpback whales feed in cold waters and migrate to warm waters to calve. Some fatten up in the North Atlantic in the summer, then make their way south to the Caribbean for the winter. Though humpbacks migrate slowly, they're very good at staying on course, probably using a combination of the Earth's magnetic field and the position of the Sun to guide them.

Sammy island-hopped through the Bahamas before landing in Cuba, where he joined up with a mixed flock of migrating birds. After a few days, the group crossed over the water to Mexico. They followed the coastline southward, stopping to forage near Mayan ruins, in fields of maize, and in monkey-filled rainforests. Eventually, they stopped to look for food near a river.

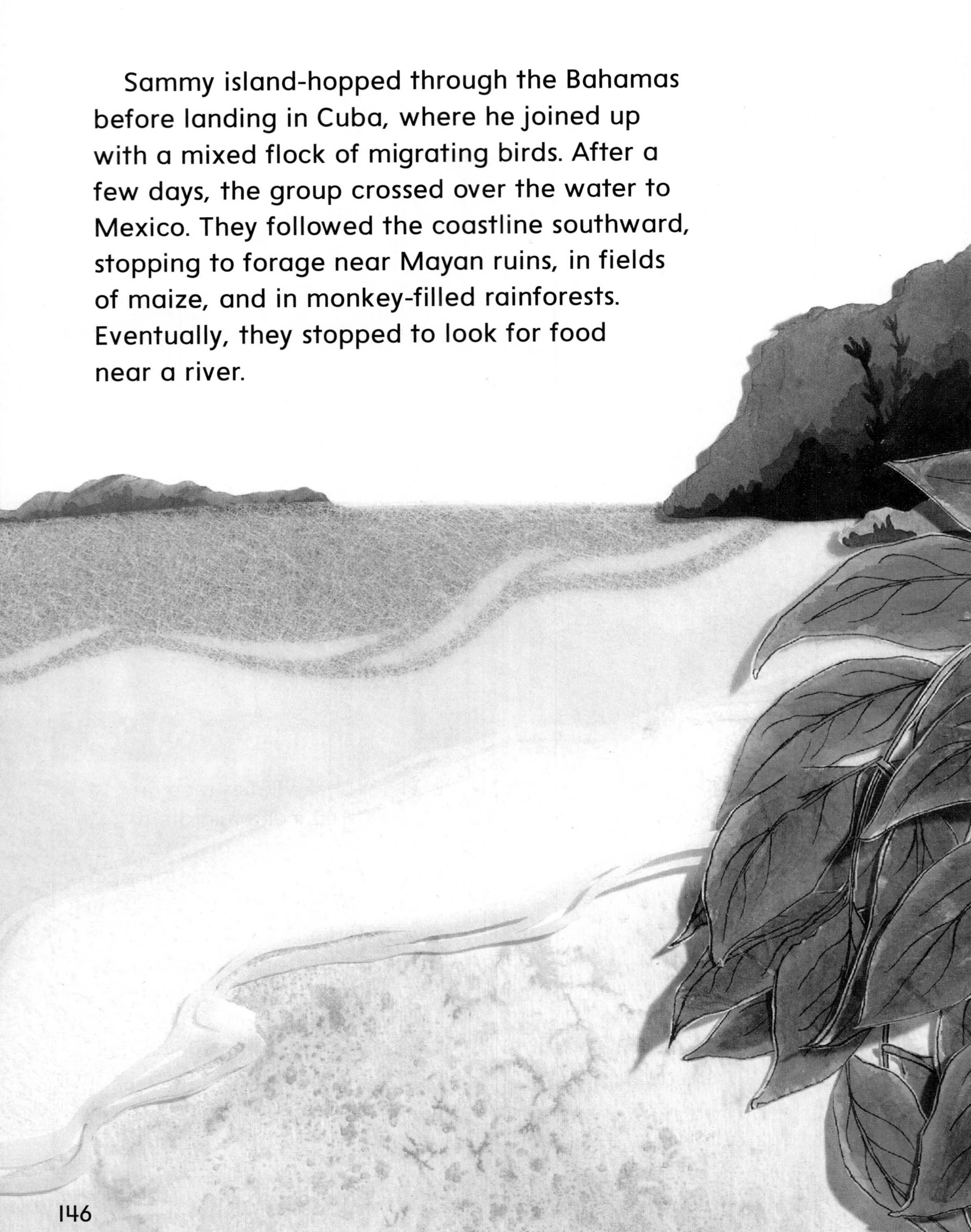

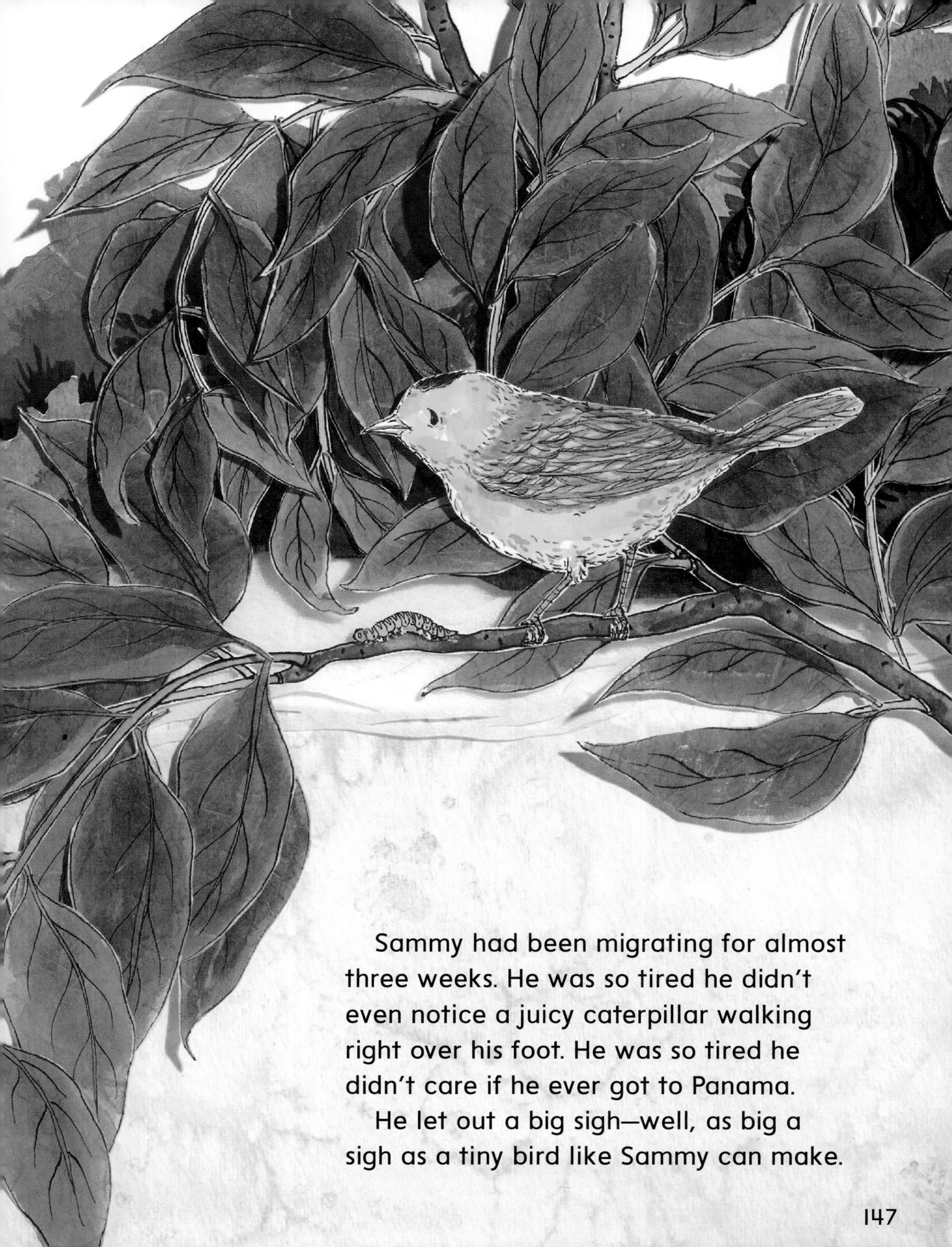

Sammy had been migrating for almost three weeks. He was so tired he didn't even notice a juicy caterpillar walking right over his foot. He was so tired he didn't care if he ever got to Panama.

He let out a big sigh—well, as big a sigh as a tiny bird like Sammy can make.

That's when he noticed something peculiar about the thicket. Sammy suddenly felt all quivery inside. And then he understood. He wouldn't have to ask anyone where he was anymore. Because he knew where he was.

Sammy was in Panama! He'd made it to his winter home.

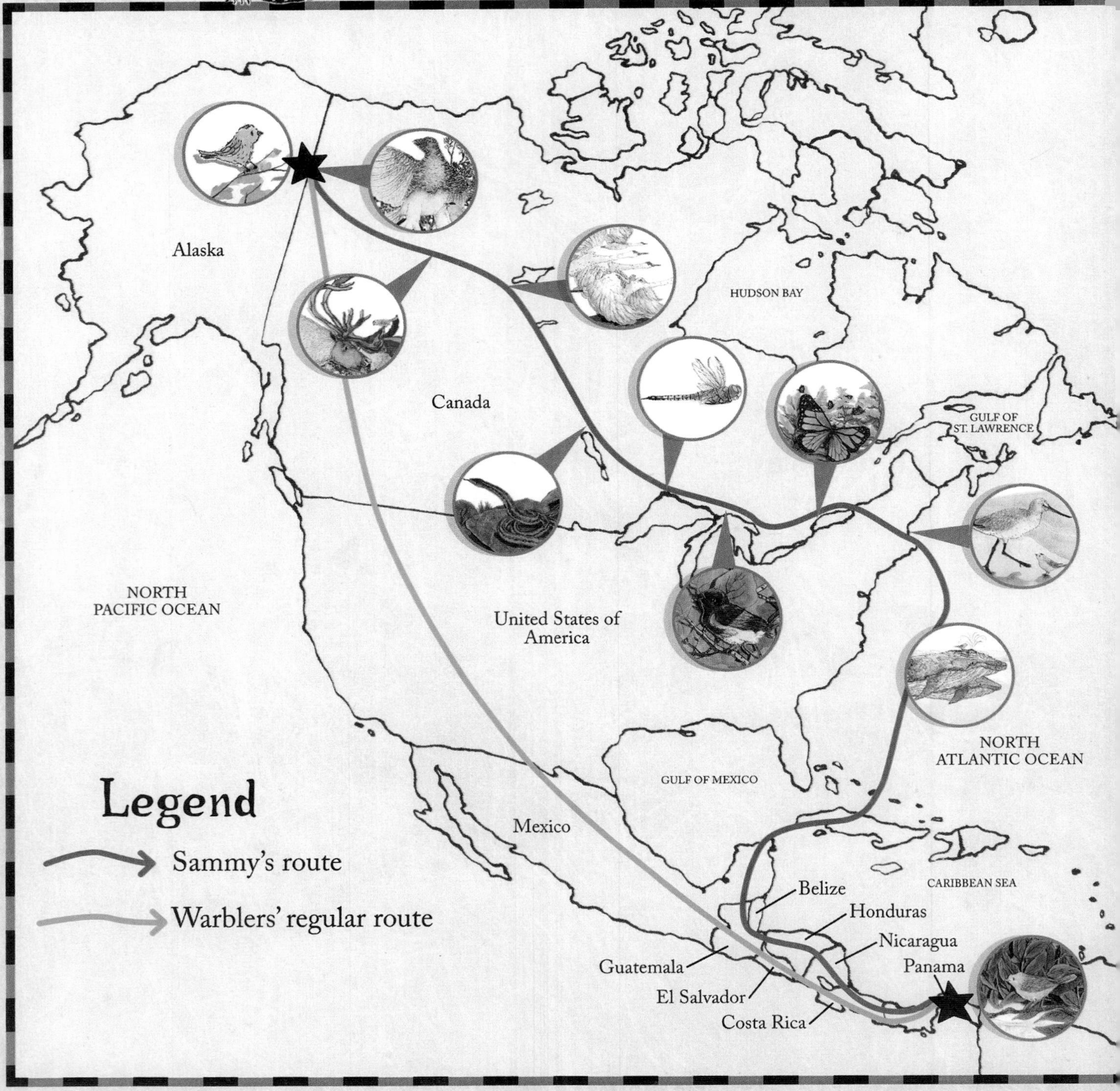

Alaska

Canada

HUDSON BAY

GULF OF ST. LAWRENCE

NORTH PACIFIC OCEAN

United States of America

NORTH ATLANTIC OCEAN

GULF OF MEXICO

Mexico

CARIBBEAN SEA

Belize

Honduras

Nicaragua

Panama

Guatemala

El Salvador

Costa Rica

Legend

Sammy's route

Warblers' regular route

Dangers of Migration

The greatest danger for migrating birds is storms, but human-made objects are dangerous, too. Millions of birds die each year by striking windows when they become confused at night by artificial lights or during the day when they see outdoor reflections in glass. Even pets are dangerous. Many millions of bird deaths could be prevented each year by keeping house cats indoors, particularly during the spring and fall migration seasons.

Wintering Grounds

Every year, millions of birds make the long round trip between their northern breeding grounds and their wintering grounds in the south. In recent years, fewer and fewer of these birds are making it back to their summer homes. This is mostly because of habitat loss in tropical countries as forests are cleared to make way for farms. One of the ways we can help is to buy bird-friendly chocolate and coffee. When cacao and coffee are grown under the shade of trees, instead of in open fields, the trees provide a more natural habitat for northern migrants.

You will answer the comprehension questions on these pages as a class.

Text Connections

1. Why does the Wilson's warbler travel from Alaska to Panama?
2. Why do you think Sammy is in Alaska at the beginning of the story?
3. Migration is an example of a behavioral adaptation, or change. Animals usually do not change their behaviors unless their survival depends on it. Think about the other selections in this unit. What is another selection in which animals changed their behavior? What was the change, and what caused it?
4. What are some ways that people can help Wilson's warblers as they migrate from Alaska to Panama?

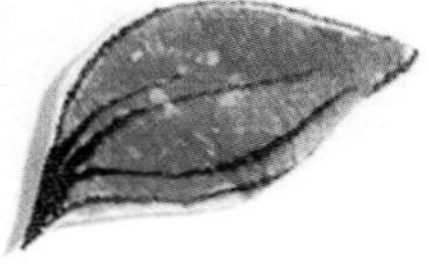

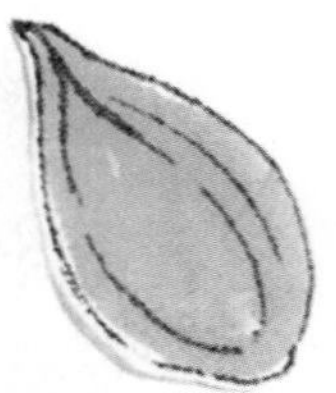

Did You Know?

Sometimes groups of Wilson's warblers are called *bouquets* or *confusions.*

Look Closer

Keys to Comprehension

1. Think about the other animals that Sammy meets during his migration. What are their reasons for migrating?
2. How do the migrating animals know where to go?

Writer's Craft

3. Some writers use a type of figurative language called *onomatopoeia*. In onomatopoeia, a word is used to imitate a sound. Reread page 136. Where is the example of onomatopoeia? What sound does it imitate?
4. A sidebar is an added section on a page that gives more information. What kinds of information are included in the sidebars for "Is This Panama?"

Concept Development

5. Look at the illustration on pages 136–137. What does it help you understand about the setting of this part of the story?

Write

Sammy met lots of other animals. Describe one of his encounters from the perspective of the animal he met.

Read the story. Then discuss it with your class.

Vocabulary Words

- chemical
- landed
- ominous
- organ
- probe
- reproduce
- routes
- ruins
- scoop
- strange
- undercoat
- vast

The Flight Home

As the airplane took off, I felt my stomach drop. The plane climbed and climbed into the air. Then finally it evened out its course, and it felt like my internal organs returned to their natural positions.

It would be four hours before we landed again, so I took out my painting sketchbook and flipped through its pages to pass the time. The pages contained scenes of ruins that I had visited and tried to reproduce. Most of the paintings were complete. However, one had been abandoned. All I had managed to paint was its undercoat. I would have to paint in the rest of the scene's details from my memory later on.

I noticed the undercoat was mottled from rain—a reminder of the storm that had blown in as I painted it. Dark clouds had gathered ominously above, so I had scooped up my belongings quickly. But I still had been caught in the cloudburst. It had been lucky that the unfinished painting was the only one that got wet.

Tired of my sketchbook, I shifted my attention to the views outside my window. The airplane's route was taking us over vast stretches of farmland. It was strangely mesmerizing to watch the fields pass below.

Now, a few hours later, the airplane has started its descent. Soon, the chemical smell of jet fuel will sting my nose as I leave the plane. My parents will greet me with probing questions about my vacation. Then finally, before I know it, I will be back home.

Concept Vocabulary

Think about the word *migration*. Would you rather be an animal that migrates over land, by air, or through the sea?

Extend Vocabulary

Answer and explain the following questions. Record your answers in your Writer's Notebook.

- What is more **ominous,** a thundercloud or a sunny day?
- What are some things you might **scoop?**
- List three things that are **vast.**

Read this Science Connection. You will answer the questions as a class.

Text Feature

Diagrams are drawings. They show the arrangement or parts of something.

Magnets and Magnetic Fields

In "Is This Panama?" you read about animals that use Earth's magnetic field to guide them. But what is a magnetic field?

A magnet is an object that attracts or repels other magnets. When a magnet *attracts,* it pulls another magnet toward it. When a magnet *repels,* it pushes another magnet away.

Every magnet has two poles, or ends. One end is its north pole, and the other end is its south pole. The north pole of one magnet repels the north pole of another magnet. Also, the south pole of one magnet repels the south pole of another magnet. However, the magnets' north and south poles attract each other.

This is where magnetic fields come in. Try this: Place two magnets near each other. Then slowly push them together. If the south pole of one magnet faces the north pole of the other, there is a point at which the two magnets will travel toward each other. They will go all by themselves and then snap together. However, if like poles face each other, there is a point at which you will feel the magnets resisting. This force is its magnetic field.

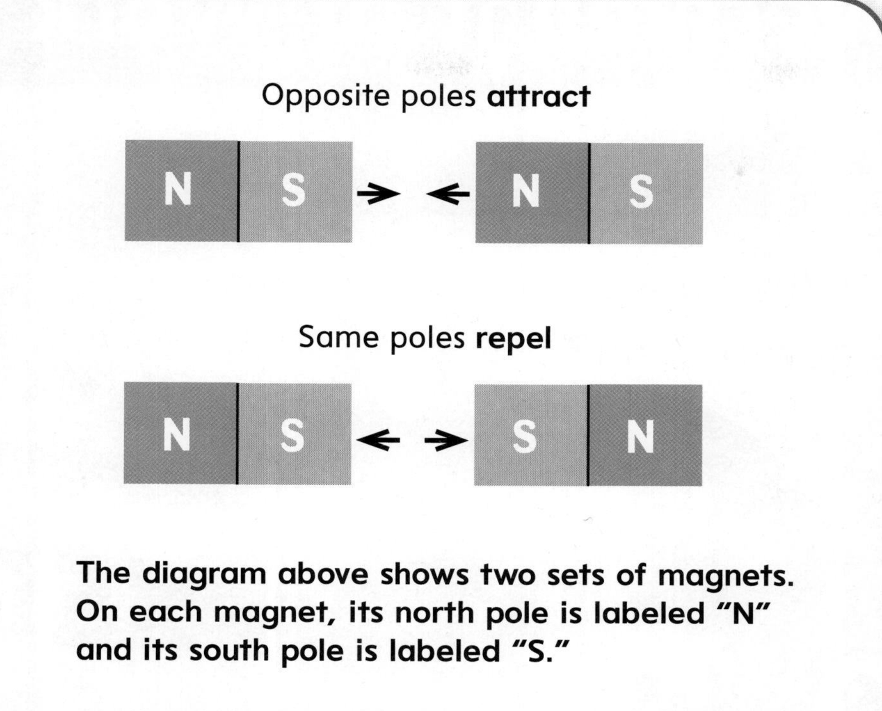

The diagram above shows two sets of magnets. On each magnet, its north pole is labeled "N" and its south pole is labeled "S."

1. Do you find this diagram to be helpful? Explain your answer.
2. Explain what "opposite poles" are.
3. The arrows in this diagram represent magnetic force. Where do the arrows point when magnets attract? Where do the arrows point when magnets repel?

Go Digital

What are magnets made of? How do magnetic fields affect life on Earth?

UNIT 5

Government at Work

Why do we need a government?

Theme Connections

What kinds of decisions are being made?

Background Builder Video
connected.mcgraw-hill.com

Genre Informational Text/Myth

Essential Questions

What are some ways that people make decisions as a group? What ways are the easiest? What ways are the most fair?

The Road to Democracy

by Chandler Tyrell

Power of the People

Democracy: a government run by the people. It sounds like such a simple idea. Yet this idea was powerful enough to change the world.

In a democracy, citizens get their power through voting. Each citizen gets one vote, and after all the votes are counted, the person, law, or plan with the most votes is the winner. It is a simple and fair way to make decisions that affect everyone. It is also a peaceful way to run a country.

Throughout much of history, leaders gave up their power only when forced to do it. It often took a war or a revolution to force a leader from power. But for more than 200 years in America, leadership has changed hands peacefully.

After each election, the men or women who were not reelected give up their power without a fight. New leaders take their places. Today, many of the world's governments are democracies. As a result, the world has become a safer place.

The Roots of Democracy

Perhaps the most important event in the history of democracy was the American Revolution. For a long time, the King of Great Britain ruled the American colonies. The colonists had little say about how they were governed. However, they felt that one person having so much power was an unfair way to run a government.

When Thomas Jefferson wrote the Declaration of Independence, he stressed that each person was important. Each person should be treated equally. Each person had rights, including the right to help make decisions about how the government was run. The new nation would be a democracy.

IN CONGRESS, JULY 4, 1776.

The unanimous Declaration of the thirteen united States of America,

When in the Course of human events, it becomes necessary for one people to dissolve the political bands which have connected them with another, and to assume among the powers of the earth, the separate and equal station to which the Laws of Nature and of Nature's God entitle them, a decent respect to the opinions of mankind requires that they should declare the causes which impel them to the separation. —— We hold these truths to be self-evident, that all men are created equal, that they are endowed by their Creator with certain unalienable Rights, that among these are Life, Liberty and the pursuit of Happiness. — That to secure these rights, Governments are instituted among Men, deriving their just powers from the consent of the governed, — That whenever any Form of Government becomes destructive of these ends, it is the Right of the People to alter or to abolish it, and to institute new Government, laying its foundation on such principles and organizing its powers in such form, as to them shall seem most likely to effect their Safety and Happiness. Prudence, indeed, will dictate that Governments long established should not be changed for light and transient causes; and accordingly all experience hath shewn, that mankind are more disposed to suffer, while evils are sufferable, than to right themselves by abolishing the forms to which they are accustomed. But when a long train of abuses and usurpations, pursuing invariably the same Object evinces a design to reduce them under absolute Despotism, it is their right, it is their duty, to throw off such Government, and to provide new Guards for their future security. — Such has been the patient sufferance of these Colonies; and such is now the necessity which constrains them to alter their former Systems of Government. The history of the present King of Great Britain is a history of repeated injuries and usurpations, all having in direct object the establishment of an absolute Tyranny over these States. To prove this, let Facts be submitted to a candid world. —— He has refused his Assent to Laws, the most wholesome and necessary for the public good. —— He has forbidden his Governors to pass Laws of immediate and pressing importance, unless suspended in their operation till his Assent should be obtained; and when so suspended, he has utterly neglected to attend to them. —— He has refused to pass other Laws for the accommodation of large districts of people, unless those people would relinquish the right of Representation in the Legislature, a right inestimable to them and formidable to tyrants only. —— He has called together legislative bodies at places unusual, uncomfortable, and distant from the depository of their public Records, for the sole purpose of fatiguing them into compliance with his measures. —— He has dissolved Represtative Houses repeatedly, for opposing with manly firmness his invasions on the rights of the people. —— He has refused for a long time, after such dissolutions, to cause others to be elected; whereby the Legislative powers, incapable of Annihilation, have returned to the People at large for their exercise; the State remaining in the mean time exposed to all the dangers of invasion from without, and convulsions within. —— He has endeavoured to prevent the population of these States; for that purpose obstructing the Laws for Naturalization of Foreigners; refusing to pass others to encourage their migrations hither, and raising the conditions of new Appropriations of Lands. —— He has obstructed the Administration of Justice, by refusing his Assent to Laws for establishing Judiciary powers. —— He has made Judges dependent on his Will alone, for the tenure of their offices, and the amount and payment of their salaries. —— He has erected a multitude of New Offices, and sent hither swarms of Officers to harrass our people, and eat out their substance. —— He has kept among us, in times of peace, Standing Armies without the Consent of our legislatures. —— He has affected to render the Military independent of and superior to the Civil power. —— He has combined with others to subject us to a jurisdiction foreign to our constitution, and unacknowledged by our laws; giving his Assent to their Acts of pretended Legislation: — For Quartering large bodies of armed troops among us: — For protecting them, by a mock Trial, from punishment for any Murders which they should commit on the Inhabitants of these States: — For cutting off our Trade with all parts of the world: — For imposing Taxes on us without our Consent: — For depriving us in many cases, of the benefits of Trial by Jury: — For transporting us beyond Seas to be tried for pretended offences: — For abolishing the free System of English Laws in a neighbouring Province, establishing therein an Arbitrary government, and enlarging its Boundaries so as to render it at once an example and fit instrument for introducing the same absolute rule into these Colonies: — For taking away our Charters, abolishing our most valuable Laws, and altering fundamentally the Forms of our Governments: — For suspending our own Legislatures, and declaring themselves invested with power to legislate for us in all cases whatsoever. — He has abdicated Government here, by declaring us out of his Protection and waging War against us. —— He has plundered our seas, ravaged our Coasts, burnt our towns, and destroyed the lives of our people. —— He is at this time transporting large Armies of foreign Mercenaries to compleat the works of death, desolation and tyranny, already begun with circumstances of Cruelty & perfidy scarcely paralleled in the most barbarous ages, and totally

Thomas Jefferson and the other founders of our country did not invent democracy. The idea of a government run by the people had been around for more than two thousand years. But during all that time, democracies were rare.

The roots of democracy reach back to the 5th century B.C. in ancient Greece. The Greek region of Attica, the birthplace of the world's first democracy, had Athens as its capital city. When decisions needed to be made, all of Attica's citizens came to Athens to vote.

According to Greek myth, the founder of democracy in Attica was a king named Theseus. In addition to being king, Theseus was a powerful and adventurous hero. He sailed the world's seas, fighting invading armies and conquering monsters. One of the most famous stories tells how Theseus defeated the Minotaur.

The Minotaur, a fierce beast, was half-man and half-bull. It lived on the island of Crete and terrorized the people of Athens. Theseus and his men sailed to Crete and defeated the monster.

Another famous myth tells how Theseus and his cousin, Heracles, bravely fought the Amazons. The Amazons, an all-female army of warriors, often attacked Athens. They appear in many Greek legends.

Although King Theseus was known for his bravery, he was also a kind and just king. He often helped the poor. He listened to the opinions of his citizens. Theseus' wisdom gave him the idea of sharing his power.

Many different tribes made up the region of Attica. These tribes often did not get along. Theseus understood that sharing some of his power could help bring peace. If the tribes worked together, they would be less likely to fight. To accomplish this, Theseus gave up his power as king, then visited every city and village. He invited all the citizens to Athens to share in his idea of unity. Democracy was born.

Democracy in the Middle Ages

Of course, the story of Theseus is just a myth, and democracy in Attica was not perfect. It did not include everyone who lived in the region. Citizens could vote, but only certain Greek men counted as citizens. Women and children did not have the right to vote. The thousands of slaves living in Attica were not allowed to vote either.

In time, other forms of government replaced democracy in Greece. During the next two thousand years, democracy was rare. When it did appear, it was limited. For example, in the Roman Empire, wealthy citizens could at times vote for leaders to represent them in the government. But usually, one person or a small group of people still had all the power to make decisions.

Types of Government

monarchy: ruled by a king or queen

dictatorship: ruled by one person

oligarchy: ruled by a small group of people

aristocracy: ruled by the wealthy

democracy: ruled by all the people

During the second half of the Middle Ages (1000–1500 A.D.), kings and queens ruled most nations in Europe. However, some of these nations allowed wealthy landowners to gather together and help decide on new laws. These assemblies of landowners were called *parliaments*.

Some nations' parliaments had more power than others. In 1215, the wealthy landowners of England—called *lords*—forced their king to sign one of history's most important documents, the Magna Carta. When King John signed the Magna Carta, or "Great Charter," it guaranteed some rights to the citizens of England, such as a limit on taxes and protection from illegal imprisonment. This document had a great influence on America's Bill of Rights.

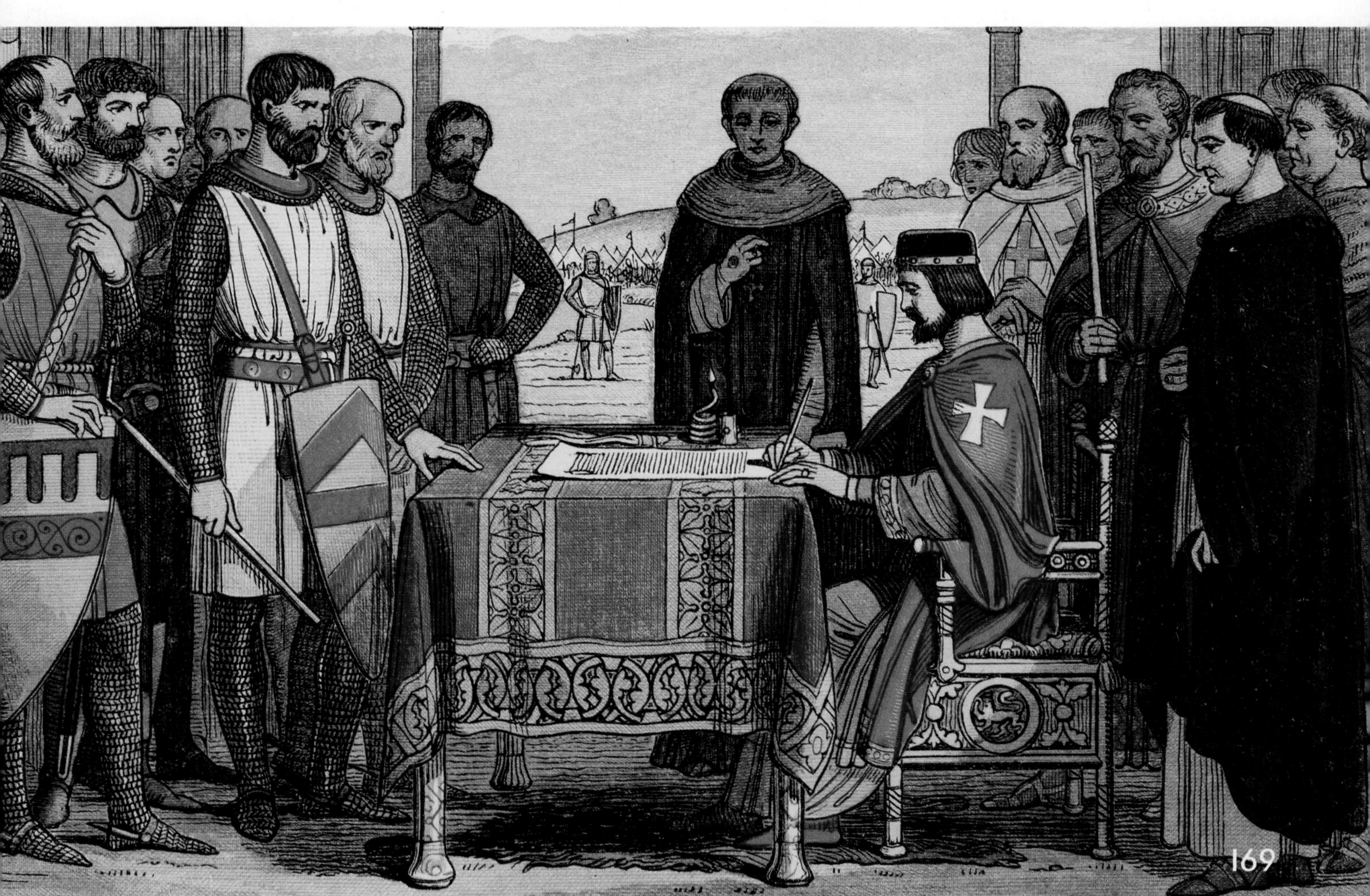

To Form a More Perfect Union

American democracy began imperfectly. Like in ancient Greece, only certain male citizens had the right to vote at first. But as the United States grew in size and population, it also grew to include more voices in its democracy.

With the end of slavery, millions of African American men gained the right to vote. The 14th Amendment to the Constitution, passed in 1868, guaranteed this right. In 1920, the 19th Amendment to the Constitution guaranteed that all women would also have the right to vote.

Voting Milestones in America

1868
The 14th Amendment gave former slaves the right to vote.

1870
The 15th Amendment guaranteed that voting rights could not be taken away because of race or religion.

1900

1920
The 19th Amendment gave women the right to vote.

1961
The 23rd Amendment gave citizens of Washington DC the right to vote for president.

1964
The 24th Amendment states that people do not have to pay a tax in order to vote.

1971
The 26th Amendment set the voting age as 18.

2000

Representative Democracy

The democracy of Ancient Greece was a direct democracy. The people took part *directly* in governing. When laws or other decisions needed to be made, all the citizens came to Athens to vote. This was possible because the population of Athens was small.

The U.S. population is much too large for a direct democracy. So, we have a *representative* democracy. We elect leaders who *represent* us in the government. They vote for us when decisions need to be made.

Even though the people do not rule directly, we have power in deciding who will or will not represent us. Representatives must listen to the people they represent. If they fail to listen, they will not be reelected. New representatives will take their place.

A Growing Trend

Just 150 years ago, the United States was one of the few democracies in the world. During the 20th century, America's wealth and power in the world increased a great deal. The rest of the world took notice. They saw that giving the people a voice and freedom can lead to great success.

During the last part of the 20th century, the number of democracies around the world grew at a fast pace. Most nations have now followed the United States' lead and given their citizens the right to vote. Today, about 60% of the world's countries are some form of democracy.

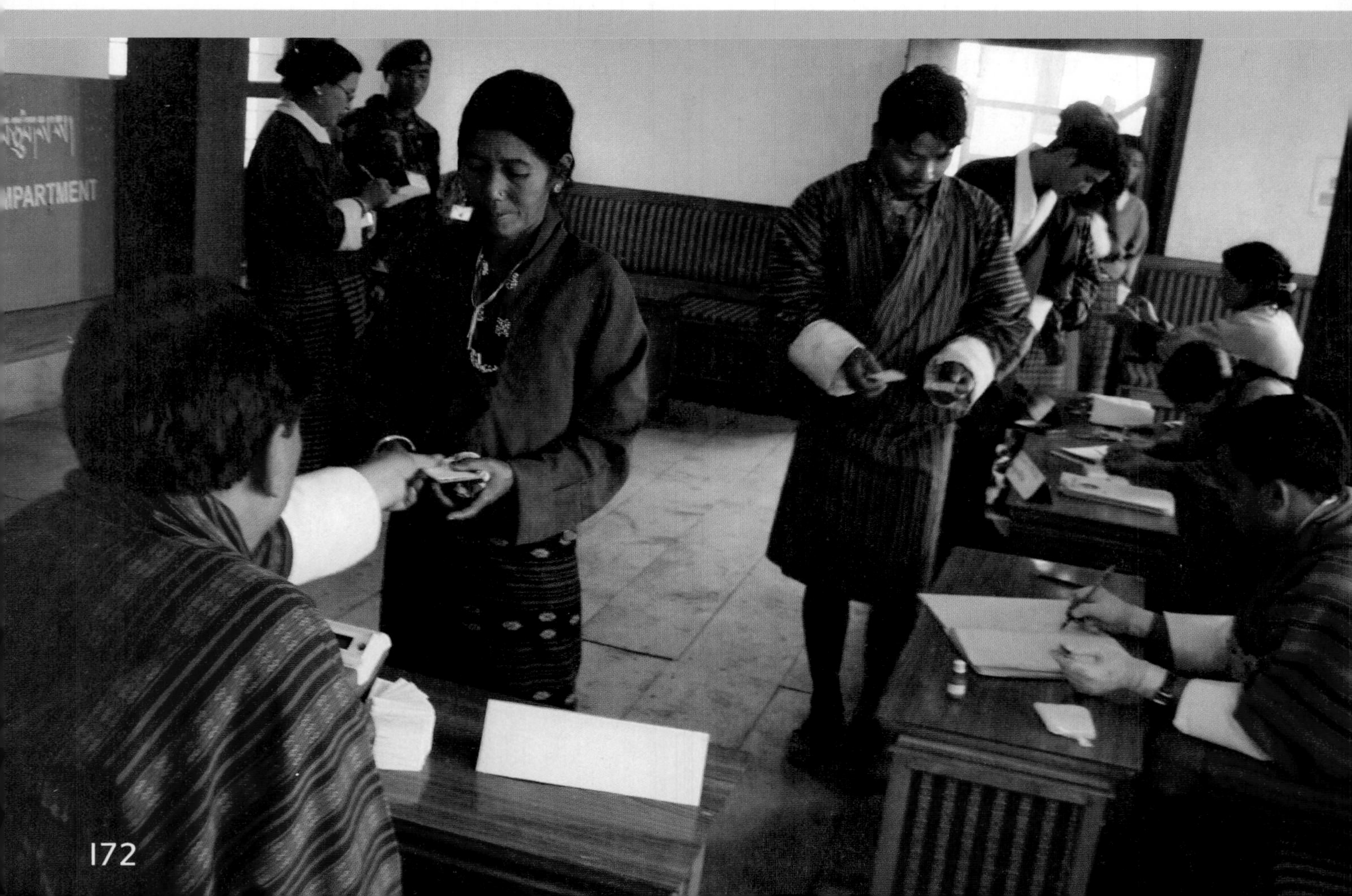

One person, one vote. It is a simple idea, but it has taken thousands of years to develop. And as democracy spreads, the world has become safer and more connected. More importantly, it has given more people a chance to have a voice in the decisions that affect their lives.

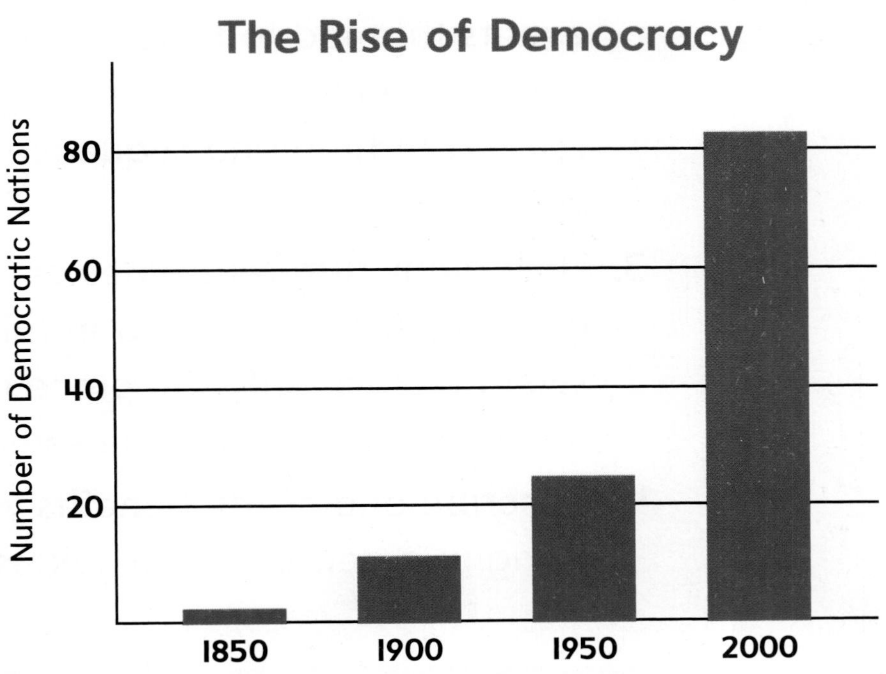

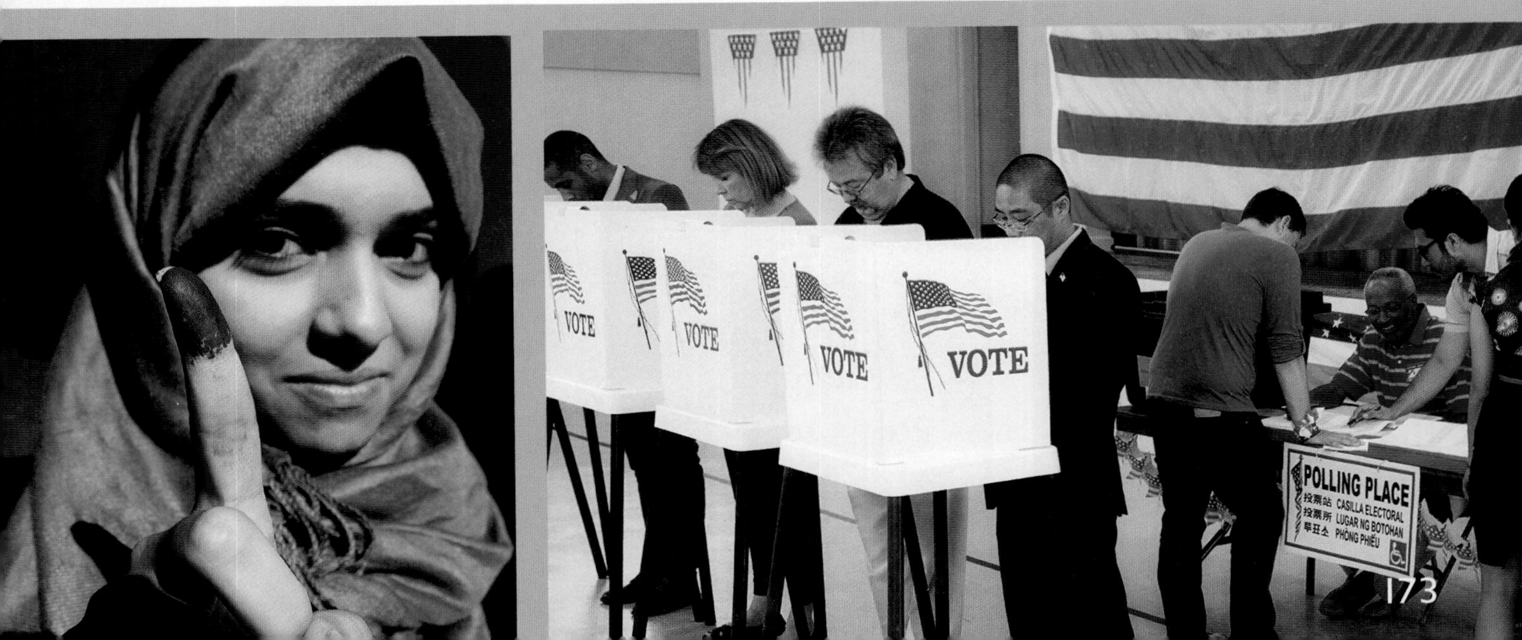

You will answer the comprehension questions on these pages as a class.

Text Connections

1. Where was the first democracy? In what century was this democracy created?
2. What are some of the historical events that led to today's growing trend of democracy? Use language related to time and sequence in your answer.
3. How many different types of government are defined in this selection? Identify the place in the text that provides your answer.
4. Describe one of the benefits you think living in a democracy provides you.

Did You Know?

The city of Athens was named after the Greek goddess Athena.

Look Closer

Keys to Comprehension

1. How does the central message of the myth of Theseus relate to the rest of this selection? Explain the key details that help you determine this message.
2. What was one of the rights guaranteed by the Magna Carta? Where did you find your answer?

Writer's Craft

3. Think about the phrase "Democracy was born" on page 167. What does this phrase mean? Is it literal language or nonliteral language?

Concept Development

4. Look at the timeline on page 170. Who was guaranteed the right to vote first, women or 18-year-olds? What voting right was protected in 1870? Do voters have to pay a tax in order to vote?
5. How are the sentences in the first paragraph on page 170 connected?

Write

Describe what King John might have felt when he was forced to sign the Magna Carta by the English lords.

Read the story. Then discuss it with your class.

Vocabulary Words

- colonists
- documents
- election
- empire
- government
- nation
- peaceful
- region
- revolution
- trend
- unity
- vote

The Struggle for Freedom

"We just want our freedom!" Josie pleaded.

Josie's social studies class was studying the thirteen colonies and their fight for independence from England. Josie and Garrett were playing two colonists, while Kyle and Lola were acting as two different English leaders.

"Why is freedom trending right now? If you want your country to have freedom, you are going to have to fight for it!" said Kyle.

"That is what we will do!" Josie declared. "Uniting our colonies as one nation is important to us."

"We would prefer to do this peacefully, too," Garrett said. "We tried writing documents, but so far England has refused to cooperate."

"You are the ones who won't cooperate!" Kyle shouted. "You continue to break our laws."

"Your laws are unfair," Josie argued. "You control all of the regions in your empire from England. You don't know what we need here."

"Fine," said Kyle. "Go ahead and revolt if you must. You will regret it. You do not have enough soldiers. Besides, even if you win you will still have a lot of work ahead of you. You will need to create your own form of government."

"In our government, everyone would vote to elect representatives from each colony to serve them," Josie explained. "That way, every person has someone to represent him or her."

"War it is, then," said Lola. "I can't believe freedom means this much to you."

"As a citizen of this new nation," Garrett said, "freedom means everything to us."

Concept Vocabulary

Think about the word *representation*. What is a way you have represented a group of people?

Extend Vocabulary

Copy the word web into your Writer's Notebook. Fill it in with words related to *nation*.

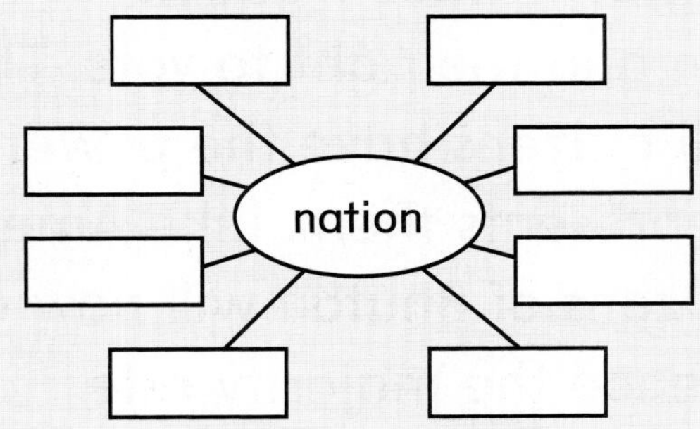

Read this Social Studies Connection. You will answer the questions as a class.

Text Feature

Parentheses can be used to separate a clarifying phrase within a sentence.

A New Democracy

Bhutan is a country that started its democracy in 2008. Unlike America, Bhutan had its first democratic election in your lifetime. Bhutan has a Parliament, which is their legislative branch. In their first election, they elected 47 new members into their National Assembly, which could be compared to the U.S. House of Representatives.

The people of Bhutan were so excited to have democracy that almost 80% of them (4 out of every 5 people) voted in the first election. In some cases, new democratic elections cause people to be angry. Sometimes, people even react violently to the change. In Bhutan, however, the first Election Day was a mostly peaceful event.

In 2008, Bhutan approved a new constitution calling Bhutan a democratic nation. Like the U.S. Constitution, the constitution of Bhutan guarantees that their citizens have freedom of speech and religion and the right to vote. This ensures that all citizens have the power to change who represents them. Like Americans, the citizens of Bhutan will now get to experience the majority rule.

Bhutanese citizens line up to vote in an election.

1. What information is in parentheses? What does it help clarify?
2. Bhutan, like America, was originally a monarchy. How is a democracy different from a monarchy?
3. What is the function of a democratic government?

Go Digital

Search for other countries with democracies. Find out if any others have been created since you were born. Look up how those countries transitioned into a democracy.

Genre Fable/Informational Text

Essential Questions

How do elections work? Why is it important for citizens to participate in elections?

Every VOTE Counts

by Lisa Kurkov
illustrated by London Ladd

One day, a miller and his son were walking their donkey to town to sell. They passed by a group of women, who laughed and pointed. "What a foolish pair, to walk when the donkey could be carrying you."

The miller urged his son to climb on the donkey's back. It wasn't long before they came to several men by the road. "What a lazy boy you have there!" shouted one. "To think that he rides while his poor old father must walk."

The boy immediately climbed down so that his father could take his place. Before long, they came to several women and children. "What is this?" shouted one woman. "You ride while your poor son must struggle to keep up with you and your donkey?"

The miller looked ashamed and pulled his son onto the donkey with him. They had settled into a steady pace when they came to a judge.

"Why must that poor old donkey carry the two of you? It would be far easier for *you* to carry *him* than the other way around!"

The miller and his son looked sheepish as they got off the donkey. They tied his feet together and hung him upside down from a pole so that they could carry him. As they crossed the bridge into town, a group of townspeople began to laugh at the sight of the two carrying the donkey. The laughter startled the donkey, and he kicked, breaking free of the ropes. He fell into the river, was quickly swept downstream, and when he finally made it to the riverbank, ran off and disappeared out of sight. The miller and his son turned, hung their heads, and walked home without their donkey.

Moral: If you try to please everyone, you will end up pleasing no one at all.

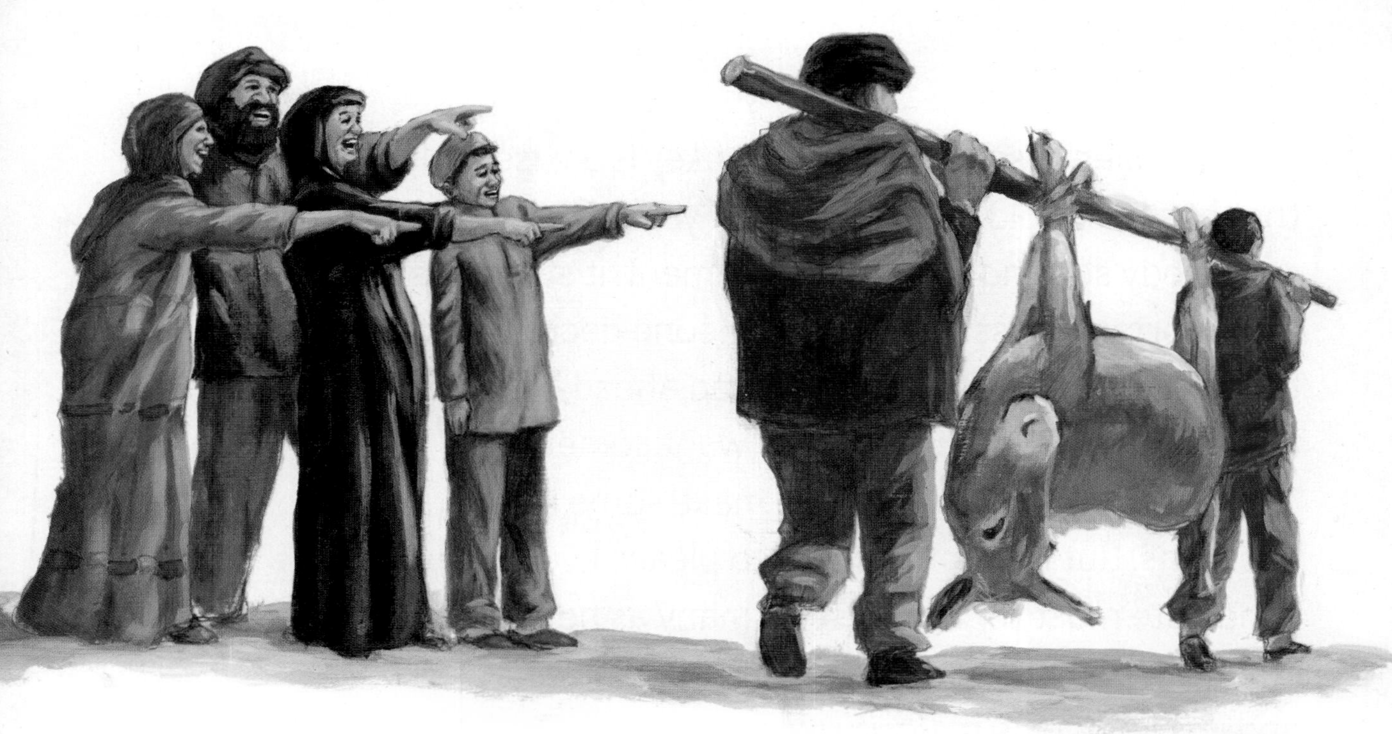

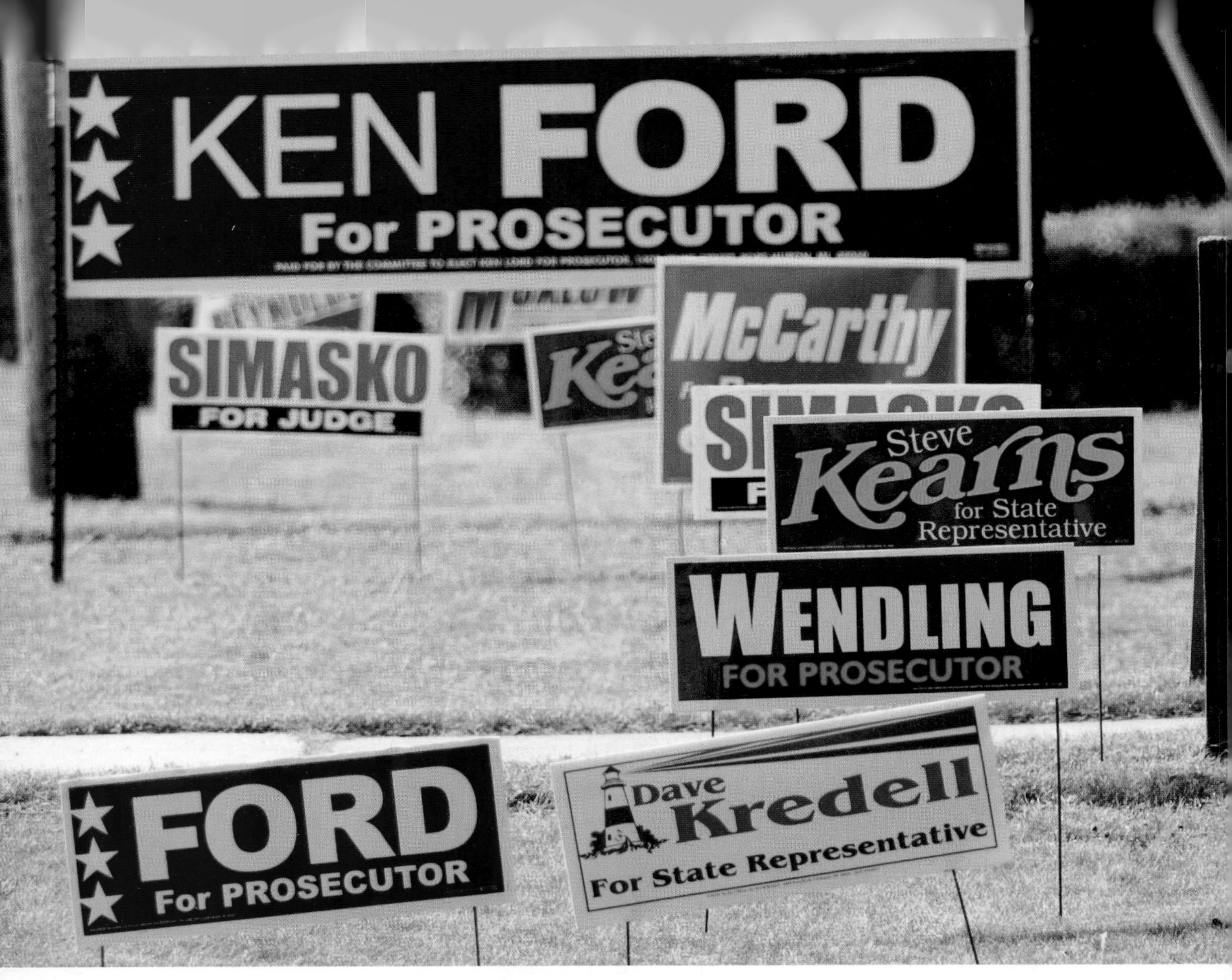

The Miller, His Son, and the Donkey is a wise fable that has been told for hundreds of years. And for somebody seeking a job in government, it still holds an important message. Once someone decides to run for office, he or she has a hard road ahead. There are many voters, and each one may want something different. The candidate has to make some tough decisions. But it is not possible to please everyone, so a candidate must try to please as many as he or she can. That is the foundation of how our government works and it is known as *majority rule.*

When Election Day draws nearer, you might notice signs on lawns and along streets. You will see numerous ads for candidates running for office. Your parents may receive phone calls from volunteers who want to talk about the candidates they support. Candidates themselves might even come to your door to say hello. They want as many voters as possible to know who they are and what they support. Election Day is coming, and every vote counts!

Many Americans take the right to vote for granted. It is good to remember, though, that we are lucky to live in a place where the voices of the citizens are heard. That is why voting and elections are so important. They give every citizen a chance to help decide how the country will be governed. Every vote is equal, regardless of who votes. Because we use majority rule, our government is guided by what the most people want.

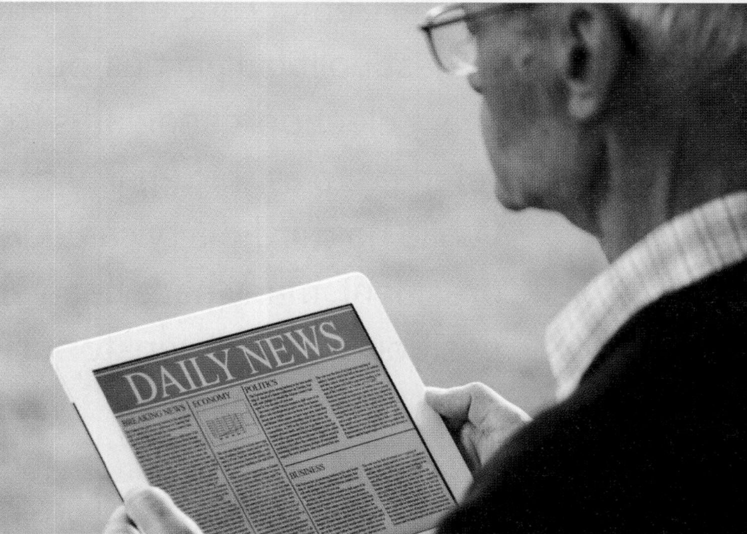

So what is voting? Why have people worked so hard to be able to participate in elections? An election is a way to choose leaders. Every four years, voters elect the next president of the United States—the most important office in our country. Many other people also play a major role in the leadership of the country, states, and towns. Voters also elect governors, senators, mayors, judges, and city council members. Even the town sheriff and dogcatcher have elected offices!

Voters need to learn as much as they can about the candidates before they vote. They can read articles in the newspaper or online. They can listen to the candidates speak. Voters look for the candidates whose views reflect their own.

Before a major election takes place, the political parties pick their candidates. Then the candidates often have a debate. A moderator asks questions. Each candidate has a chance to answer. This helps voters get a clear idea of where the candidates stand and what kind of leaders they might be.

The Democratic and Republican parties are the two largest political parties, but they are not the only ones. Every election, candidates from other parties, often referred to as third-party candidates, run for office. While no third-party candidate has been elected president, many have been elected to prominent positions such as senator or state governor.

People vote for more than just leaders. They can also vote for or against issues. Should a new highway be built through town? Should taxes be raised to pay for schools? Should an area be developed for a shopping mall? The voters decide these issues too.

On Election Day, voters cast their ballot for the candidates and issues they support. But did you know that when you vote in a presidential election, your vote does not go directly to the president? Instead, it goes to an elector. An elector is a member of the Electoral College, the group that decides who will be the next president. After citizens have voted, their elector votes for president. The elector chooses the candidate his or her voters want.

Each state has a certain number of electors. States with larger populations have more electors. For example, Florida has a large population. It has many more electors than North Dakota, which has a much smaller population.

There are 538 electoral votes in all. A candidate has to receive the majority of the votes—at least 270—to win an election.

Electors are supposed to vote for the candidate that voters want, but sometimes they don't! When an elector chooses a different candidate, he or she is known as a faithless elector. Faithless electors go against majority rule. Most voters feel betrayed by faithless electors. Many states have laws that punish electors who do not vote for the candidate that voters want.

ELECTORAL VOTES BY STATE, 2010–2020

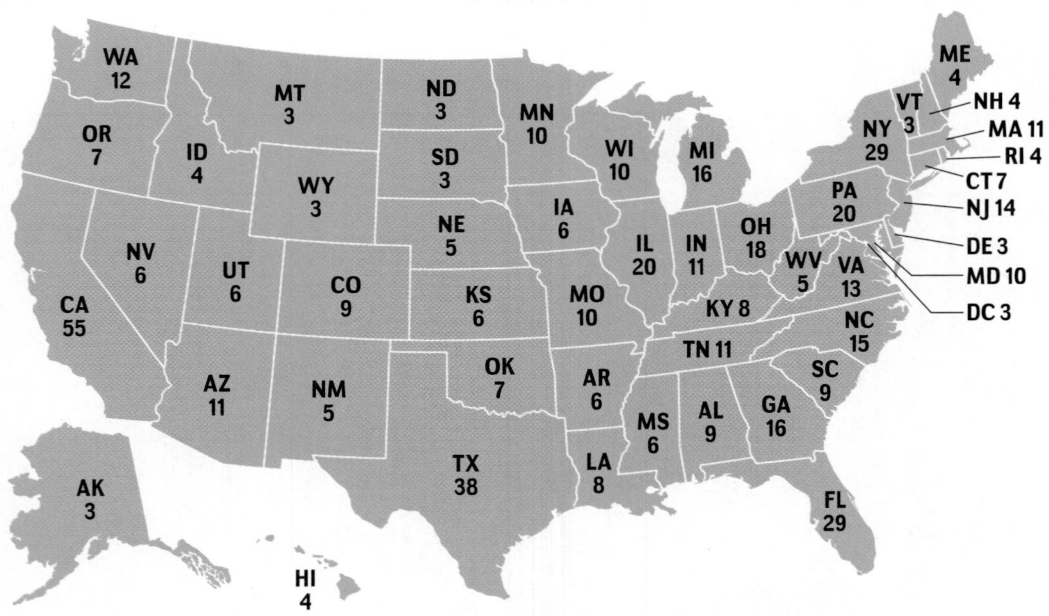

THE STEPS OF RUNNING FOR PRESIDENT

A person decides to run for president.

↓

He or she travels to get the word out, raise money, and campaign.

↓

In primary elections, Democrats and Republicans in each state vote for a candidate in their party to run for president.

↓

Democrats and Republicans separately hold huge national conventions. At each convention, delegates from each state vote for the candidates they want for president. The candidate with the most votes becomes the party's choice to run for president. These candidates will run against each other in the presidential election.

↓

The nominees for each party begin to travel around the country. They give speeches, meet the citizens, have debates, raise money, and let the people know where they stand on the issues.

↓

In November, citizens go to the polls and cast their votes for the candidate that best represents their views.

It may seem strange, but a candidate for president can win the election without receiving the most votes! In 2000, Al Gore received more total votes than George Bush. But Bush received more electoral votes, so he won the presidency.

After citizens have cast their vote and polling places have closed, the votes are counted. This can take some time, depending on how close the election is. In the election of 2000, it took 36 days for the votes to be counted and recounted! It was a close race between Al Gore and George Bush. Bush was finally declared the winner.

Although you will be too young to vote for a number of years, you can still get involved now. You can support a candidate you like by putting up posters or yard signs. Organize a mock election in your school where students can vote in the next election. If you feel strongly about an issue, contact an elected official to tell him or her your views. Even if you cannot vote yet, you are still a citizen and your voice can be heard!

Essential Question
What would happen if nobody voted?

Election Day

by Angela Parker
illustrated by Luciana Powell

Today it is election day,
and at the polls we're free
to cast a vote and celebrate
our democracy.

Today we'll exercise a right
that our forefathers wrote.
The future of this nation
still depends on every vote.

Are you ready? Now it's time
to make a careful choice.
Today it is election day,
a day to use your voice.

vote for JUAN!
Katie For CLASS President
Haiying wants YOUR vote!
VOTES

You will answer the comprehension questions on these pages as a class.

Text Connections

1. Why does the selection say that "every vote counts"?
2. What are the two most popular political parties in the United States?
3. What is something else that voters vote for in this country, besides candidates to fill job positions? Use evidence from the text to support your answer.
4. In what ways does the poem "Election Day" relate to the selection "Every Vote Counts"?

Did You Know?

Presidential elections are held every four years on the first Tuesday *after* the first Monday in November. That means the election will always be between November 2 and November 8.

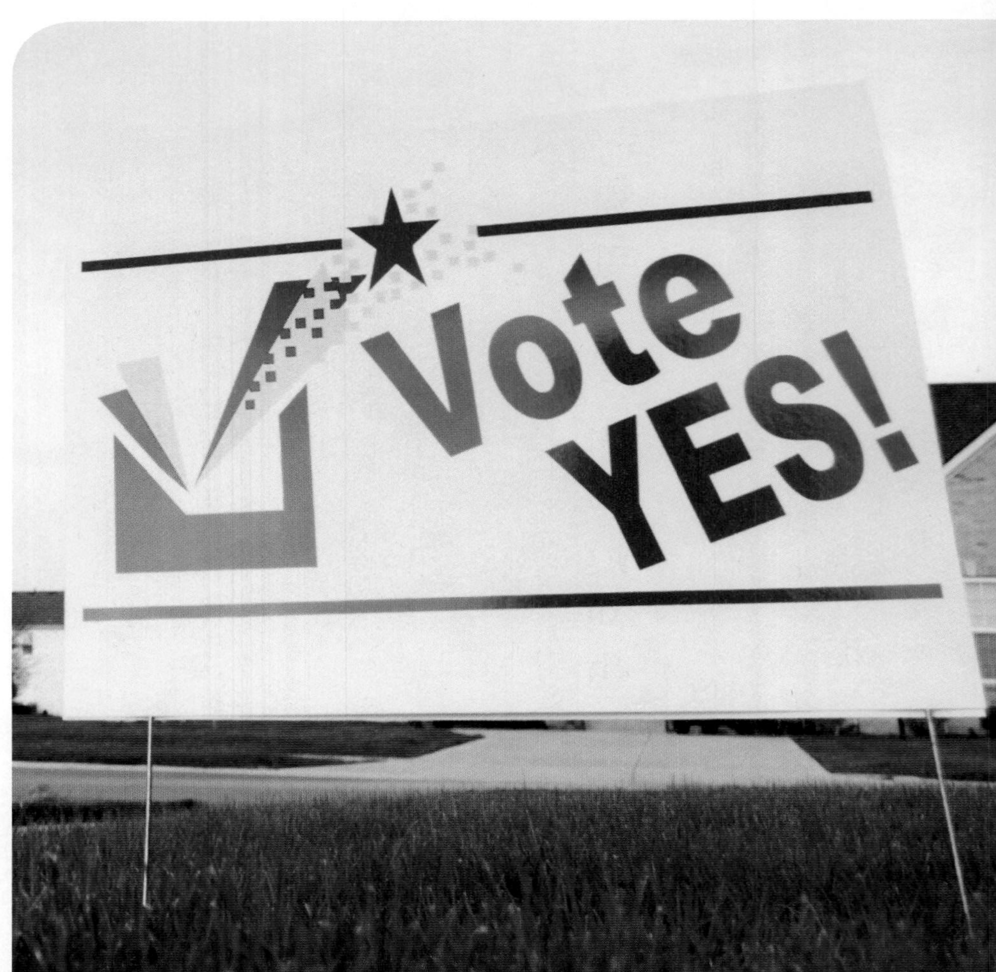

Look Closer

Keys to Comprehension

1. What are some things you can do to get involved in our democracy?
2. What is the moral of "The Miller, His Son, and the Donkey"? What are the key details that convey this moral?

Writer's Craft

3. What is the meaning of the phrase "a day to use your voice" in the poem? Why do you think the speaker uses this phrase?
4. Where would you look in "Every Vote Counts" to find out more information about what happened in the 2000 presidential election?

Concept Development

5. Which state has the highest amount of electoral votes? How many votes do they get? Which state has the lowest amount? How many do they get? What does the map tell you about each state's population?

Write

Continue the fable from the beginning of this selection. What do you think the miller and his son said to each other as they returned home? Do you think they learned a lesson? Explain it in their dialogue.

Read the story. Then discuss it with your class.

Vocabulary Words

- **ashamed**
- **candidate**
- **decisions**
- **foundation**
- **immediately**
- **moral**
- **numerous**
- **pace**
- **participate**
- **populations**
- **prominent**
- **volunteers**

Door to Door

"Hi, my name is Angela. I hope you'll support my father, Michael McCann, on Tuesday. He is a candidate for City Council," I say proudly to the woman standing in her doorway.

"Wow, he is a very prominent politician," the woman says. Numerous people tell me this when I talk about my father.

"Yes, he is!" I agree. I have been volunteering for my father for the past few months. Today we are going door to door handing out flyers about my father's political foundation. One thing he wants to do is work with a group to clean up the river. He wants to help make many decisions for the city. We are trying to talk to the entire population of our city by Tuesday!

"How many people are helping you today?" the woman asks.

"It's just me and my father today," I tell her. I ashamedly admit that more people are not participating today. "But we're working very hard!" I'm working so hard, my father can't keep up with my pace. He is two houses behind me.

When I hear him shout for me to wait up, I immediately turn around.

"Okay!" I shout back. The woman laughs.

"I guess the moral you learned is that faster isn't always better," she says.

"Maybe not!" I say with a laugh.

Concept Vocabulary

Think about the word *leadership*. What does it mean to be a leader?

Extend Vocabulary

For each of the vocabulary words that follow, provide one antonym, synonym, or related word.

- ashamed
- numerous
- prominent
- leadership

Read this Social Studies Connection. You will answer the questions as a class.

Text Feature

A **map** shows the location, size, and shape of an area.

Party Time

Democrats and Republicans have not always been the two main political parties in America.

In 1834, the Whig party was formed. The Whigs named themselves after the political party in England that was opposed to the monarchy. They did this because they feared that President Andrew Jackson was gaining too much power. They even called him "King Andrew" to mock him.

The Whig party has been called supporters of businesses, free education, and a strong national government. However, they did not support the expansion of U.S. lands. In 1834, there were only 24 states in the union.

Between 1836 and 1860, the Whigs had ten candidates run for president. Four Whigs served as president; they were William Henry Harrison, John Tyler, Zachary Taylor, and Millard Fillmore.

In the 1850s, the Whig Party lost prominence and merged into the newly-formed Republican Party. Though the Whigs are no longer around, their legacy lives on in the presidents that were elected from their party.

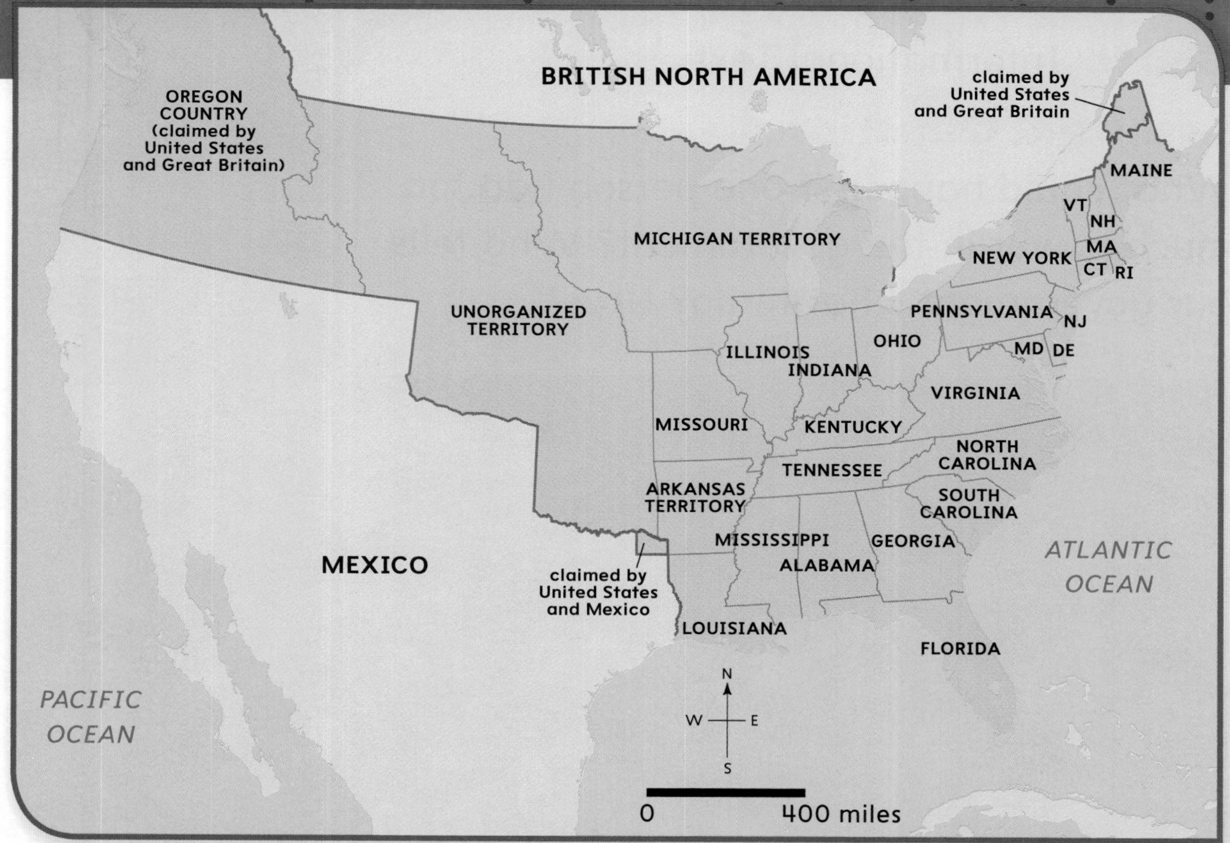

In 1834, there were only 24 states. The Whigs opposed creating more because there was a risk of going to war with other countries that had a claim on the land.

1. What does this map show? What does it add to your understanding of the Whig Party?
2. What can we learn from past political parties?
3. What sorts of events might change the way a nation views a certain political party?

Go Digital

Find out more about the Whig Party. Discover what their political views were and when they were popular. Find more notable politicians from that party.

Genre Informational Text

Essential Questions

What could happen if one person had too much power in the government? Who tells our government what to do? How?

How Congress Works

by Phillip Jackson

In the United States, citizens elect leaders. Some of the leaders we elect make laws. For example, we have laws that protect our health and laws that make sure people are treated fairly. Where do these laws come from? They are created by the part of government called Congress. Congress is also known as the legislative branch of government. *Legislative* means "relating to making laws." There are two other branches of government: the executive branch and the judicial branch. The president and the vice-president lead the executive branch. They enforce the laws. The Supreme Court leads the judicial branch. They interpret the laws, or make decisions about when a law should or should not be followed.

The Supreme Court Building is part of the judicial branch of government.

Congress is made up of two chambers, or parts. The founders of the United States designed Congress this way for a reason. They wanted power to be shared and important decisions about new laws to be considered by both groups. This keeps one group from becoming too powerful and taking over control of the government. The founders of the United States called this a system of "checks and balances." The two chambers of Congress that keep a check on each other are the Senate and the House of Representatives.

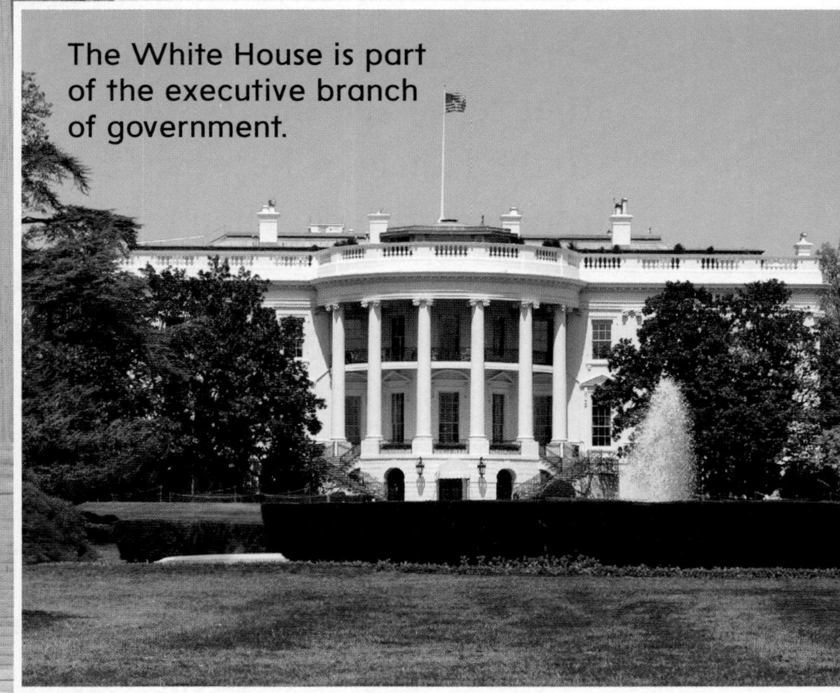

The White House is part of the executive branch of government.

People elected to serve in the Senate are called senators. Each state has two senators that represent it, which means we have 100 senators that represent the 50 states. People elected to the House of Representatives are called representatives. They might also be called congressmen or congresswomen. The number of representatives for each state depends on the state's population. For example, Vermont has only one member in the House of Representatives. Texas, a much larger state with many more people, has 36 members in the House of Representatives. The total number of members in the House of Representatives is 435.

To be elected to the Senate, a person must be at least 30 years old. A senator must have been a U.S. citizen for at least nine years and live in the state he or she represents. All of the people who live in a particular state vote for a candidate for senator.

Members of the House of Representatives must be at least 25 years old. They must have been a U.S. citizen for at least seven years and live in the state they represent. Representatives are voted on by only the people who live in their district. A district is a section of a state.

Senators serve a term that lasts six years. Representatives serve a term that lasts only two years. This helps Congress stay balanced. The longer term for senators helps make Congress stable. Senators are not as affected by public pressure on current issues. However, the shorter terms for representatives drives them to respond quickly to current issues and changes in public opinion. Because representatives have to run for office every two years, they must campaign a lot. During this process, they meet people in their districts and hear about citizens' immediate concerns. Currently, no limit exists on the number of times a senator or representative can be elected.

It would be impossible for a member of Congress to become an expert on every subject that might come up. A congressional committee allows members of Congress to develop specialized knowledge about a subject. They use this knowledge to review information and recommend policies to the other members of Congress.

The most important work of Congress is forming and passing laws. A suggestion for a new law is called a bill. Members of Congress work on committees that present, discuss, and revise bills. Congress has many different types of committees. For example, they have committees on banking, natural resources, and housing. Each chamber of Congress has its own set of committees.

Neither the Senate nor the House of Representatives can make a law on its own. The two chambers have equal power, and both must vote to approve a law.

Much of the work of Congress takes place in the U.S. Capitol. Here, members of the Senate and the House of Representatives meet. They present and debate bills, deciding which ones will become laws. In the Capitol building, the House of Representatives meet in the House Chamber. This room has hundreds of chairs arranged in a semicircle facing a speaker's platform. The Senate meets in the Senate Chamber. This room has 100 desks arranged in a semicircle facing a speaker's platform. In each of these assembly halls, visitors may sit in the balcony around the top of the room. Citizens can watch their elected officials at work.

United States senators and representatives are responsible for making laws for the country. But regular citizens can get involved, too. They can write to or call their elected officials to share their thoughts about proposed laws. They can tell their elected officials what issues are important to them. Members of Congress are supposed to represent their constituents, or the people in their states and districts. Those citizens have the right—and the responsibility—to participate in government also.

Members of Congress are elected to represent us and need to hear from the public in order to learn what is important to them.

Essential Question
What is the purpose of the government?

The Preamble of the United States Constitution

The United States Constitution is the supreme law of our country. It is a document that sets up our system of government. The Constitution separates power into three branches: legislative, executive, and judicial. It describes the relationship between the states and the federal government. And it describes our basic rights, including our freedom of speech and our voting rights.

Before it does any of that though, it offers an introduction, known as the Preamble. The Preamble is only 52 words long, but those words say a lot. The Preamble states the basic purpose of the Constitution as well as its guiding principles. Often thought of as the "spirit" of the Constitution, the Preamble gives us an idea of what the nation's founders hoped the Constitution would accomplish. For over 200 years, it has done just that. It has also inspired people around the world to believe that democracy, or "government of the people, by the people, for the people," can work.

We the People of the United States,
in Order to form a more perfect Union,
establish Justice,
insure domestic Tranquility,
provide for the common defence,
promote the general Welfare,
and secure the Blessings of Liberty
to ourselves and our Posterity,
do ordain and establish this Constitution
for the United States of America.

Respond

Comprehension

You will answer the comprehension questions on these pages as a class.

Text Connections

1. Why did the founders of the United States design a Congress that has two chambers?
2. Do you think a system of checks and balances makes it harder or easier for the United States' legislative branch to form and pass new laws? Explain your answer.
3. Think about what you read in "The Road to Democracy." How is the U.S. Congress an example of a representative democracy?
4. Think about the rules that govern your school, such as dress codes and cell phone policies. What groups of people worked together to decide these rules? If one group dislikes a rule or thinks the rule is unfair, what can they do?

Did You Know?

In order for a bill to become law, both chambers of Congress must agree on it. Then the president must decide whether to sign the bill into law.

Look Closer

Keys to Comprehension

1. What are the three branches of the United States government? Who leads each branch? What is the purpose of each branch?
2. More people are elected to serve in the House of Representatives than in the Senate. Why is this?

Writer's Craft

3. Reread the paragraph on page 211. What opinion does the author state in this paragraph? Do you agree with the author's opinion? Why or why not?

Concept Development

4. Reread the paragraph on page 208. Does this paragraph make comparisons and contrasts, or does it describe a sequence of events? What are some signal words that help you understand the structure and purpose of this paragraph?
5. Reread the caption on page 209. Why does Congress have special committees on subjects such as banking, natural resources, and housing?

Write

If you could write a new law, what would it be? Who would the new law help, and how would it help them?

Read the story. Then discuss it with your class.

Vocabulary Words

- **current**
- **debate**
- **fairly**
- **interpret**
- **process**
- **proposed**

Speaker of the House

The Speaker of the House is the elected leader of the United States House of Representatives. He or she is voted upon by the members of the House. In my house, though, the current speaker is my mother.

"Gather around, gather around," she shouted throughout the house.

Today, we are debating the household chores that my mother and father assigned. My sister Ana believes that I am supposed to clean the kitchen alone. I interpreted the chore differently, and think that we should clean it together.

We all sit down in the living room. My mother and father make sure the process is just.

"Each party will present his or her side," my father explained. "Luke, you can go first."

"Thank you. I believe that Ana should help me clean the kitchen. That's the fairest way to do it," I said.

“But I have to clean my room first!” Ana interrupted. “I can’t help it that Luke already cleaned his room. You should probably check to make sure he did a good job.”

“Of course I did a good job! Actually, I’m willing to help you clean your room if you help me clean the kitchen,” I offered.

My mother and father looked at Ana. “That sounds fair to me,” my mother told her.

“Fine, but I propose that Luke has to clean the dishes!” Ana said.

It turns out that our house can hold a fair debate, too!

Concept Vocabulary

Think about the phrase *checks and balances.* How do checks and balances work in a school?

Extend Vocabulary

Provide one synonym or related word for the following words:

- debate
- current
- interpret
- propose

Read this Social Studies Connection. You will answer the questions as a class.

Text Feature

Parentheses are used around words that add information.

State Governments

In "How Congress Works," you learned about the national (also called *federal*) government's legislative branch. However, states have their own governments, and they work somewhat differently.

Each state has its own constitution, as well as legislative, executive, and judicial branches. The legislative branch is usually made up of two parts, like the legislative branch of the national government. Only one state (Nebraska) has a legislature that is not broken up into two parts.

The state executive branch is run by a governor. In most states, a Lieutenant Governor serves as the second in command of the executive branch. Only five states do not have a Lieutenant Governor position.

Like the federal government, the state government's judicial branch is led by a Supreme Court. They interpret their state's laws. Unlike the U.S. Supreme Court justices, who are appointed by the president, the state Supreme Court justices are elected by the people of their state.

The state governments have a system of checks and balances, like the one you learned about in the national government.

The Texas State Capitol is where its state government is based.

1. What information is found in parentheses? Why do you think the author put it in parentheses?
2. Why are checks and balances important at any level of government?
3. What purpose does state government serve that national government might not be able to?

Go Digital

Search for how the legislature works in your state. Find out if it has one or two parts and whether one of those parts is called a "House of Representatives" or an "Assembly."

Genre Informational Text

Essential Questions

What are symbols of our government? What do these symbols stand for? Why are they important?

THE UNITED STATES CAPITOL

by Holly Karapetkova

The United States Capitol Building is located in America's capital city, Washington, D.C. The magnificent domed building is known around the world as a symbol of American government and democracy. It is the place where the Legislative Branch, the Senators and Representatives elected by the American people, works to make the country's laws. It is also a museum where the nation's art, architecture, and history are on display.

The Capitol Complex includes the Capitol, the Office Buildings of the Senate and House of Representatives, the Library of Congress, the Supreme Court Building, and other buildings and grounds.

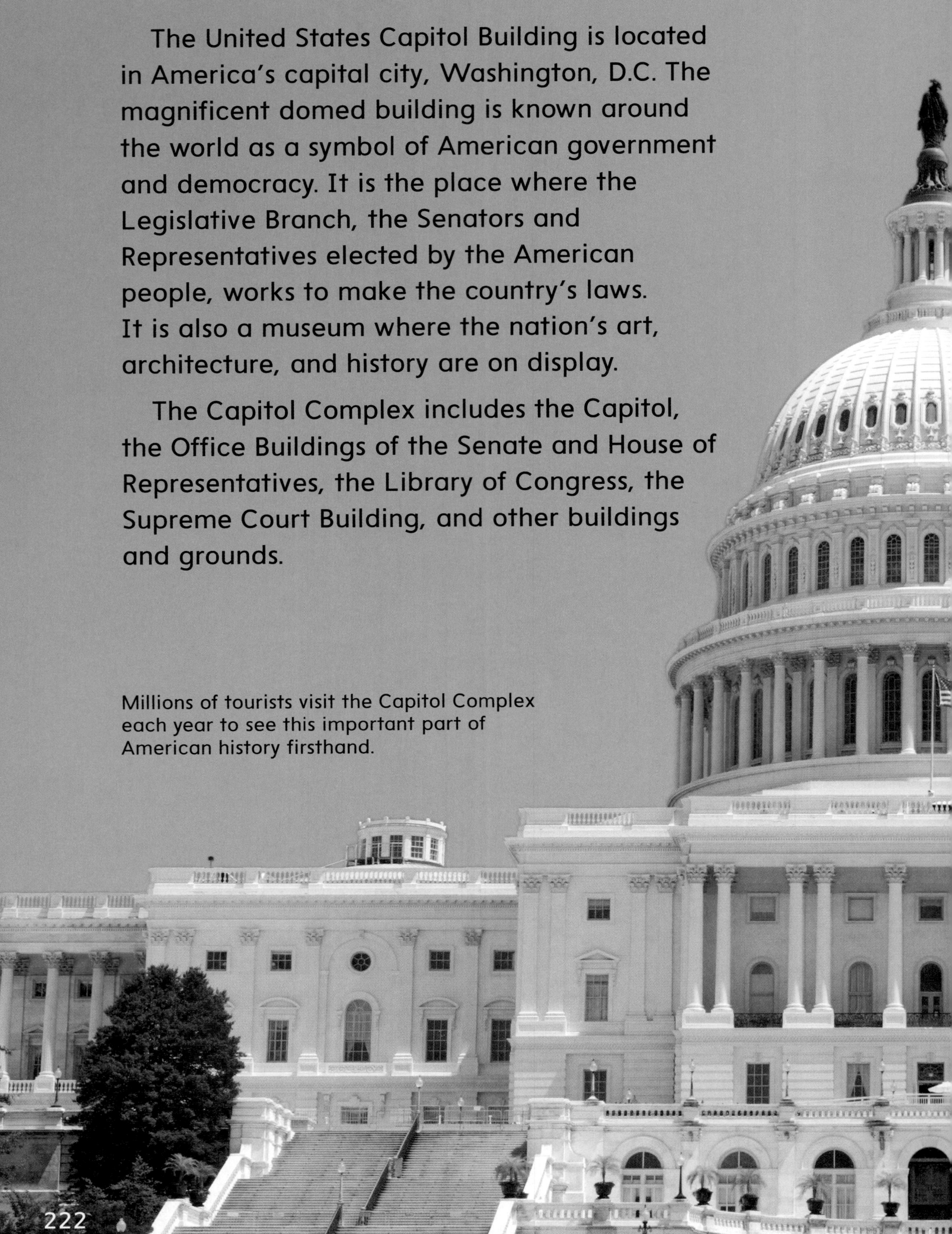

Millions of tourists visit the Capitol Complex each year to see this important part of American history firsthand.

The history of the Capitol is closely connected to the history of the United States itself. The Capitol has been part of some of the most important events in American history, like the War of 1812 and The Civil War. It has also grown and expanded with the country. Its changes over the years reflect the changing nature of the nation.

America's first president, George Washington, began constructing the Capitol in 1793. He held a contest to see who could come up with the best Capitol design and William Thornton, a physician and amateur architect, won.

The North Wing was ready in 1800, and both Houses of Congress met in the same wing for a while. The South Wing was finished several years later.

This painting of the Capitol's North Wing was completed by William Birch in 1803.

Disaster struck the Capitol during the War of 1812. In 1814, the British set the Capitol on fire. Most of the inside of the building was destroyed, but a rainstorm put the fire out and saved some of its outer walls.

During the War of 1812, the British burnt the Capitol, along with many other important buildings, including the White House, the Library of Congress, and the Treasury.

Many people felt the Capitol should be rebuilt in a new location, but others felt that rebuilding the Capitol from the surviving walls would prove that the nation itself had survived and was standing strong.

The government decided to use the old walls and reconstruct the Capitol on its original spot. In 1819, it was ready for the Congress to move back in. The central dome (also called the Rotunda) was completed in 1824.

America grew rapidly over the next few decades. The population increased and new states joined the Union. This meant that more representatives and senators were becoming part of Congress. The Capitol was too small to hold all of them, so in 1850 the government decided to expand the two wings on either side of the building. The government also decided to raise the central dome, making it larger and more noticeable.

Thomas Walter, an architect from Philadelphia, designed a new elevated dome for the Capitol.

The new dome was made of iron and was lifted into place by steam-powered machines called derricks.

The dome was still under construction during President Lincoln's inauguration in 1861.

The new construction was going well until 1861 when the Civil War began. For a time, the Capitol became a military barracks and a hospital for wounded soldiers. At one point, as many as 4,000 soldiers slept in the Capitol.

Money and labor were scarce, but President Lincoln insisted that the construction of the Capitol go on. He wanted people to know that the United States was strong and would persevere. "If the people see the Capitol going on," he said, "it is a sign that we intend the Union shall go on."

In 1863, the new dome was completed and American artist Thomas Crawford's statue was raised piece by piece to the top. The statue, named *Freedom*, symbolized the strength of the country and the freedom of all people living within it.

The Statue of Freedom

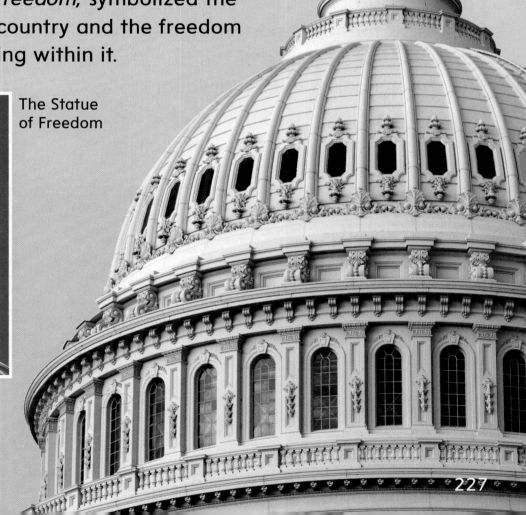

THE ROTUNDA

One of the paintings on display in the Rotunda is John Trumbull's *Declaration of Independence*.

Millions of visitors tour the Capitol every year. The tour begins in the Rotunda, the large circular room at the center of the Capitol beneath its great dome. The Rotunda is filled with paintings of important moments in the nation's history, including the reading of the Declaration of Independence and scenes from the American Revolution. These paintings were created by John Trumbull, a famous American painter.

STATUARY HALL

The Statuary Hall is another important part of the Capitol. It contains bronze and marble statues of important figures in the history and culture of the fifty states. The statues donated by individual states represent political and military heroes, religious leaders, and even popular icons.

The walls of the Rotunda contain a frieze depicting events in American history from The Landing of Columbus to The Birth of Aviation.

THE HOUSE CHAMBER

The House Chamber is where our 435 Representatives meet to make our nation's laws.

Many Americans see the House Chamber on television each year when the President gives his State of the Union Address. The tradition of the State of the Union Address comes from the U.S. Constitution, which declares that the president "shall from time to time give to the Congress information of the state of the union." Presidents use this opportunity once a year to tell Congress and the American people about their plans and goals for the country.

THE SENATE CHAMBER

The Senate Chamber is where our Senators meet to make laws. Each state has two Senators, and the citizens of each state get to vote to decide who will represent them in the Senate. Like the House of Representatives, the Senate votes on whether ideas for new laws should become bills.

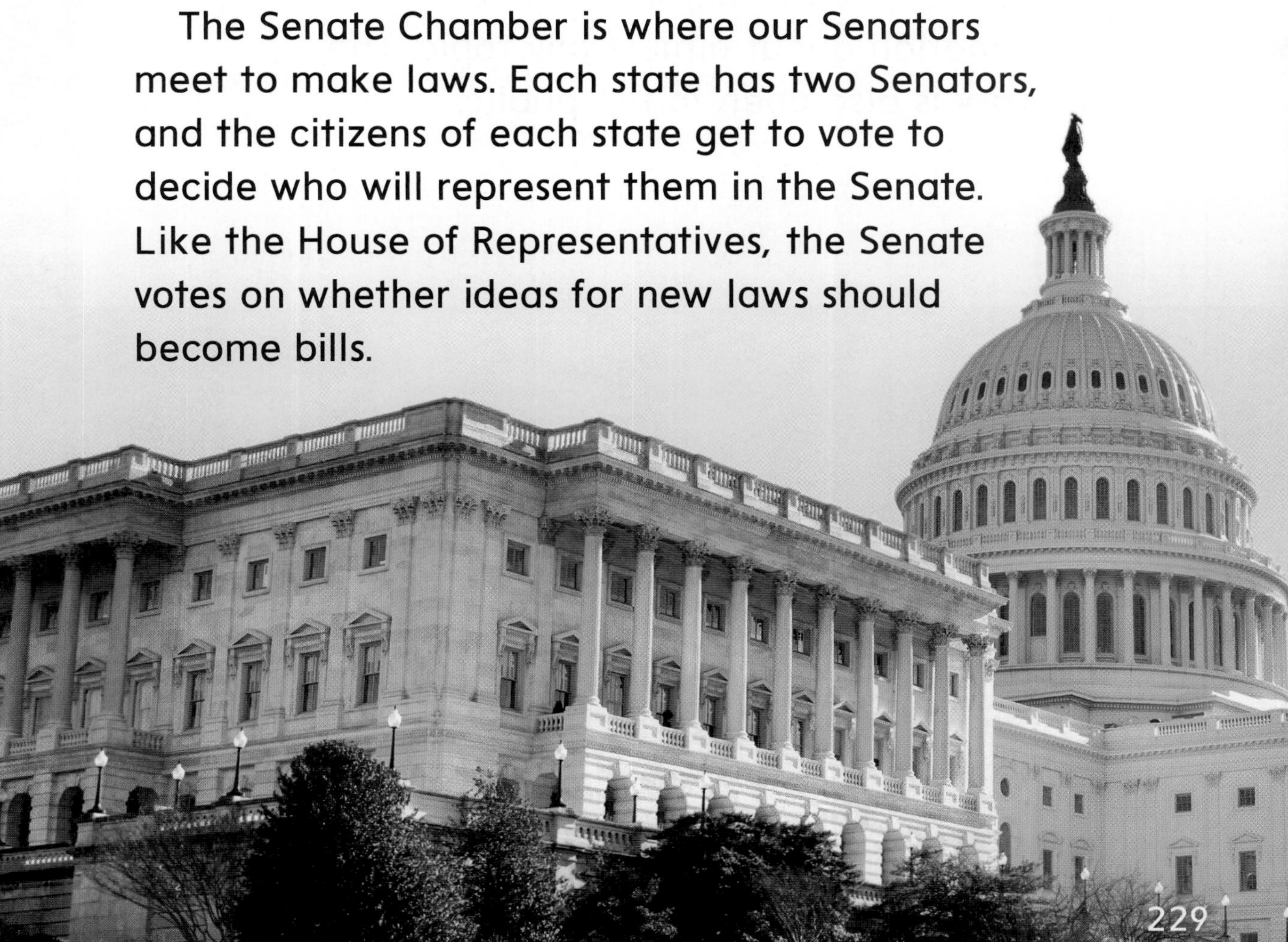

THE LIBRARY OF CONGRESS

In 1800, Congress decided to establish a reference library with books on all sorts of subjects. As Thomas Jefferson wrote, "there is, in fact, no subject to which a Member of Congress may not have occasion to refer." The Library grew so rapidly that by 1867 the shelves were full, and books were stacked on the floor. In 1897, the Library moved into its own building. Today, the Library of Congress takes up three huge buildings and is the largest library in the world. It contains 530 miles of bookshelves! It also holds large collections of newspapers, films, maps, and other resources. Members of Congress can use the Congressional Research Service of the Library in order to find information about almost any topic. The Library is also open to the public.

The interior of the Library of Congress is richly decorated.

Many people work in the Capitol. There are 535 members of Congress in both chambers combined, but these 535 people do not perform their jobs alone. They have tens of thousands of staff members and other workers who help keep Congress running smoothly.

In addition, the Capitol does not just provide members of Congress and their staff with a place to conduct business. It provides them with many types of services and support. The Capitol contains a post office, souvenir shops, snack bars, restaurants, barbershops, and banks. Television studios and control rooms monitor sessions of Congress and provide spaces for interviews with members of Congress. All of these operations make the Capitol seem like a small city in itself.

You will answer the comprehension questions on these pages as a class.

Text Connections

1. What are some different things that the Capitol building has symbolized over the years?
2. What information do the photographs and captions provide that help you understand the text?
3. Think about what you know of the House of Representatives and the Senate from "How Congress Works." Why do you think the House and the Senate have separate chambers in the Capitol?
4. Why might the Capitol be a good resource for people who want to know more about American history? Find evidence in the text to support your answer.

Did You Know?

Although the dome of the Capitol Building is made of cast iron, it has been carefully painted to look like the stone that the rest of the building is made of.

Look Closer

Keys to Comprehension

1. Reread pages 223–227. The main idea of this section is that the history of the Capitol is closely connected to the history of the United States. In what ways has the Capitol reflected the nation's struggles?
2. In what ways is the Capitol like a small city?

Writer's Craft

3. Sometimes writers use apposition to help clarify new words introduced in a piece of writing. Reread page 222. Which sentence on this page contains an example of apposition?

Concept Development

4. Reread the last paragraph on page 223. Which was built first, the Capitol's North Wing or South Wing?
5. Reread the paragraph on page 226. Does this paragraph tell about causes and effects or comparisons and contrasts? Explain your answer.

Write

What part of the Capitol's history do you think is the most inspiring, and why does it inspire you?

Read the story. Then discuss it with your class.

Vocabulary Words

- **amateur**
- **architecture**
- **chamber**
- **persevere**
- **scarce**
- **wing**

Mr. Vice President

"Mr. Vice President, Mr. Vice President!" I shout loudly to try to get his attention. I'm an amateur reporter for a news website. I'm in Washington, D.C., trying to write a story about the vice president.

He hurries into the chamber where the Senate meets while I stand in one of the wings of the Capitol building and wait with the other reporters. I take this time to look around the building. It is architecturally beautiful. People have worked very hard over the years to make the U.S. Capitol building what it is today.

Finally, the vice president comes back out. The other reporters surround him, shouting, hoping for an interview. But I imagine getting shouted at all day grows tiresome. And I know that the vice president scarcely gives out interviews, so I stay back. I try to think of ways I can write my story without an interview with the vice president. Maybe I can find a staff member to talk to. My story might not be as good, but if I persevere, I know I can get it right.

As I walk away, I hear a voice saying "Hey, you." I turn around and see the vice president walking toward me. The other reporters are behind him, still shouting for an interview.

"I appreciate that you are not shouting for my attention," the vice president tells me. "If you'd like a short interview, I'd be happy to answer a few questions for you."

"That would be great!" I tell him. "I guess sometimes it pays not to be the loudest person in the room."

After my interview, the vice president walked away without talking to another reporter. It turns out my story was the best one after all!

Concept Vocabulary

Think about the word *symbol.* What are some symbols you know? What do they stand for?

Extend Vocabulary

Answer the following questions about the vocabulary words.

1. Besides a reporter or an architect, what profession might have an **amateur?**
2. What would make a good **symbol** for **perseverance?**
3. Why might the structure attached to the side of a building be known as a **wing?**

Read this Science Connection.
You will answer the questions as a class.

Text Feature

Numbered lists can be used to provide step-by-step instructions for an experiment.

Under Pressure

In "The United States Capitol," you learned that the Capitol building was once reconstructed after a fire. Constructing a building takes knowledge of the rules of motion and stability.

When equal force is placed on all sides of an object, the object cannot move. When force is placed on only one side, the object can move. An architect knows that walls will only stay standing if there is force put on them from multiple sides. Try this experiment.

1. Build a stack of ten coins or similar objects on a table.
2. Lay a pencil on the table beside the stack, then slide the pencil along the table and hit the stack of coins. What happened to the stack of coins?
3. Restack the coins and press down on the top of the stack with one finger.
4. Slide the pencil along the table until it hits the stack. What happened this time?

This experiment shows that equal force on two sides (from the table on bottom and your finger on top) can stop something from moving even when it is hit.

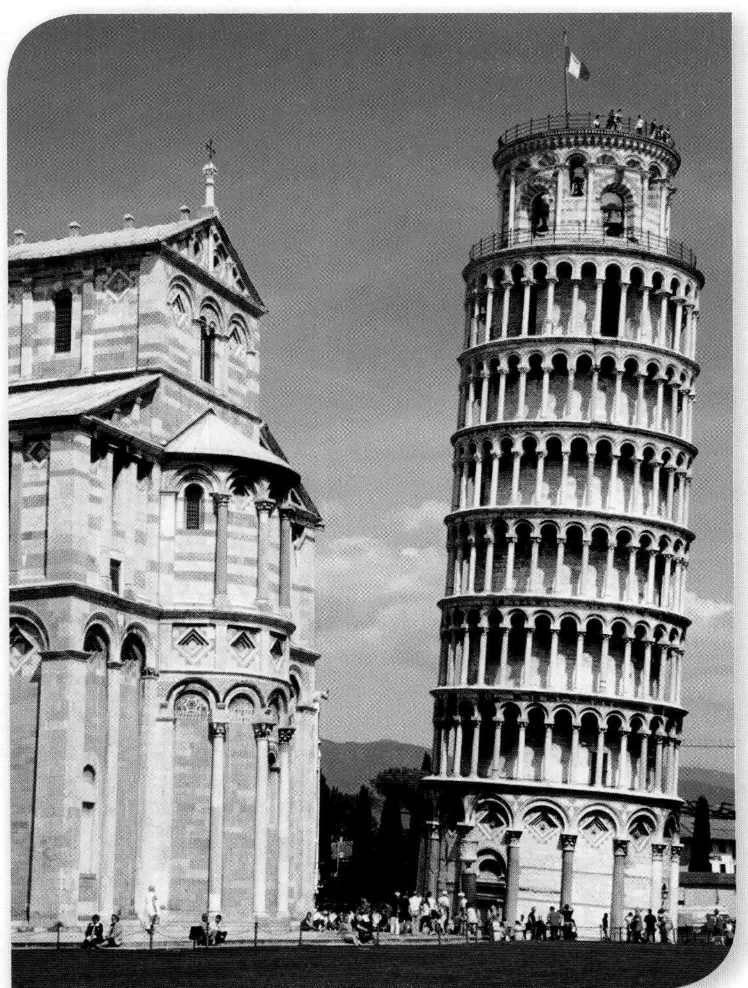

Buildings rely on the physics of balance and stability to stay standing. If they become unbalanced, they could tilt like the Leaning Tower of Pisa, or even fall apart completely.

1. What information does the numbered list contain? How does it present this information?
2. Why do you think the stack of coins moved when it was hit by the pencil the first time?
3. What is another example of an unbalanced force placed on one side of an object, causing it to move?

Go Digital

Search for time-lapse videos of a house constructed from start to finish and observe how builders keep the walls balanced.

Genre Historical Fiction

Essential Questions

How do we change the laws? Why do people value their right to vote? What are some ways to let the government know your opinion?

MARCHING WITH AUNT SUSAN:

SUSAN B. ANTHONY AND THE FIGHT FOR WOMEN'S SUFFRAGE

by Claire Rudolph Murphy
illustrated by Stacey Schuett

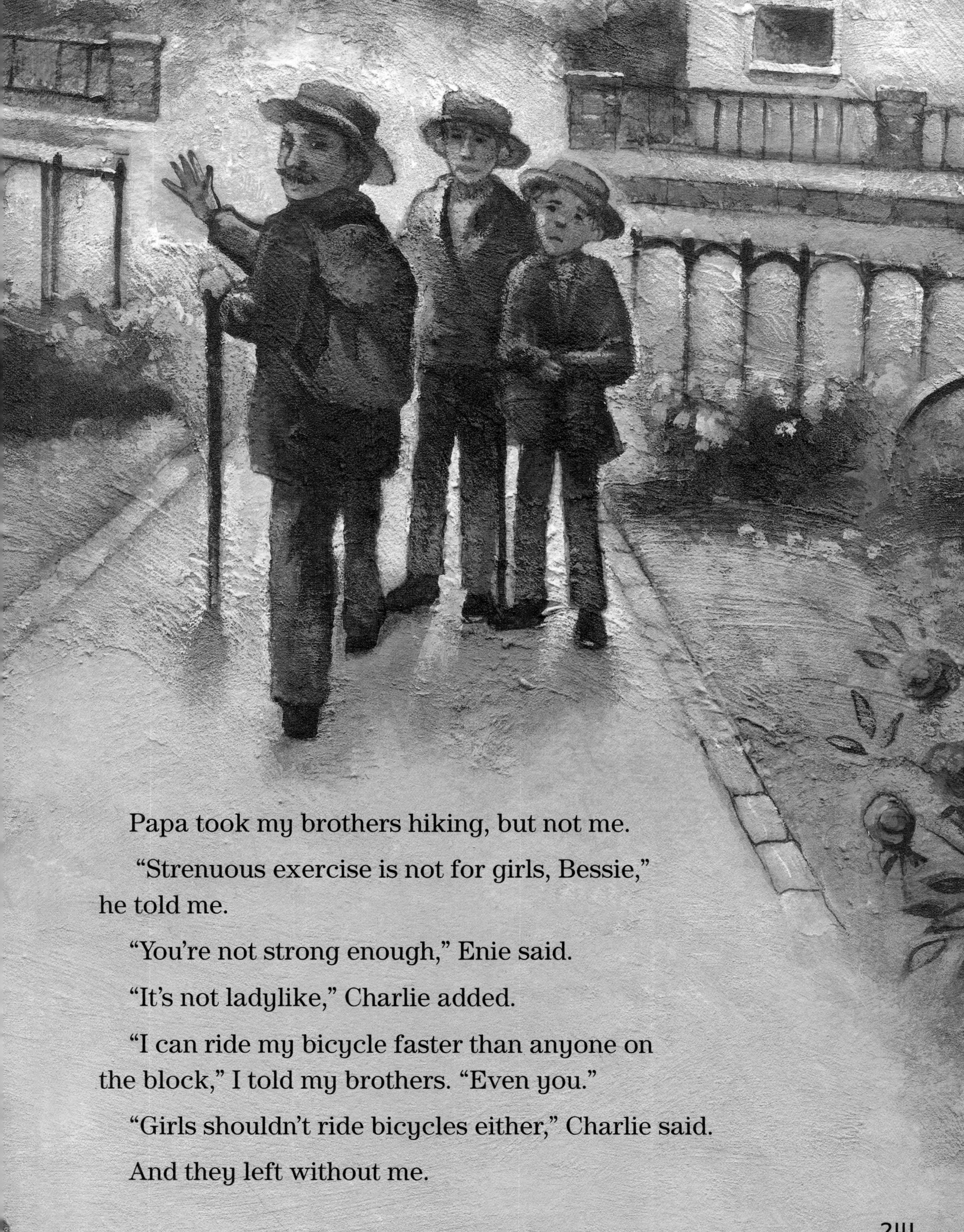

Papa took my brothers hiking, but not me.

"Strenuous exercise is not for girls, Bessie," he told me.

"You're not strong enough," Enie said.

"It's not ladylike," Charlie added.

"I can ride my bicycle faster than anyone on the block," I told my brothers. "Even you."

"Girls shouldn't ride bicycles either," Charlie said.

And they left without me.

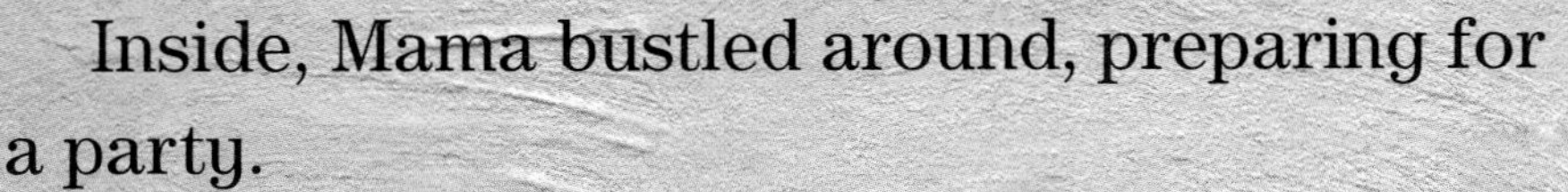

Inside, Mama bustled around, preparing for a party.

"I'm strong enough to hike," I said. "Papa wouldn't take me along, just because I'm a girl."

"You can help me get ready for the suffrage tea," Mama said. "Aunt Mary will be arriving soon with our guest of honor, Miss Susan B. Anthony."

"Suffrage? I'm the one who's suffering." I picked up the newspaper and stared at Miss Anthony's photo. "She looks like a crabby old lady."

"A crabby old lady who has fought fifty years for women's rights," Mama said, "even when people threw garbage at her and called her names."

At the tea, everybody swarmed around Miss Anthony. They called her Aunt Susan, even though they weren't related to her.

She spoke about the long fight for equal rights. She told us that children should grow up in a world where both men and women were free.

Later, Aunt Mary introduced me to Aunt Susan.

"Why can't girls do the same things as boys?" I asked her.

She shook her head. "When I was your age, my teacher thought only boys were smart enough to learn long division."

"That's not right," I said.

"Come to the rally in San Francisco tomorrow, Bessie. Women's votes can help change the world."

Golden Gate Auditorium was so crowded that I could barely breathe. Aunt Susan stood on a stage, surrounded by hundreds of roses. Her voice thundered across the hall. "The votes of all the people, including women with men, will surely bring about the wisest and best government the world has ever seen."

I pulled a white handkerchief out of my purse and joined the sea of flags waving in the air.

The day after the rally, I rode my bicycle over to my best friend Rita's house. "You should have heard Aunt Susan speak yesterday," I told her.

"My papa says ladies shouldn't speak in public," Rita said.

"Aunt Susan says that girls are just as smart as boys. We should get to help make decisions too."

"Papa decides everything in our family," Rita said.

"That's not right." I looked at my best friend. "Someday I want to vote. Let's see if we can help out at suffrage headquarters."

All through the summer, Rita and I wrote letters, licked envelopes, and painted posters. As we worked, we listened to women talk.

"Men decide everything. They even decide if we should get to vote."

"Men decide how the children are raised."

"Men decide how the household money is spent."

"I don't understand," I said to Rita. "I get to spend my allowance any way I want. And Mama makes decisions about lots of our purchases."

"Not at our house." Rita shook her head. "Papa keeps track of every penny."

The week before the election, we visited a factory in San Francisco. Rows and rows of girls sat hunched over, sewing in a dark room. Aunt Susan encouraged them to come to our suffrage parade.

Afterward, a girl walked up. “Me and my sister did some extra sewing to help the campaign.” She handed Aunt Susan two dimes. “If women win the vote, will I be able to go to school?”

I couldn’t imagine not learning how to read and write. I leaned against the wall and tried to catch my breath.

Back at headquarters, I asked Aunt Susan why those girls didn't go to school.

"Many parents can't make enough money to feed their families," she told me. "So the children have to work."

"Can women getting the vote change that?" I asked.

Aunt Susan nodded. "We can work to pass laws that will help adults *and* children."

I dumped out all the coins in my purse and handed them to her. "If those girls can give money, I should too."

Later I painted a picture of the factory girl on a banner for the parade. Rita printed the letters.

Sunday afternoon before the vote, Rita, Mama, and I marched along, carrying our banner. The crowd cheered as we sang new lyrics to "My Country, 'Tis of Thee."

Our country, now from thee,
Claim we our liberty,
In freedom's name.
Guarding home's altar fires,
Daughters of patriot sires,
Their zeal our own inspires,
Justice to claim.

VOTES FO
SCHOOL FO
GIRLS

But then men began shouting. "Women belong in the kitchen! Girls belong at home!"

Rita's father appeared and dragged her away. "No daughter of mine will parade in the streets!"

A boy splattered an egg down the front of my white dress. "What do you want to be—a man?" he yelled.

I stood frozen, watching the oozing yellow stain spread, until Mama picked up Rita's end of the banner and we marched on.

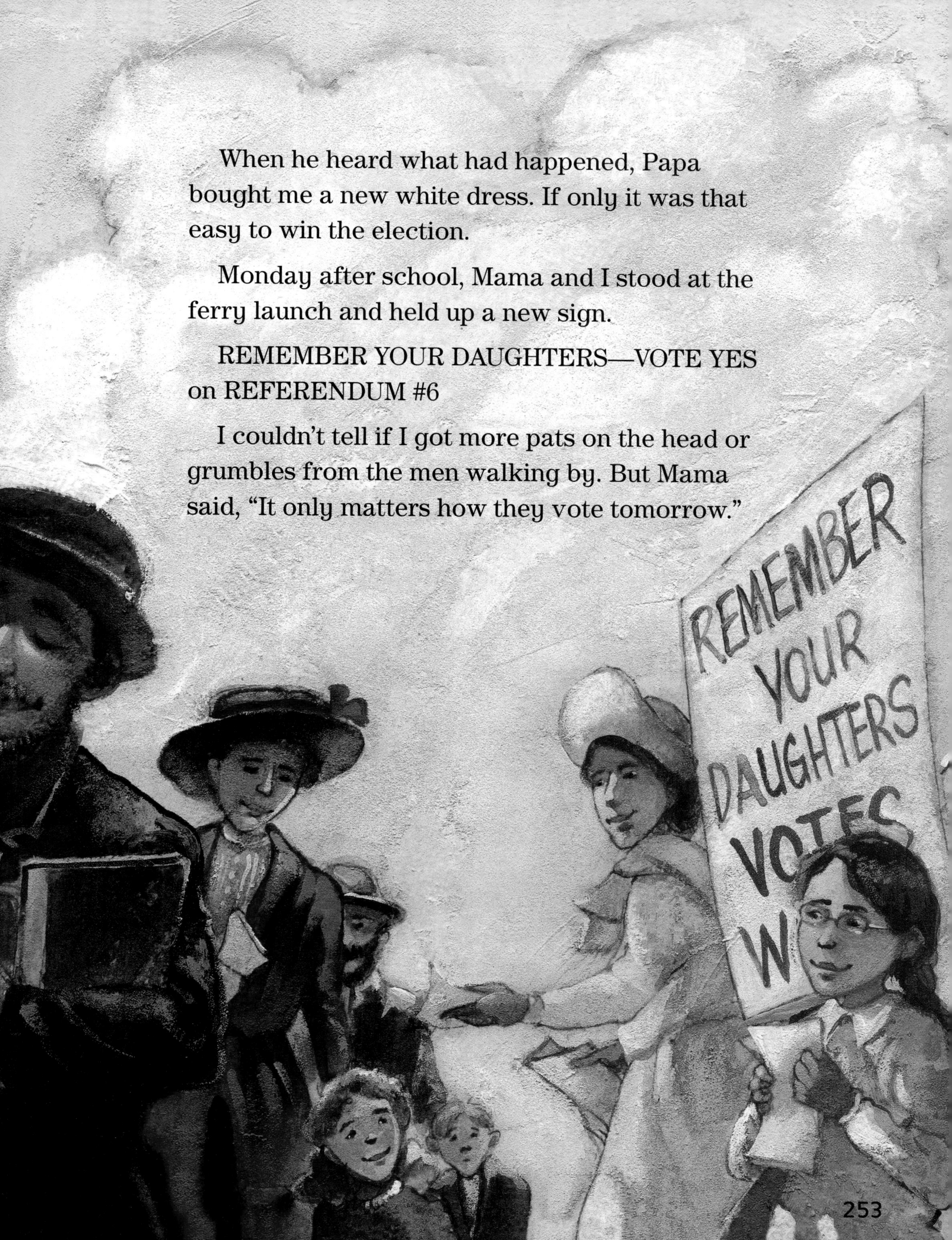

When he heard what had happened, Papa bought me a new white dress. If only it was that easy to win the election.

Monday after school, Mama and I stood at the ferry launch and held up a new sign.

REMEMBER YOUR DAUGHTERS—VOTE YES on REFERENDUM #6

I couldn't tell if I got more pats on the head or grumbles from the men walking by. But Mama said, "It only matters how they vote tomorrow."

The day after the election, my brothers raced me home from school. Charlie grabbed the newspaper off the front porch.

"Women Lose the Vote!" he shouted.

I leaned my bicycle against the house and snatched the newspaper out of his hand.

"What are you so mad about?" asked Enie.

"Someday you'll get to vote and you don't even care. Mama is as smart as Papa, and I'm as smart as you. We should get to vote too."

Mama came out and picked up my bicycle. "Aunt Susan says that a bicycle gives a woman freedom. Teach me how to ride, Bessie."

"It's hard to do," I said, sitting down on the steps.

"When you first tried to ride, you kept falling and scraping your knees," she reminded me. "But you didn't give up."

Finally I showed her what to do—how to mount the bicycle, balance, pedal, and drag her feet to stop.

When Papa arrived home, Mama was wobbling up and down the street. "I'm sorry about the election, Bessie," he said.

"Girls should be allowed to do the same things as boys, Papa."

"Why don't we go hiking this Saturday?" he asked.

"Thanks, Papa," I said, grabbing his hand. "And Sunday there's a rally for the next suffrage campaign. Come march with Mama and me."

Suffrage History

Our Constitution states that citizens should be allowed to vote, but it doesn't spell out who is considered to be a citizen. That was left up to each state to decide. In the early days of our country, only male landowners were allowed to vote. Men of color won the right to vote with passage of the Fifteenth Amendment in 1870, but women still could not vote.

Beginning with the first suffrage convention in Seneca Falls, New York, in 1848, women in every state worked to get the vote. The seventy-two-year campaign stretched through two wars and sixteen presidents. It included 56 state referendum campaigns, 480 campaigns to get legislatures to consider suffrage amendments, 47 campaigns for constitutional conventions, 277 campaigns directed at state party conventions, and 30 campaigns to get national parties to put suffrage in their platforms.

In 1878, the Susan B. Anthony amendment was first introduced in Congress. But it wasn't until 1919 that it finally passed both houses of Congress. In August 1920, Tennessee became the thirty-sixth state to ratify the Nineteenth Amendment. One hundred years after Susan B. Anthony's birth, women from every state finally gained the vote.

The Nineteenth Amendment to the United States Constitution

The right of citizens of the United States to vote shall not be denied or abridged by the United States or by any state on account of sex.

Congress shall have power to enforce this article by appropriate legislation.

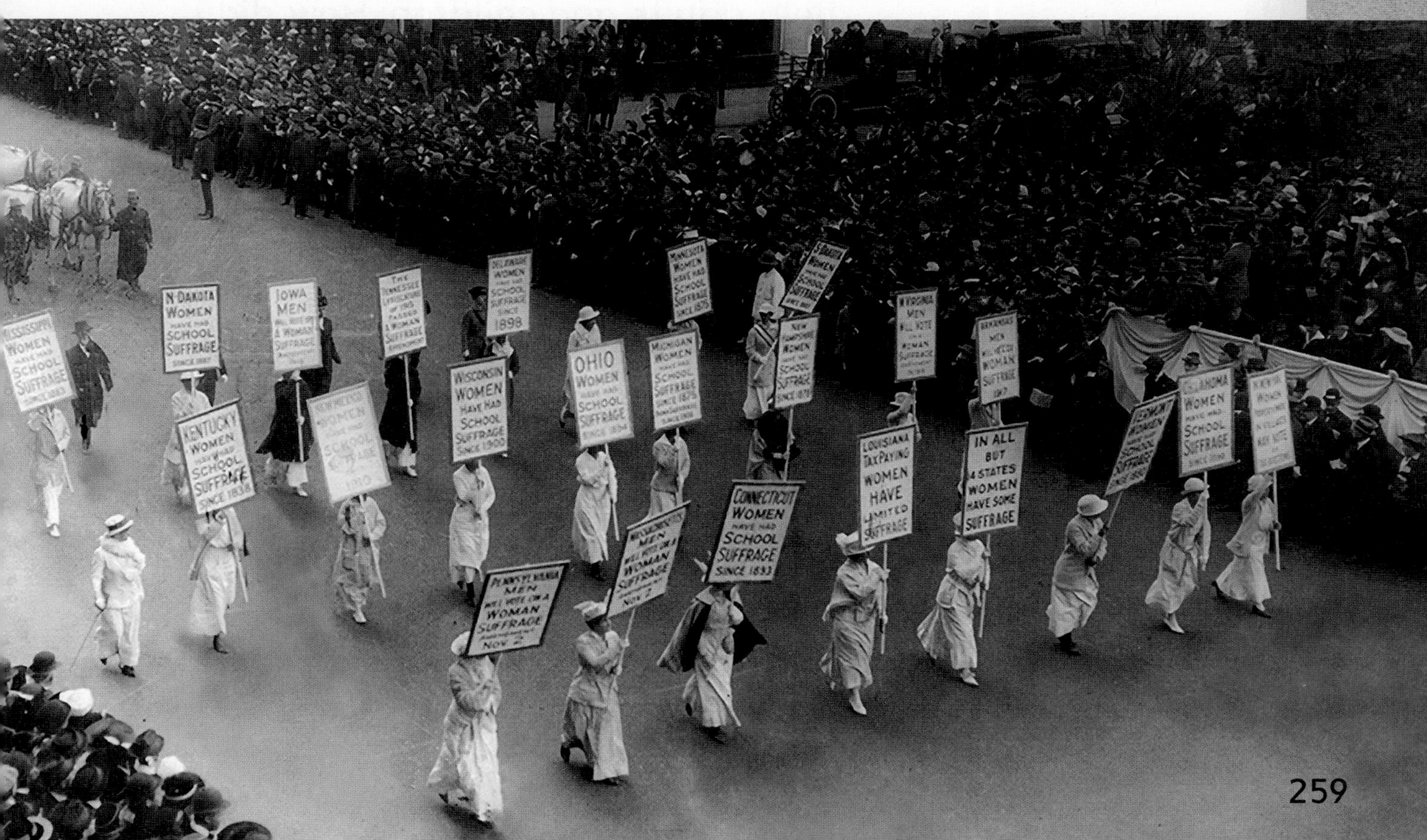

You will answer the comprehension questions on these pages as a class.

Text Connections

1. When did the women's suffrage movement begin in the United States? When did it end and why?
2. Why do you think Susan B. Anthony was called "Aunt Susan" by so many women?
3. Recall what you read about *majority rule* in "Every Vote Counts." Was majority rule a fair way to govern before women had the right to vote? Explain your answer.
4. On page 249, Susan B. Anthony tells Bessie that if women are able to vote, they will be able to pass laws that help adults *and* children. How did Bessie hope laws would help children? Do present-day laws help children in the way Bessie hoped they would?

Did You Know?

Susan B. Anthony was the first real woman to be depicted on United States currency.

Look Closer

Keys to Comprehension

1. What are some wrong ideas about women that the story's men have? How do these ideas affect women and girls in their everyday lives?
2. How does Papa feel about Bessie at the beginning of the story? Do Papa's feelings about Bessie change? How do you know?
3. How does Bessie feel about Susan B. Anthony at the beginning of the story? How and why do Bessie's feelings change?

Writer's Craft

4. A metaphor compares two different things that are alike in an important way. Reread page 245. What are the handkerchiefs compared to? Do you think Bessie's description is meant to be taken literally? Explain your answer.

Concept Development

5. Look at the illustration on page 248. What does this illustration help you understand about how Bessie feels after visiting the factory?

Write

Imagine new laws that could improve the lives of people like you and your friends. What might those laws be?

Read the story. Then discuss it with your class.

Vocabulary Words

- **appropriate**
- **campaign**
- **factory**
- **liberty**
- **marched**
- **mount**
- **power**
- **rally**
- **ratify**
- **strenuous**
- **suffrage**
- **zeal**

The Liberty Parade

My father and I finished campaigning for the day so we could attend the popular Liberty Parade downtown. Passing out flyers to everyone in town was strenuous and stressful work, but the parade was the perfect way to celebrate a hard day's work.

The parade was full of men, women, and children dressed in historic clothes. A zealous band marched behind them playing popular patriotic tunes. My father spotted Mrs. Mendes walking in the parade wearing a large dress.

"Look, Angela! It's Councilwoman Mendes," my father said as he pointed her out amongst the other parade walkers. I saw Mrs. Mendes whenever I visited my father's office. We both waved to her. "It looks like she's supposed to be Susan B. Anthony. She fought for women's suffrage, which means—"

"That's the right to vote!" I said. I had learned a lot about suffrage in school.

"Exactly! Susan B. Anthony's father worked in a factory, so she was not from an important family. And she wasn't in the government, but she had a lot of power anyway. In fact, she played an important role in getting the 19th Amendment ratified. That amendment gave women the right to vote."

Mounting one parade float was a tall statue of Susan B. Anthony, which had community members rallying around it. Some even wore shirts with Susan B. Anthony's face on it.

"It seems like this year's parade is all about Susan B. Anthony!" I said.

"I think that's an appropriate choice, indeed!" my father said.

Concept Vocabulary

Think about the word *progress.* What is something you have made progress on recently?

Extend Vocabulary

Answer the following questions about the vocabulary words.

- If you feel **zeal** for something, do you love it or dislike it?
- If a job is **strenuous,** is it easy for you to do or difficult?
- If you have **power,** can you influence a lot or very little?

Read this Social Studies Connection. You will answer the questions as a class.

Text Feature

A **timeline** shows the order in which important events have happened.

Educational Progress

An institution is an organization created for a specific purpose, normally to serve people. School is an important institution that has changed over time. In "Marching with Aunt Susan," you read that some girls did not get to attend school because they had to work in factories. For a long time, girls did not receive the same education as boys did.

In the 1700s, young girls were taught to sew, cook, and clean so they could help around the home. If they attended school with boys, they were in a separate classroom. Even then, women were calling for a change in the education of girls.

In 1841, teacher Catharine Beecher wrote that girls should be taught math, reading, and history. Her idea was not popular. At the time, many teachers were men. But she wound up having the power to influence change.

Eventually, girls and boys began going to school in the same classrooms. Many people did not like this change. Some feared it would make girls more like boys!

The institution of the school reflects the beliefs of America. As one changes, so does the other.

1790	1800	1810	1820	1830	1840	1850

1792,
Sarah Pierce opened her Connecticut home to educate young girls.

1833
Oberlin College in Ohio became the first college to admit women.

1841
Catharine Beecher published a book about the importance of education for girls.

1848
At the Seneca Falls Convention, over 300 people gathered to discuss equality in education.

Here are some notable events in the history of education for girls.

1. What does the timeline show? How does it help you locate information quickly?
2. How did change for institutions like schools begin from the inside?
3. How do institutions affect your life?

Go Digital

Search for countries where girls still do not get a good education. Discover how girls from around the globe have struggled for access to fair and equal schooling.

Genre Biography

Essential Questions

What kind of person could become the president? What do you think all presidents should have in common?

So You Want to Be President?

by Judith St. George
illustrated by David Small

There are good things about being President and there are bad things about being President. One of the good things is that the President lives in a big white house called the White House.

Another good thing about being President is that the President has a swimming pool, bowling alley, and movie theater.

The President never has to take out the garbage.

The President doesn't have to eat yucky vegetables. As a boy, George Bush had to eat broccoli. When George Bush grew up, he became President. That was the end of the broccoli!

One of the bad things about being President is that the President always has to be dressed up. William McKinley wore a frock coat, vest, pin-striped trousers, stiff white shirt, black satin tie, gloves, a top hat, and a red carnation in his buttonhole every day!

The President has to be polite to everyone. The President can't go anywhere alone. The President has lots of homework.

People get mad at the President. Someone once threw a cabbage at William Howard Taft. That didn't bother Taft. He quipped, "I see that one of my adversaries has lost his head."

Lots of people want to be President. If you want to be President, it might help if your name is James. Six Presidents were named James. (President Carter liked to be called Jimmy). Four Johns, four Williams (President Clinton liked to be called Bill), two Georges, two Andrews, and two Franklins—all became President.

James Monroe
James Polk
James Buchanan
James Garfield
James Carter
CALL ME JIMMY
John Quincy Adams
John Tyler
JOHN
John Kennedy
GEORGE
George Washington
George Bush
FRANKLIN
Franklin Pierce
Franklin Roosevelt

Zachary Taylor
James Polk
Andrew Jackson
Millard Fillmore

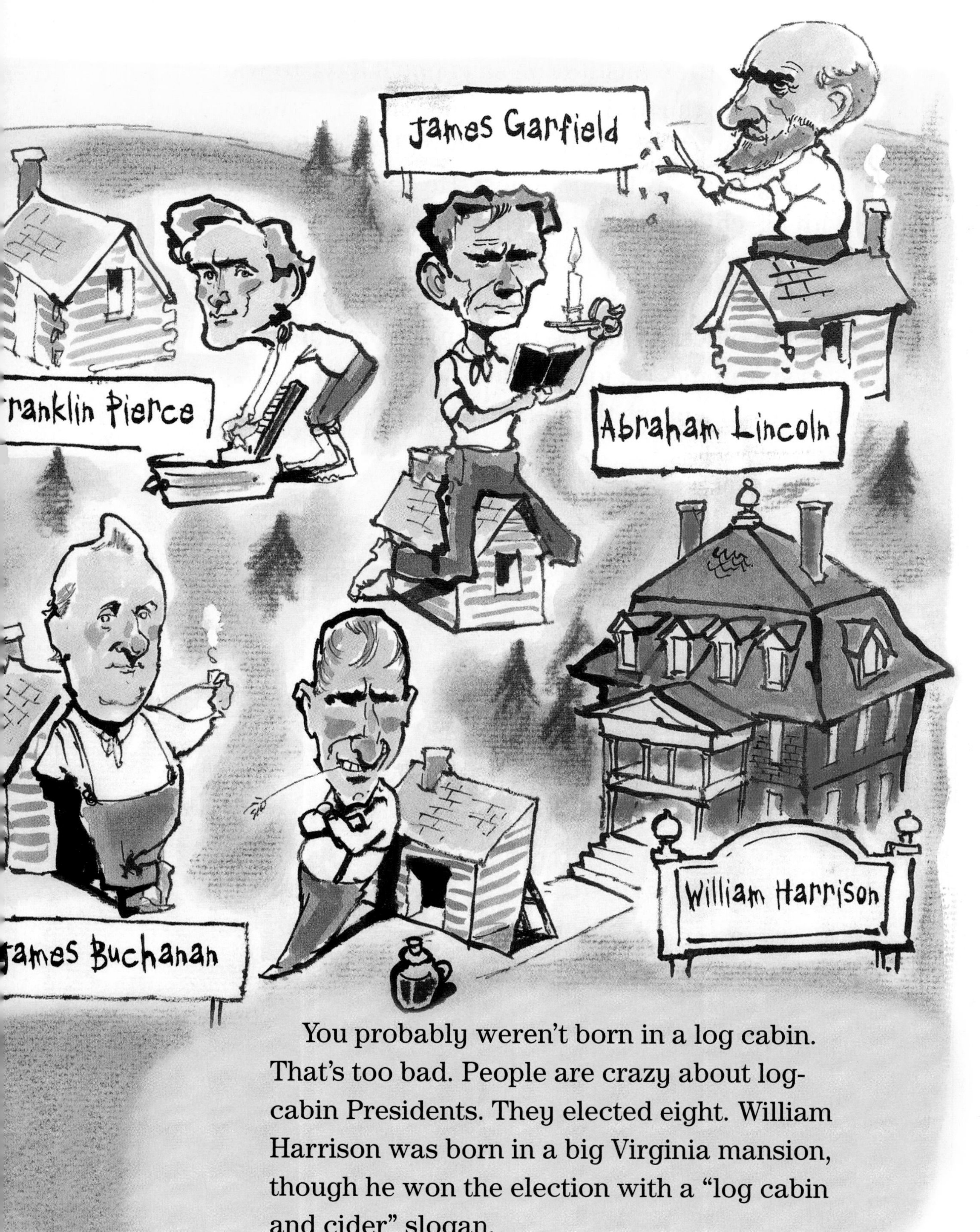

You probably weren't born in a log cabin. That's too bad. People are crazy about log-cabin Presidents. They elected eight. William Harrison was born in a big Virginia mansion, though he won the election with a "log cabin and cider" slogan.

Though the Constitution says you'll have to wait until you're thirty-five, young, old, and in between have become President. Theodore (Teddy) Roosevelt at forty-two was the youngest. He had pillow fights with his children and played football on the White House lawn. "You must always remember that the President is about six," a friend said. Ronald Reagan was the oldest. When he first ran for President, he was sixty-nine. He joked that it was the thirtieth anniversary of his thirty-ninth birthday.

Some Presidents joked and some didn't—Presidents' personalities have all been different. William McKinley was so nice that he tried to stop a mob from attacking the man who had just shot him. Benjamin Harrison was so cold that one senator said talking to Harrison was like talking to a hitching post. Calvin Coolidge was so shy and quiet that a dinner guest once made a bet that she could get him to say more than two words. "You lose," he told her. Andrew Jackson certainly wasn't shy. When he ran for President, his opponents printed a list of his duels, fights, shootings, and brawls. Fourteen in all!

Don't worry about your looks. Abraham Lincoln was a homely man, but he was one of our best Presidents. (He reunited the country by winning the Civil War.) Someone once called Lincoln two-faced. "If I am two-faced, would I wear the face that I have now?" Lincoln asked.

Warren Harding was a handsome man, but he was one of our worst Presidents. (He gave government jobs to his crooked friends.) “I am not fit for this office and never should have been here,” he admitted.

Do you have pesky brothers and sisters? Every one of our Presidents did. Benjamin Harrison takes the prize—he had eleven! (It's lucky he grew up on a six-hundred-acre farm.) James Polk and James Buchanan both had nine. George Washington, Thomas Jefferson, James Madison, and John Kennedy each had eight. (Two Presidents were orphans, Andrew Jackson and Herbert Hoover.)

A President in your family tree is a plus. John Quincy Adams was John Adams' son. Theodore Roosevelt and Franklin Roosevelt were fifth cousins. Benjamin Harrison was William Harrison's grandson. James Madison and Zachary Taylor were second cousins.

Some Presidents threw money around and some were penny pinchers. James Monroe ordered French silverware, china, candlesticks, chandeliers, clocks, mirrors, vases, rugs, draperies, and furniture for the White House. Ninety-three crates in all!

William Harrison was thrifty. He walked to market every morning with a basket over his arm.

Do you have a pet? All kinds of pets have lived in the White House, mostly dogs. Herbert Hoover had three dogs: Piney, Snowflake, and Tut. (Tut must have been a Democrat. He and his Republican master never got along.) Franklin Roosevelt's dog, Fala, was almost as famous as his owner.

George Bush's dog wrote *Millie's Book: Adventures of a White House Dog* (as reported to Mrs. Bush!). Ulysses Grant had horses, Benjamin Harrison's goat pulled his grandchildren around in a car, the Coolidges had a pet raccoon, Jimmy Carter and Bill Clinton preferred cats.

Theodore Roosevelt's children didn't just have pets, they ran a zoo. They had dogs, cats, guinea pigs, snakes, mice, rats, badgers, raccoons, parrots, and a Shetland pony called Algonquin. To cheer up his sick brother, young Quentin once took Algonquin upstairs in the White House elevator.

You don't have to be musical to be President. Ulysses Grant certainly wasn't. He knew only two tunes. "One is 'Yankee Doodle'," he said, "and the other one isn't."

But many Presidents were musical. Thomas Jefferson, John Tyler, and Woodrow Wilson played the violin; John Quincy Adams, the flute; Chester Arthur, the banjo; Harry Truman and Richard Nixon, the piano; Bill Clinton, the saxophone, and Warren Harding almost any brass instrument, including the sousaphone.

Some Presidents knew how to dance and some didn't. Our first President did a mean minuet. At his inaugural ball George Washington danced with every lady but his wife. (Mrs. W. had stayed home!) James Madison's opinion of his inaugural ball? "I would much rather be in bed." Abraham Lincoln wasn't much of a dancer. "Miss Todd, I should like to dance with you the worst way," he told his future wife. Miss Todd later said to a friend, "He certainly did." Woodrow Wilson liked to do the jig step while singing silly ditties.

Not all Presidents danced, but most had a sport. John Quincy Adams was a first-rate swimmer. Once when he was swimming in the Potomac River, a woman reporter snatched his clothes and sat on them until he gave her an interview.

Ulysses Grant raced his rig through the streets of Washington (and was arrested for speeding!). Rutherford Hayes played croquet on the White House lawn. Ronald Reagan split wood. William McKinley's idea of exercise was to sit under a tree with a good book.

Golf has been big with Presidents. Dwight Eisenhower and John Kennedy were especially good. But when Gerald Ford, George Bush, and Bill Clinton teamed up for a golf game, three of their shots clobbered spectators!

Though most Presidents went to college, nine didn't: George Washington, Andrew Jackson, Martin Van Buren, Zachary Taylor, Millard Fillmore, Abraham Lincoln, Andrew Johnson, Grover Cleveland, and Harry Truman. (Andrew Johnson couldn't read until he was fourteen! He didn't learn to write until after he was married!)

Thomas Jefferson was top-notch in the brains department—he was an expert on agriculture, law, politics, music, geography, surveying, philosophy, and botany. In his spare time he designed his own house (a mansion), founded the University of Virginia, and whipped up the Declaration of Independence.

If you want to be President, you might consider joining the army. George Washington, Andrew Jackson, William Harrison, Zachary Taylor, Ulysses Grant, Rutherford Hayes, James Garfield, Chester Arthur, Benjamin Harrison, and Dwight Eisenhower were all generals.

If you can't be a general, be a hero like Theodore Roosevelt or John Kennedy. (Roosevelt's Rough Riders charged up Kettle Hill to help win the Spanish-American War. Kennedy led his crew to safety in World War II when the Japanese sank his PT boat.)

Don't be a Franklin Pierce. In his very first battle, Franklin Pierce's horse bucked, he was thrown against his saddle and fainted, his horse fell, broke its leg, and Pierce hurt his knee. (He got elected anyway!)

Another route to the White House is to be Vice President, though most don't think much of the job. Truman's Vice President, Alben Barkley, told about a man who had two sons. One son went to sea, the other was elected Vice President. Neither was ever heard from again. (Who's ever heard of Alben Barkley?)

Other Vice Presidents have been heard from. John Adams, Thomas Jefferson, Martin Van Buren, Richard Nixon, and George Bush were all elected President. (Gerald Ford became President when Richard Nixon resigned.) John Tyler, Millard Fillmore, Calvin Coolidge, and Harry Truman moved up when a President got sick and died. Andrew Johnson, Chester Arthur, Theodore Roosevelt, and Lyndon Johnson became top man when guns were drawn, bullets flew, and a President was assassinated!

Almost any job can lead to the White House. Presidents have been lawyers, teachers, farmers, sailors, engineers, surveyors, mayors, governors, congressmen, senators, and ambassadors. (Harry Truman owned a men's shop. Andrew Johnson was a tailor. Ronald Reagan was a movie actor!)

SCREEN STARS

One thing is certain, if you want to be President—and stay President—be honest. Harry Truman paid for his own postage stamps. Grover Cleveland was famous for his motto: "Tell the truth."

Other Presidents weren't so honest. Democrat Bill Clinton was impeached for lying under oath. Republican Richard Nixon's staff broke into Democratic headquarters to steal campaign secrets. He covered up the crime and then lied about it. (That was the end of Richard Nixon as President!)

There they are, a mixed bag of Presidents! What did they think of being head man? George Washington, who became our very first President in 1789, worried about his new line of work. “I greatly fear that my countrymen will expect too much from me,” he wrote to a friend. (He was a howling success.) Some loved the job. “No President has ever enjoyed himself as much as I,” Theodore Roosevelt said. Others hated it. “The four most miserable years of my life,” John Quincy Adams complained.

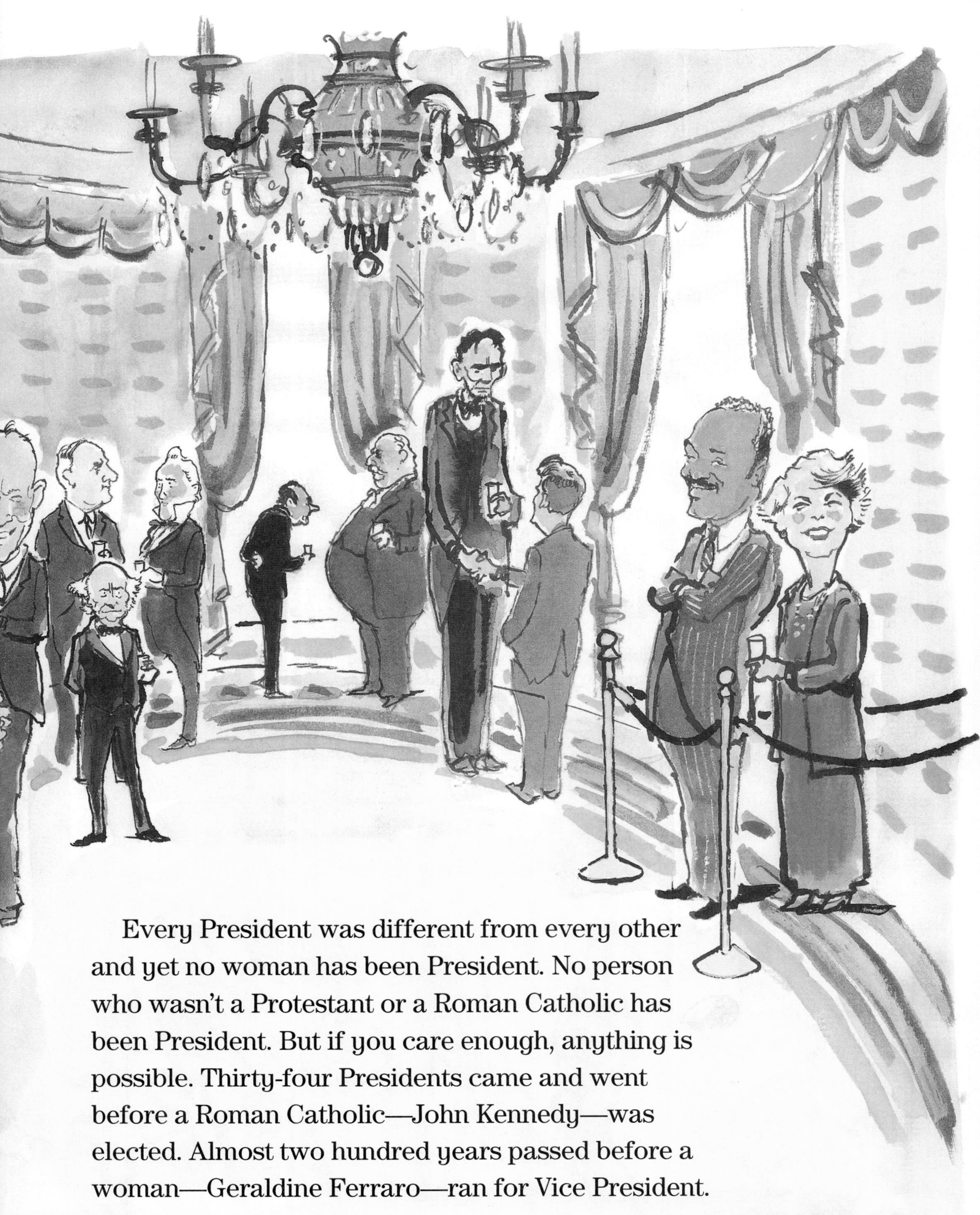

Every President was different from every other and yet no woman has been President. No person who wasn't a Protestant or a Roman Catholic has been President. But if you care enough, anything is possible. Thirty-four Presidents came and went before a Roman Catholic—John Kennedy—was elected. Almost two hundred years passed before a woman—Geraldine Ferraro—ran for Vice President.

It's said that people who run for President have swelled heads. It's said that people who run for President are greedy. They want power. They want fame.

But being President can be wanting to serve your country—like George Washington, who left the Virginia plantation he loved three times to lead the country he loved even more.

It can be looking toward the future like Thomas Jefferson, who bought the Louisiana Territory and then sent Lewis and Clark west to find a route to the Pacific. (They did!)

It can be wanting to turn lives around like Franklin Roosevelt, who provided soup and bread for the hungry, jobs for the jobless, and funds for the elderly to live on.

It can be wanting to make the world a better place like John Kennedy, who sent Peace Corps volunteers around the globe to teach and help others.

Every single President has taken this oath: “I do solemnly swear (or affirm) that I will faithfully execute the office of President of the United States, and will to the best of my ability, preserve, protect, and defend the Constitution of the United States.”

Only thirty-five words! But it’s a big order when you’re President of this country. Abraham Lincoln was tops at filling that order. “I know very well that many others might in this matter as in others, do better than I can,” he said. “But… I am here. I must do the best I can, and bear the responsibility of taking the course which I feel I ought to take.”

That's the bottom line. Tall, short, talkative, quiet, vain, humble, lawyer, teacher, or soldier—this is what most of our Presidents have tried to do, each in his own way. Some succeeded. Some failed. If you want to be President—a good President—pattern yourself after the best. Our best have asked more of themselves than they thought they could give. They have had the courage, spirit, and will to do what they knew was right. Most of all, their first priority has always been the people and the country they served.

You will answer the comprehension questions on these pages as a class.

Text Connections

1. The author of this selection finds a lot of things the presidents have had in common. What are some examples?
2. What is the main idea of "So You Want to Be President?" How do the details in the text support this idea?
3. According to the selection "How Congress Works," what branch of government does the president lead and what is its role? What does this selection say the role of the president is? How do these roles compare?
4. What does the term *thrifty* on page 285 mean? How does William Harrison demonstrate he is thrifty?

Did You Know?

George Washington was the only president to be unanimously elected.

Write

What qualities do you have that would help you perform the role of president? How would these qualities help you?

Look Closer

Keys to Comprehension

1. The author answers the question *so you want to be president?* by writing a piece about "a mixed bag of presidents." What message does this send to readers?
2. To people who want to become president, the author recommends: "pattern yourself after the best." What ideals do presidents uphold, in the author's opinion?

Writer's Craft

3. Reread the second paragraph on page 306. Do you agree with the author when she says that Abraham Lincoln was "tops" at being the president? Why or why not?
4. Reread the first paragraph on page 306. What is an oath? What clues in the text help you determine the meaning of the word?

Concept Development

5. Reread pages 304–305. How are the paragraphs on page 305 connected to the text on page 304?

Read the story. Then discuss it with your class.

Vocabulary Words

- adversaries
- ambassadors
- anniversary
- execute
- interview
- pesky
- philosophy
- preferred
- priority
- slogan
- spectators
- vain

For the Win

"The Princes can't execute a play out there today!" my big brother Frank shouted from the stands. My mom and I were visiting him at college today, and we decided to see a football game before we left. The Princes were playing their rival, the Purple Pirates, on the big anniversary of their first football game. The Princes' pesky purple adversaries were very talented. As a spectator, it was hard to watch because I preferred to see the Princes win.

Before the start of a new play, Frank told my mom and me about his campaign to be student council president. He had to do three interviews and prove that he had good priorities, like education and leadership. He talked about getting an A+ in a tough philosophy class and being an ambassador for several different groups on campus.

"It's not easy, but I'm glad I'm doing it. It would be great to be student council president," he said.

Just then, the Princes scored. Their opponents, who had been acting vainly by celebrating before the game ended, quickly hung their heads. The game was tied, and the crowds on both sides cheered loudly.

My brother got up and walked to the front of the stands. He started cheering the Princes' unofficial slogan, "Only Princes get the crown!" and soon, all of the students and families in the stands started cheering along. The football players must have heard them, because they scored again and won the game!

"They love you! You're going to make a great student council president," I told him when he returned to his seat.

Concept Vocabulary

Think about the word *service*. What are ways you can provide a service to your community?

Extend Vocabulary

Think of a related word for each of the following vocabulary words.

- anniversary
- spectators
- preferred
- pesky

Read this Social Studies Connection. You will answer the questions as a class.

Text Feature

A **quote** is a written statement of a person's exact words.

Community Service and You

The people you read about in "So You Want to Be President?" served the country in a very important way. But you can, too. One of the core democratic ideals in our country is to serve the community by volunteering our time and abilities.

There are many ways to serve the community. Some people prefer to volunteer at places that they see a lot. You can pick up litter at your favorite park or volunteer to clean up trash around your school. Or you can plant flowers in an empty field you see every day.

Others like to help elderly people or the homeless. You can create cards to send to men and women in nursing homes or in homeless shelters. Hearing encouraging words can brighten someone's day.

President John F. Kennedy famously said to "ask not what your country can do for you, ask what you can do for your country." When citizens volunteer, they improve not only their community, but themselves and their country, as well. And by participating in community service, they live up to the ideals of some of our greatest presidents, too.

1. What does Kennedy's quote mean? How does it relate to community service?
2. How does community service help a democracy run smoothly?
3. How can you serve communities around the world? How does this serve the American democracy?

Go Digital

Look up a schedule of service opportunities in your community. Find ways to serve an institution that has served you.

UNIT 6 Art on the Move

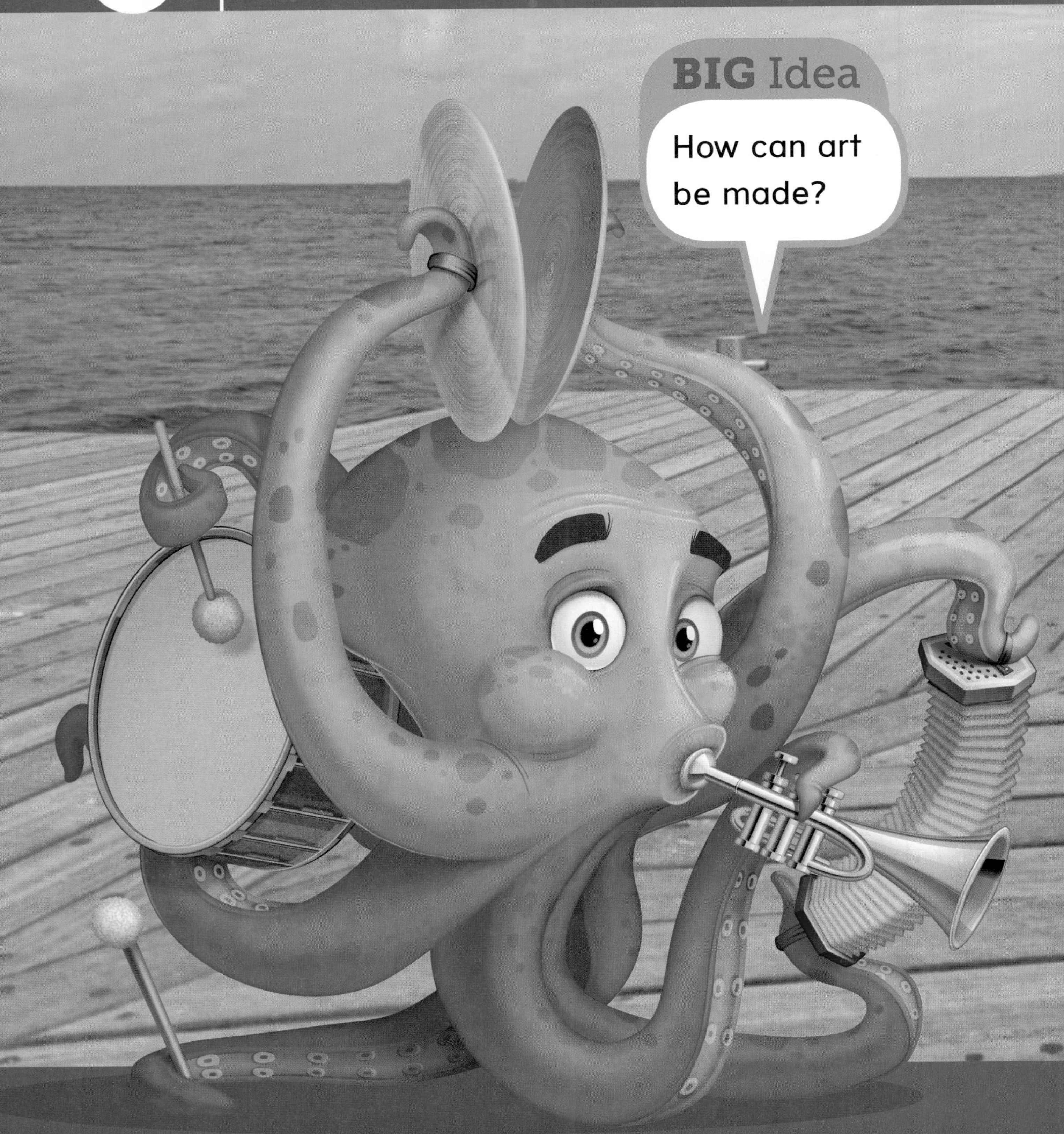

BIG Idea
How can art be made?

Theme Connections

What can be considered a performance?

Background Builder Video
connected.mcgraw-hill.com

Genre Myth/Informational Text

Essential Questions

Why do you think ancient people valued music so highly? What myths, legends, fairy tales, or other stories have you heard about music?

The Power of Music

by Karen E. Martin
illustrated by Leslie Hawes

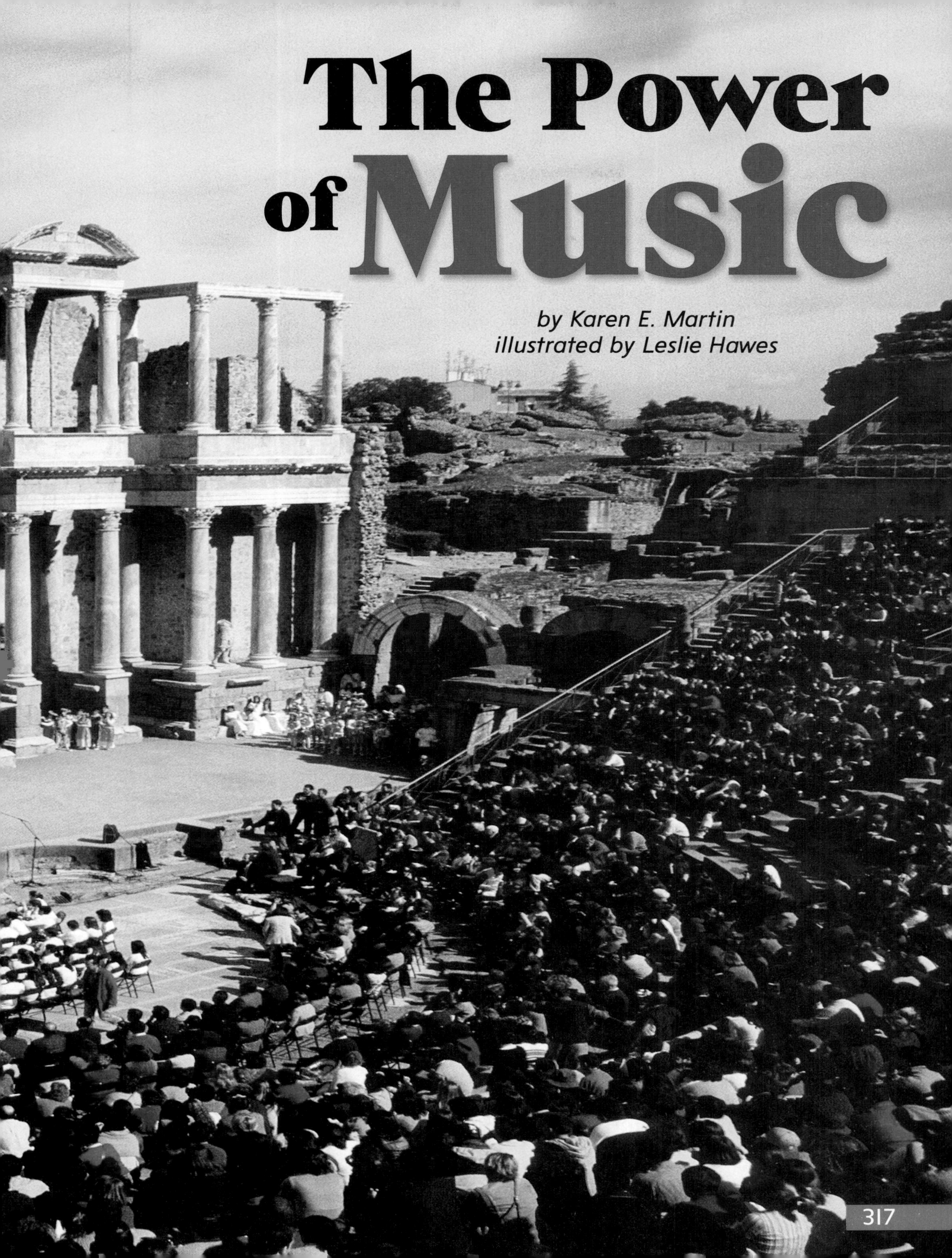

Myths have inspired humankind for thousands of years. One myth in particular speaks to us of the power of music: Orpheus, "the father of songs." His story is retold to this day through art, music, and literature.

The Myth of Orpheus

In ancient Greece lived a man named Orpheus. Born with the gift of music, he played the lyre and sang more beautifully than any living creature.

Orpheus often wandered through the forest, singing and playing. Wild animals followed wherever he led. Rivers changed their course so they could flow near him. So special was his music that even the stones could not resist his song. All living and nonliving things on Earth loved to listen to Orpheus sing. Word of his superb music spread quickly throughout the land.

Also living in Greece at that time, the hero Jason was preparing for a dangerous journey. King Pelias had ordered Jason and his crew on a risky sea voyage to Colchis. Their mission: to capture the Golden Fleece. By recovering this blanket, made from the wool of a golden-winged ram, Jason would be made the rightful ruler of a kingdom stolen from him.

Upon hearing of the power of Orpheus' music, Jason entreated him to join his crew, the Argonauts. Orpheus agreed. Soon, they set off on the famed ship *Argo* for the distant shore of Colchis.

Each day as the men rowed, Orpheus sang to them. The oars rose and fell to the steady rhythm of his chants. Even the sea was calmed by his lovely melodies.

The Argonauts endured many perils on the sea. As they neared Colchis, they came upon the Clashing Rocks. These giant stones rose to great heights from the sea. They crushed any ship that passed between them. The sea boiled and the waves crashed furiously as the *Argo* sailed closer. Thinking quickly, Orpheus grabbed his lyre. He began to play a soft, soothing melody. He sang the stones into stillness, and the ship slipped through unharmed.

At last, the *Argo* arrived in Colchis. After completing three heroic tasks, Jason seized the Golden Fleece. With his prize in hand, Jason dashed back to the ship and away the Argonauts sailed, victorious.

Unfortunately, more obstacles stood between the crew and the safety of home. The most treacherous of these obstacles was the Sirens. These alluring, deadly creatures lived on rocky islands in the sea. There, they sang to ships passing by. No sailor who heard their lovely song could resist it. The shores were littered with the bones of sailors the Sirens had lured to their deaths on the rocks. But Jason and his crew could not veer around the Sirens. The *Argo's* path sailed directly through their waters.

The islands grew large on the horizon. The Sirens' song began to drift across the waves. Who could save the crew but Orpheus? He struck up his lyre and sang, loudly and from the depths of his soul, more beautifully than ever before. The beauty of his song drowned out the enchanting melody of the Sirens. The ship sailed onward to safety.

Music in Ancient Greece

As the myth of Orpheus shows, music held great power for the ancient Greeks. Even the word *music* comes from the Greek Muses. The Muses inspired people to create art, to dance, to write, and to make music. One of those Muses was Orpheus' mother!

Music was a part of everyday life in ancient Greece. Shepherds played pipes in the fields. Soldiers marched in time to music. Women sang as they worked around the home. And like Orpheus, many people sang as they played an instrument.

This ancient tile mosaic shows Orpheus playing his lyre.

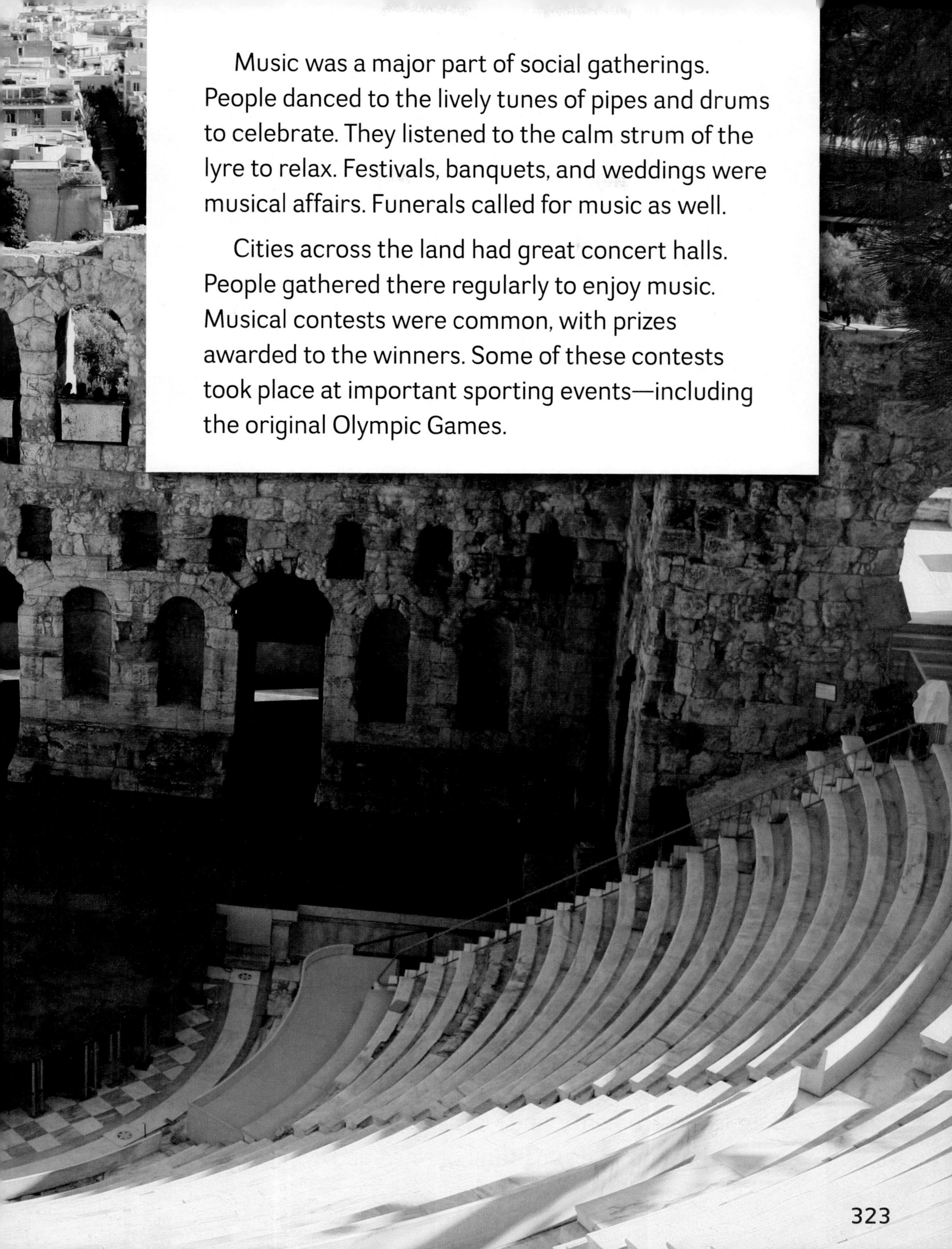

Music was a major part of social gatherings. People danced to the lively tunes of pipes and drums to celebrate. They listened to the calm strum of the lyre to relax. Festivals, banquets, and weddings were musical affairs. Funerals called for music as well.

Cities across the land had great concert halls. People gathered there regularly to enjoy music. Musical contests were common, with prizes awarded to the winners. Some of these contests took place at important sporting events—including the original Olympic Games.

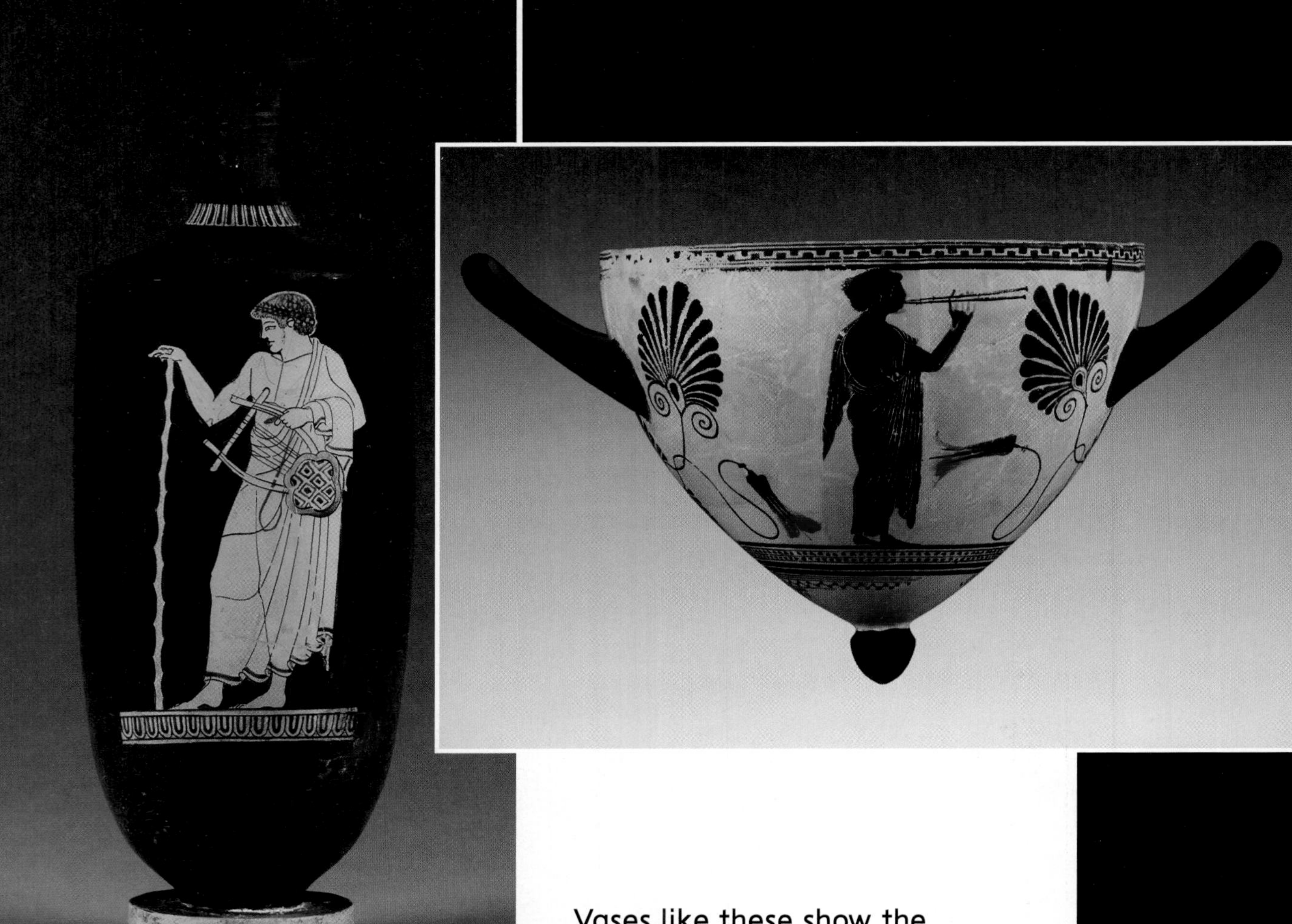

Vases like these show the variety of instruments that ancient Greeks played.

The Greeks played many of the same instruments we play today. How do we know? Archaeologists have found the remains of vases and other art from ancient Greece that show people playing music. We can see how the instruments were held and played. One instrument, the hydraulis, was a kind of water organ. It had pipes and a keyboard. The Greeks also played long, curved horns and flute-like instruments. And just as we do today, musicians set the beat using drums, tambourines, and cymbals.

A New Form of Art Emerges

The ancient Greeks also combined music with drama. In fact, their plays inspired later generations to create a new form of art: opera.

Operas are dramatic plays set to music. They are written by a composer, who writes the music, and a librettist, who writes the words of the opera. Once held only in palaces, operas are now held in large concert halls. The performers sing nearly all of their characters' lines. Large orchestras fill the concert hall with beautiful music. People who go to operas usually love the music as much as the story the opera tells.

Orpheus Lives On in Opera

Many of the earliest opera composers decided to use Greek myths as the subject of their operas. Their audience already knew these myths and what to expect from the story. What story could be more compelling than that of Orpheus? The power of his music to move hearts made him the perfect subject.

In the 1600s, at least 20 operas were written about Orpheus. Dozens more have been written since then. Incredibly, many of these historic operas are still staged today. New versions of the opera continue to be written as well. The story has also been the basis for films, ballets, popular music, and even comic books.

The myth of Orpheus is more than two thousand years old. But its message about the power of music to move humankind lives on.

You will answer the comprehension questions on these pages as a class.

Text Connections

1. Why was Jason sent to Colchis? How many heroic tasks did Jason have to complete before receiving his prize?
2. Who were the Sirens? What could they do and when did the Argonauts face them?
3. How do we know today the types of instruments the ancient Greeks used?
4. What is the difference between a composer and a librettist?

Did You Know?

Colchis was located where the country of Georgia currently is, on the east coast of the Black Sea.

Look Closer

Keys to Comprehension

1. How would you describe Orpheus from the myth in this selection? How do his actions influence the sequence of events?
2. What is the main idea of "The Power of Music"? Identify some of the key details from the selection that helped you determine this main idea.
3. Briefly retell the myth of Orpheus. What do you think the central message is? Explain how key details support the central message.

Writer's Craft

4. While reading this selection, how did the photographs help you better understand the text? What information did the captions add that was not present in the main text?

Concept Development

5. How does the illustration on page 321 help you better understand what the Sirens were?

Write

The myth about Orpheus mentions that the Argonauts faced many perils while they were at sea, but it gives the details about only two dangers. Describe another danger the crew may have faced.

Read the story. Then discuss it with your class.

Vocabulary Words

- archaeologists
- banquets
- basis
- endured
- entreated
- humankind
- lively
- lyre
- Muses
- orchestras
- palaces
- remains

An Enduring Instrument

Did you know that lyres are still played today? This was a complete surprise to me! I came upon this information while doing some research on the Internet.

I had been wondering how people played these early instruments. So, I asked my music teacher about it, and he entreated me to go online. As I started my Internet search, I expected to find only paintings. (Old pottery pieces found on archaeological digs sometimes have pictures of lyre players on them.) However, to my surprise, I found *videos* of lyre players!

Apparently, humankind's fascination with the lyre has been an enduring one. Like me, other modern-day people saw pictures of the lyre and wanted to know how it sounded, so some constructed lyres of their own! They used ancient paintings as the bases for their designs. Then they built the lyres. After that, all that remained was to play the lyres!

As it turns out, the lyre doesn't play the liveliest music I have ever heard. Nor can it play the loud, grand-sounding tunes you might hear from an orchestra. However, one man played a lyre song so sweet and mesmerizing that it could have come straight from a Muse. It sounded regal in a way, like the background music for a fine banquet hosted in a palatial home. But at the same time, I could imagine a shepherd playing it on a hillside. It was lovely! I wonder if the lyre music from ancient times sounded the same way.

Concept Vocabulary

Think about the word *epic.* What are some examples of epic stories that you know? Have you ever had an adventure that you would describe as *epic?*

Extend Vocabulary

Synonyms are words with similar meanings. For example, think about these words: *entreated, requested, implored, demanded, urged.* All are synonyms for *asked.* However, each word implies a different state of mind for the person who is doing the asking. Copy these words into your Writer's Notebook. Then write a sentence for each word that uses the word in the correct context. If you need help, use a dictionary to clarify the precise meaning of each word.

Read this Science Connection. You will answer the questions as a class.

Text Feature

A **caption** tells about a picture and adds information to an article or story.

Fossils

Imagine you are on an archaeological dig. You are looking for artifacts from a bygone era, and you expect to find pieces of pottery. However, what you actually find is even more incredible—fossils!

Fossils are the rock hard remains or evidence of once-living plants and animals. Usually plants and animals decay after they die. This means that they break down and become part of the soil or seafloor. However, something special happens to create a fossil. Perhaps an animal or insect got caught in something sticky, such as tar or tree sap. The sticky substance became very hard. It protected parts of the animal or insect from decay.

Or, maybe parts of a leaf or animal made an imprint on wet ground. Over time the ground hardened and became rock and kept the imprint.

Fossils are created in a number of ways! All share the ability to teach us about how plants and animals looked and lived very long ago.

This fossil was found in the desert.

This modern-day animal lives in the sea.

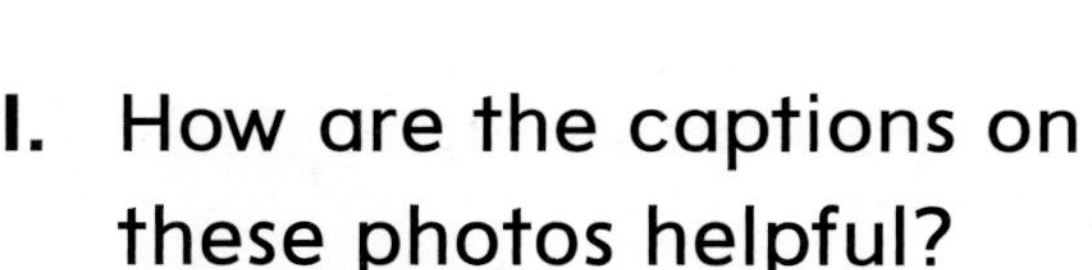

1. How are the captions on these photos helpful?
2. What features do the fossil and the modern-day sea animal share?
3. In what kind of environment was the fossil found? What does the fossil help you understand about this environment?

Go Digital

What kinds of plants and animals become fossils? Where are fossils usually found?

Genre Biography

Essential Questions

What role does natural talent play in a performer's success? How can talent help a performer overcome adversity?

Little Melba and Her Big Trombone

by Katheryn Russell-Brown
illustrated by Frank Morrison

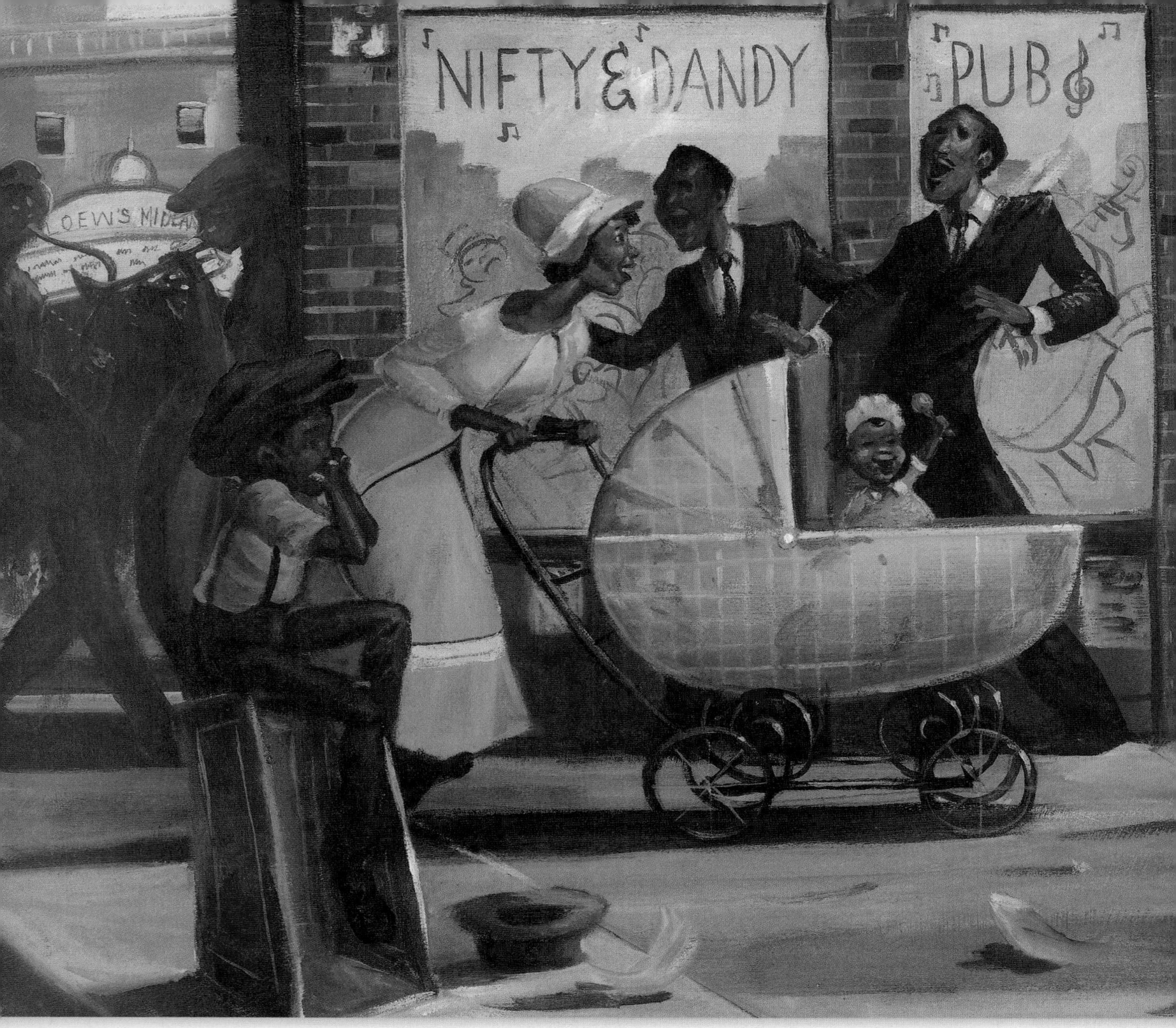

SPREAD THE WORD! Little Melba Doretta Liston was something special.

The year she was born was 1926. The place was Kansas City, where you could reach out and feel the music. The avenues were lined with jazz clubs, street bands, and folks harmonizing on every corner. All the hot music makers made sure they had a gig in KC.

From as far back as her memory would go, Melba loved the sounds of music. Blues, jazz, and gospel rhythms danced in her head—

the *plink* of a guitar,

the hummmmm of a bass,

the **thrum-thrum** of a drum,

the *ping-pang* of a piano,

the tremble of a sweet horn.

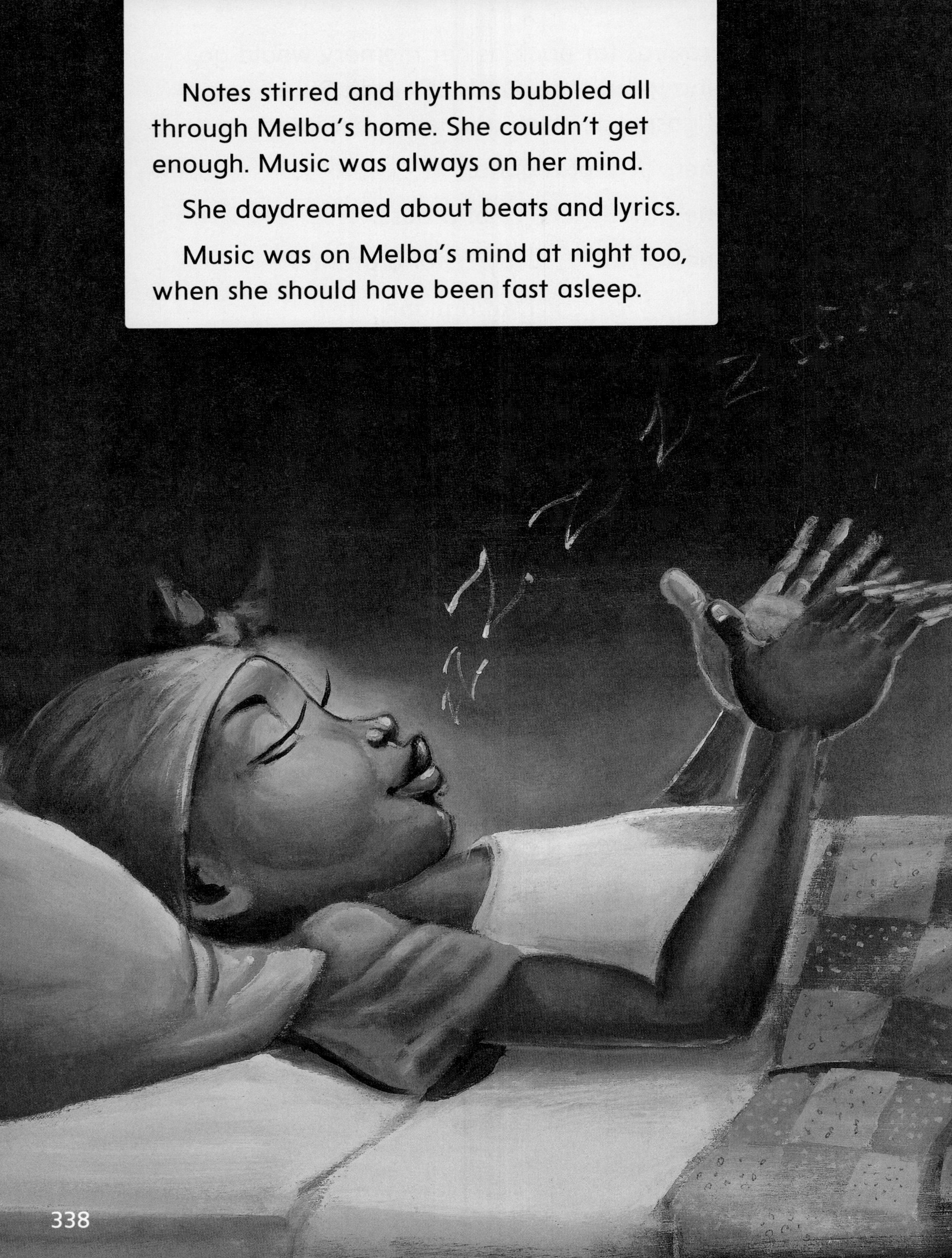

Notes stirred and rhythms bubbled all through Melba's home. She couldn't get enough. Music was always on her mind.

She daydreamed about beats and lyrics.

Music was on Melba's mind at night too, when she should have been fast asleep.

Melba loved to hum along with the radio. Sometimes the music sounded so good she cupped her ear to the Majestic and closed her eyes. She especially loved Fats Waller, with his growly voice and booming piano.

The player piano came alive when Melba's kinfolk stopped by. While Melba pedaled, her aunties danced around the room.

With all that music flying by, Melba wanted to create her own sounds. When she was seven years old, she decided to sign up for music class at school.

What instrument could I play? Melba wondered.

At the traveling music store, Melba eyed a long, funny-looking horn.

"That one!" she cried. "It's beautiful!"

"A trombone?" Momma Lucille frowned. "It's big, and you're a little girl."

"Pleeeeease," Melba begged.

Momma Lucille bought the shiny trombone on the spot. She couldn't say no to her only child. Melba beamed from ear to ear and squeezed her new friend.

That night on the porch, Melba listened to Grandpa John play his guitar. This time she had her own music maker.

Grandpa John showed Melba how to cradle the horn. She tried to push out the slide, but her arm was too short. She had to tilt her head sideways and *streeeeeetch* out her right arm.

Melba gave the horn a mighty blow.

HOoooooooNK!

HAAAAAAAAHNNNNK!

It sounded bad, like a howling dog.

"I'm no good, Grandpa," Melba said, tearing up.

"If you can blow, you can play," Grandpa John said. "Now stand up straight and blow steady."

Melba stayed up real late and practiced until she could play a simple tune all by herself.

Even with her keen ear, teaching herself to play the trombone was no piece of cake. But Melba kept blowing her horn, getting better day by day. The cool brass of the horn felt swell on her fingers.

Before long, Melba and her horn were making magic. She was only eight when the local radio station invited her to play a solo. Momma Lucille and Grandpa John were so proud as they watched little Melba play her big trombone.

Hard times hit rock bottom in 1937. That's when Melba and her mother moved to Los Angeles. The long train ride took them five states west and worlds away from Kansas City.

Melba's new teachers discovered that she was as smart as a whip. Her test scores were so high, the principal skipped her up from sixth grade to eighth.

In high school Melba joined Alma Hightower's famous after-school music club. Melba quickly became the star player in the club's band, The Melodic Dots.

The other club members struggled to keep up with Melba. Jealous boys called her bad names. She tried not to care, but way down deep the names hurt. Melba used her horn to turn all those hurt feelings into soulful music.

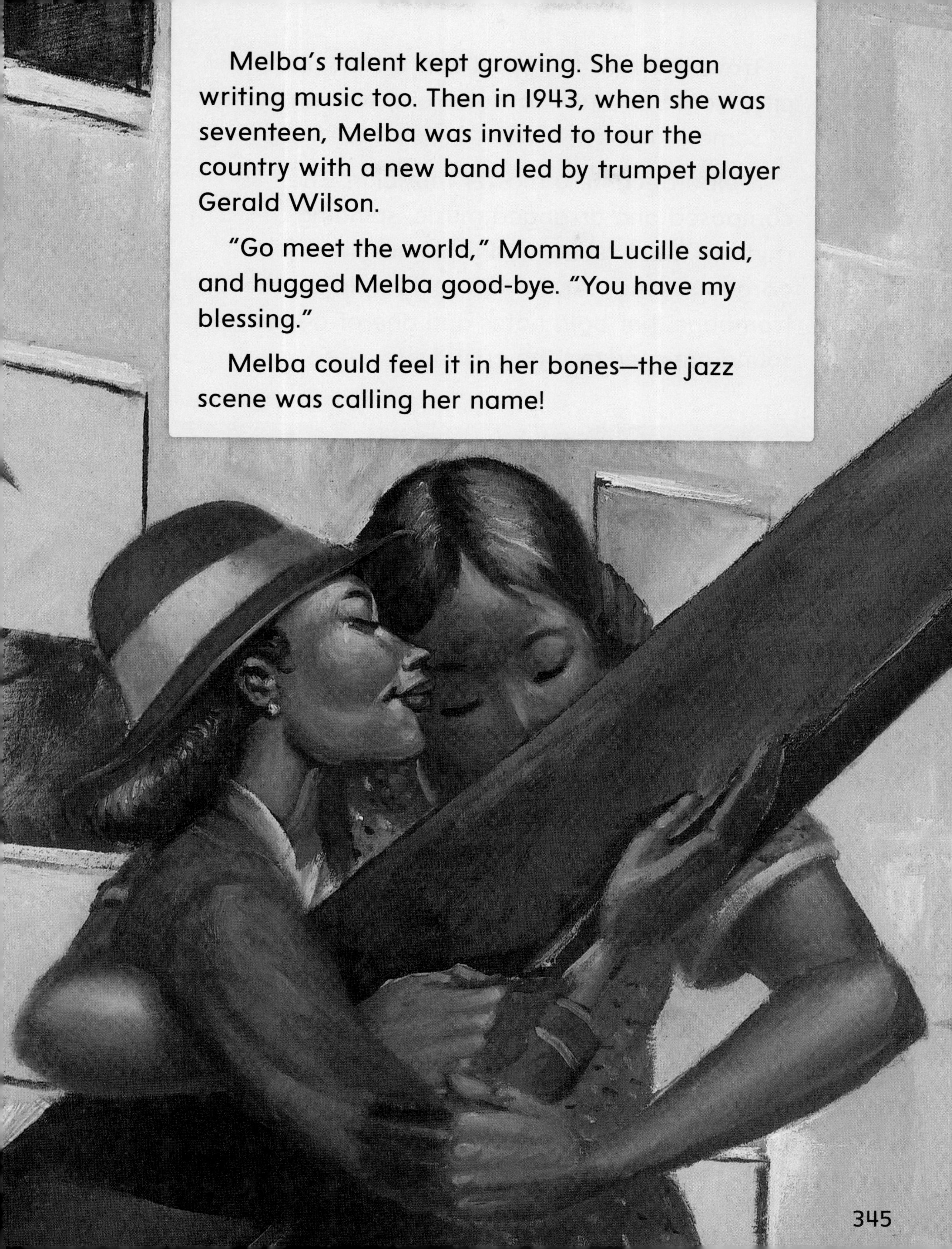

Melba's talent kept growing. She began writing music too. Then in 1943, when she was seventeen, Melba was invited to tour the country with a new band led by trumpet player Gerald Wilson.

"Go meet the world," Momma Lucille said, and hugged Melba good-bye. "You have my blessing."

Melba could feel it in her bones—the jazz scene was calling her name!

Traveling with the band was a thrill. Each city, from Salt Lake to New York, was an eyeful of something new.

Melba became a master musician. She composed and arranged music, spinning rhythms, harmonies, and melodies into gorgeous songs. And when Melba played the trombone, her bold notes and one-of-a-kind sound mesmerized the crowd.

Still, Melba was lonely. She was the only woman in the band. Some of the men were cruel. Others acted as if she wasn't there. Melba let the music in her head keep her company.

Rough times came when Melba traveled down South with singer Billie Holiday and her band. Some white folks didn't show good manners toward folks with brown skin. Hotel rooms were hard to come by, and the band members often had to sleep on the bus. Restaurants didn't always want their business. In the clubs, audiences sometimes just sat and stared at the band, or didn't show up at all.

Discouraged, Melba almost walked away from her trombone for good.

But Melba's fans wouldn't let her quit!

By the 1950s, all the cool jazz musicians wanted some Melba magic: Dizzy Gillespie, Duke Ellington, Quincy Jones, and more. They wanted to be on the bandstand with Melba and her divine horn. They wanted to play Melba's music.

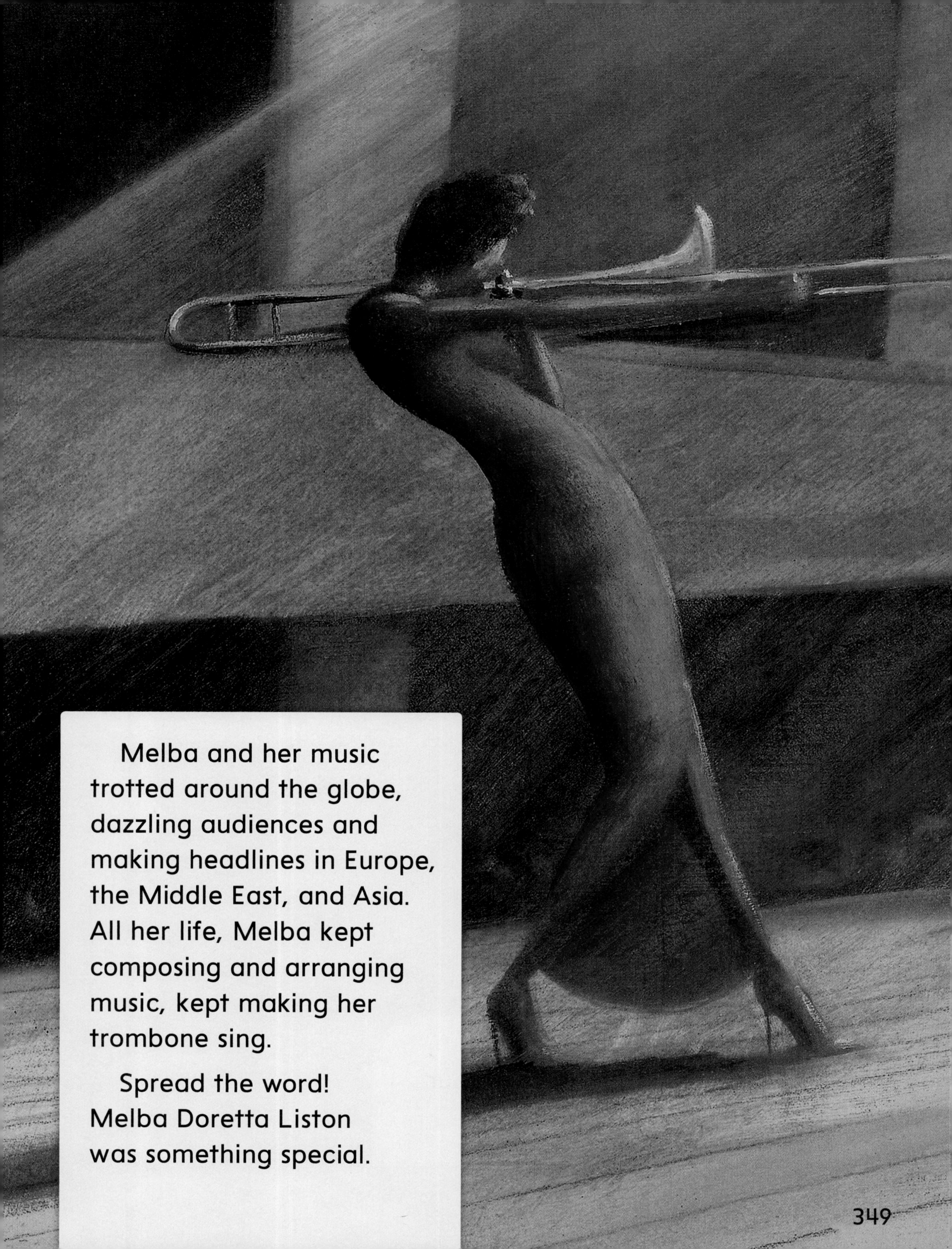

Melba and her music trotted around the globe, dazzling audiences and making headlines in Europe, the Middle East, and Asia. All her life, Melba kept composing and arranging music, kept making her trombone sing.

Spread the word! Melba Doretta Liston was something special.

Essential Question

What rhythms do you hear in your everyday life?

Jazz Is Everywhere

by Maggie Smith-Beehler

I hear the drum,
the *snap-hiss-snap-hiss*
of sticks and brushes striking,
the rhythm like a ball
bouncing on blacktop.

I hear the saxophone,
its voice deep and rich
like my father's
when he comes home smiling
and calls my name.

I hear the piano,
its sweet notes racing
to and fro, high and low,
on that long street of keys,
like me, running free.

You will answer the comprehension questions on these pages as a class.

Text Connections

1. What kinds of music did Melba like to listen to as a girl? What kind of music did she play when she grew up?
2. What type of music do you like the best? Does music move you in the same way it moved Melba? Explain your answer.
3. In "The Power of Music," what was the effect of Orpheus's music? In what ways was the effect of Melba's music similar?
4. Playing the trombone helped Melba endure many challenges. What kinds of challenges did Melba face? Why do you think playing the trombone helped her?

Did You Know?

The first trombones were called sackbuts. The name *sackbut* comes from the Middle French words *sacquer,* meaning "pull," and *bouter,* meaning "push."

Look Closer

Keys to Comprehension

1. The main idea of "Little Melba and Her Big Trombone" is that Melba Doretta Liston was a great musician. What details from the text support this idea?
2. Reread page 347. What is the main idea? How do the details on this page support this main idea?
3. What traits enabled Melba to become a success?

Writer's Craft

4. Some writers use idioms to add personality to their writing. An idiom is a phrase that means something more than is suggested by the definitions of its words. Find the following idioms on pages 342 and 343: *no piece of cake* and *smart as a whip*. What do these idioms mean? Use context clues to help you decide.

Concept Development

5. Reread page 338. How does the illustration help you understand the text on this page?

Write

Describe a time when determination helped you or someone you know achieve something special.

Read the story. Then discuss it with your class.

Vocabulary Words

- **beamed**
- **blessing**
- **company**
- **composed**
- **daydreamed**
- **discouraged**
- **melodic**
- **rhythms**
- **solo**
- **steady**
- **thrill**
- **tilt**

Choir Enthusiast

As a singer, I'm kind of an anomaly in my family—neither of my parents are musical. However, both know I've daydreamed of becoming a soloist. So, they gave me their blessings when I joined my school's choir.

There are so many things I love about choir! One is the songs we get to sing. Our choir director, Mr. Weber, arranges favorite songs from the radio for us. This means he remakes the songs into musical compositions that are in four-part harmony. Choir arrangements have four parts because a choir has four groups: sopranos, altos, tenors, and basses. Each group sings different notes of a song.

One challenge of being in a choir is learning to sing your group's part. Another is singing in rhythm with everyone else. Mr. Weber helps with this. He waves his hands in a steady beat that we all try to match with our voices.

Even harder than staying in rhythm is staying on pitch. When people sing a little higher or lower than they should, it makes Mr. Weber cringe. "That's not the melody!" he says, while tilting his head and screwing up his face in a look of pain.

It is discouraging when we can't get a song right. But Mr. Weber helps us practice, and then he beams when we finally hit all the notes correctly. It is always thrilling to see him smile at the end of a song. Even better, though, is singing in the company of music lovers like me.

Concept Vocabulary

Think about the word *groundbreaking.* What are some ideas or inventions that you would call groundbreaking?

Extend Vocabulary

Some words, such as *thrill,* describe an effect on one's state of mind. How is the effect described by *thrill* different from the effect described by these synonyms: *grip, delight, exhilarate, inspire.* Copy these words into your Writer's Notebook. Then write a sentence for each word that uses the word in the correct context. If you need help, use a dictionary to clarify the precise meaning of each word.

Read this Science Connection. You will answer the questions as a class.

Text Feature

A **diagram** adds to information provided in a text. Some diagrams show a process.

Force

Think about how a trombone works. A trombone has two basic parts, a horn and a slide. The horn is where sound is produced. The slide controls the pitch of the sound. In order for the slide to work, motion is required. A trombone player *pulls* the slide in or *pushes* the slide out. These pulling and pushing actions are examples of *force*.

Force and motion are always related. For a resting object to move, something must pull or push it. Also, for a moving object to stop or change speed, something must pull or push it. Now think about that for a moment. Does that seem like a true statement? If you push a ball away from you, does the ball keep moving at the steady speed with which you sent it? No, the ball slows down and then comes to a rest. What is the cause of this?

Scientists say that an object is at rest whenever balanced forces act on it. When the forces on an object are balanced, there is an equal amount of pushing or pulling on every side of the object. In order for an object to change position, the forces on that object must become unbalanced.

This diagram shows the effects of Earth's gravity on a ball. Because of gravity, this ball will roll down the hill.

1. How is the diagram helpful?
2. What parts of the diagram represent force? How is the strength of a force illustrated? Are the forces applied to this ball balanced or unbalanced?
3. What kind of force is gravity? Does it push or pull?

Go Digital

What is friction, and how does it affect the motion of an object?

Genre Realistic Fiction

Essential Questions

What goes into a performance that the audience does not see? Who works to make performances possible?

Marshall's Role

by Sam Estrada
illustrated by Cheryl Mendenhall

Marshall so wanted to be Peter Pan. Once he saw the notice about tryouts for the play, he set his heart on winning the part. As Peter Pan, he would fly through the air. He would rescue Wendy and her brothers. Best of all, he would defeat Captain Hook!

At the audition, Marshall did his very best. He read some lines of dialogue just as he thought Peter would say them. He showed his sword fighting moves.

But when Marshall walked off the stage, his heart sank. He overheard the director say to her assistant, "He was really good. It's too bad he's too young for the role."

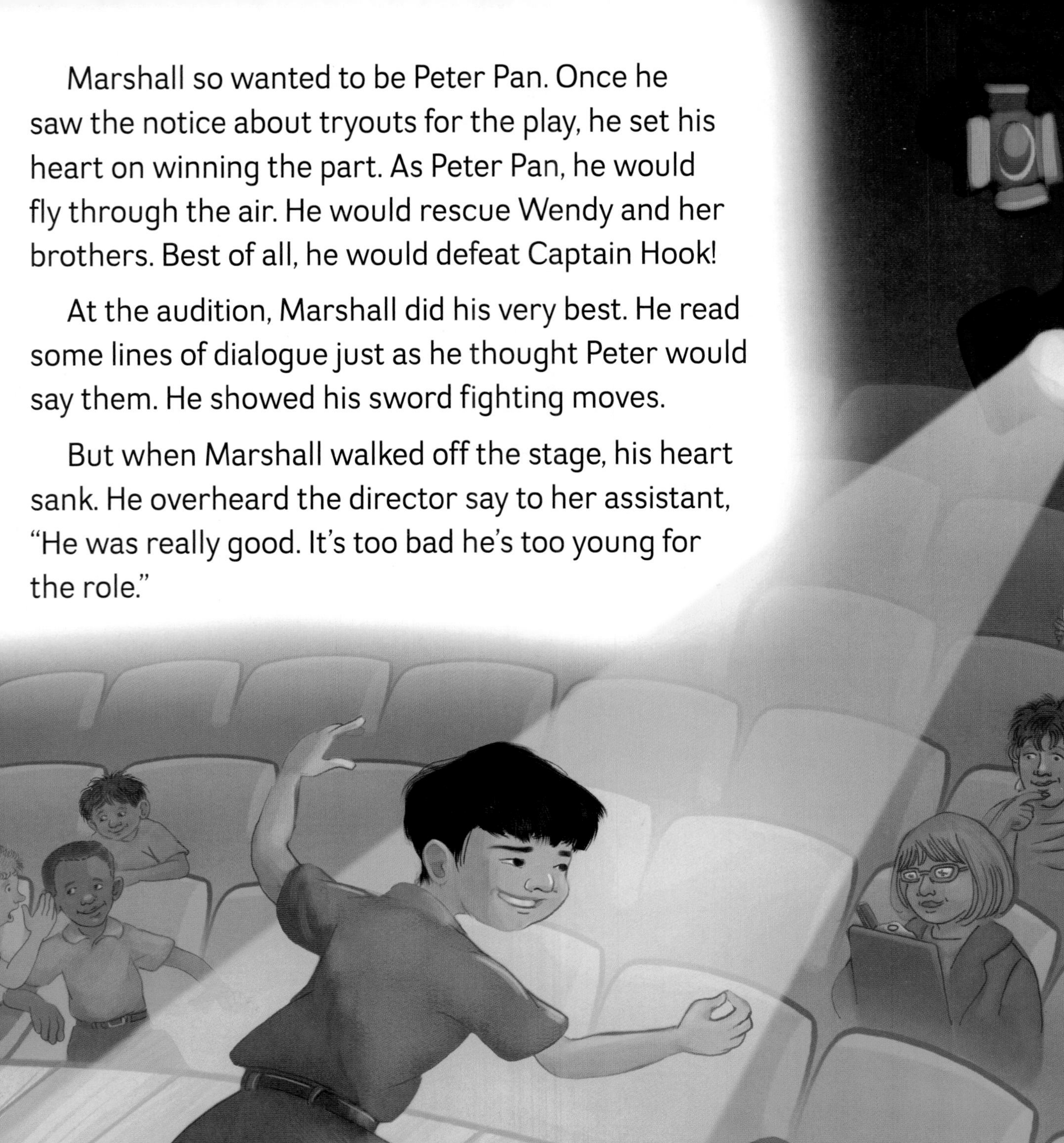

Sure enough, when the list of actors chosen for the play was posted, Marshall's name was not there. Not as Peter, not as a pirate, not even as one of Peter's group of Lost Boys.

Instead, Luke Scott won the role of Peter. Luke was three years older than Marshall. "Just watch!" Luke said. "I'm going to be great!"

A girl who had also tried out for a part nudged Marshall's arm. "You didn't get a role either, did you?" she asked

"No," said Marshall sadly.

"Well, we can still be part of the play," the girl said. "We can work backstage on one of the tech crews."

Marshall's first thought was to say *No way!* But then he reconsidered.

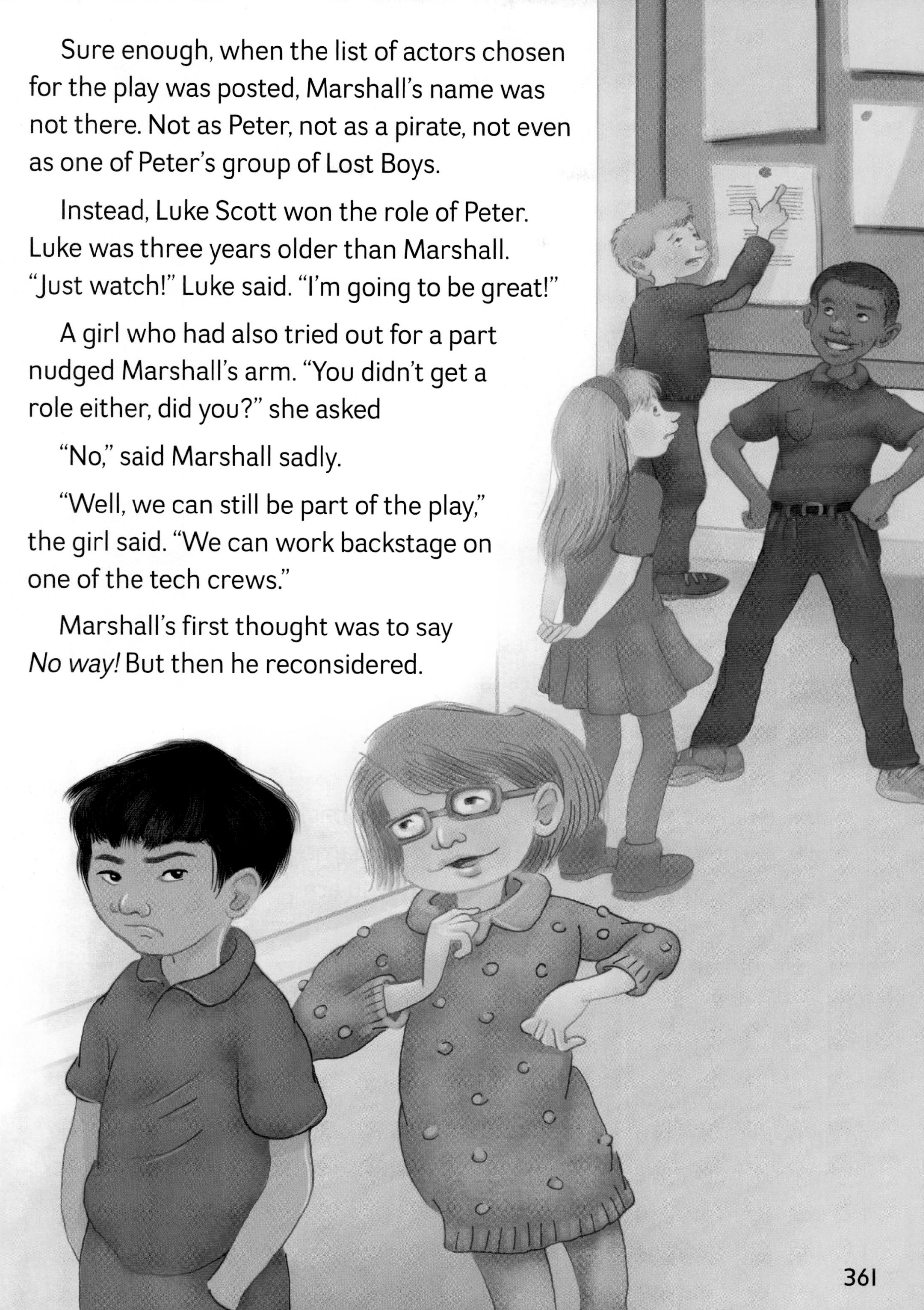

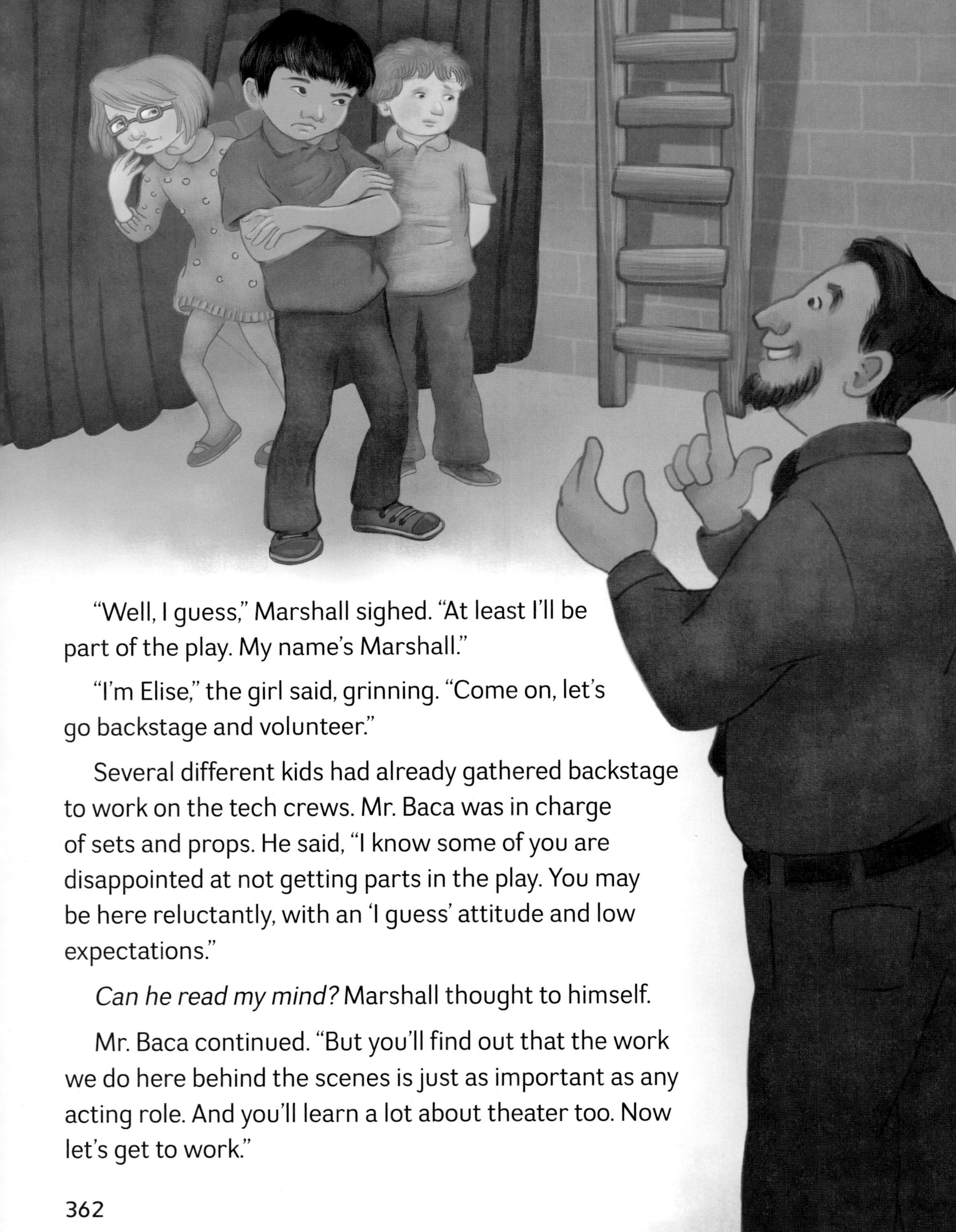

"Well, I guess," Marshall sighed. "At least I'll be part of the play. My name's Marshall."

"I'm Elise," the girl said, grinning. "Come on, let's go backstage and volunteer."

Several different kids had already gathered backstage to work on the tech crews. Mr. Baca was in charge of sets and props. He said, "I know some of you are disappointed at not getting parts in the play. You may be here reluctantly, with an 'I guess' attitude and low expectations."

Can he read my mind? Marshall thought to himself.

Mr. Baca continued. "But you'll find out that the work we do here behind the scenes is just as important as any acting role. And you'll learn a lot about theater too. Now let's get to work."

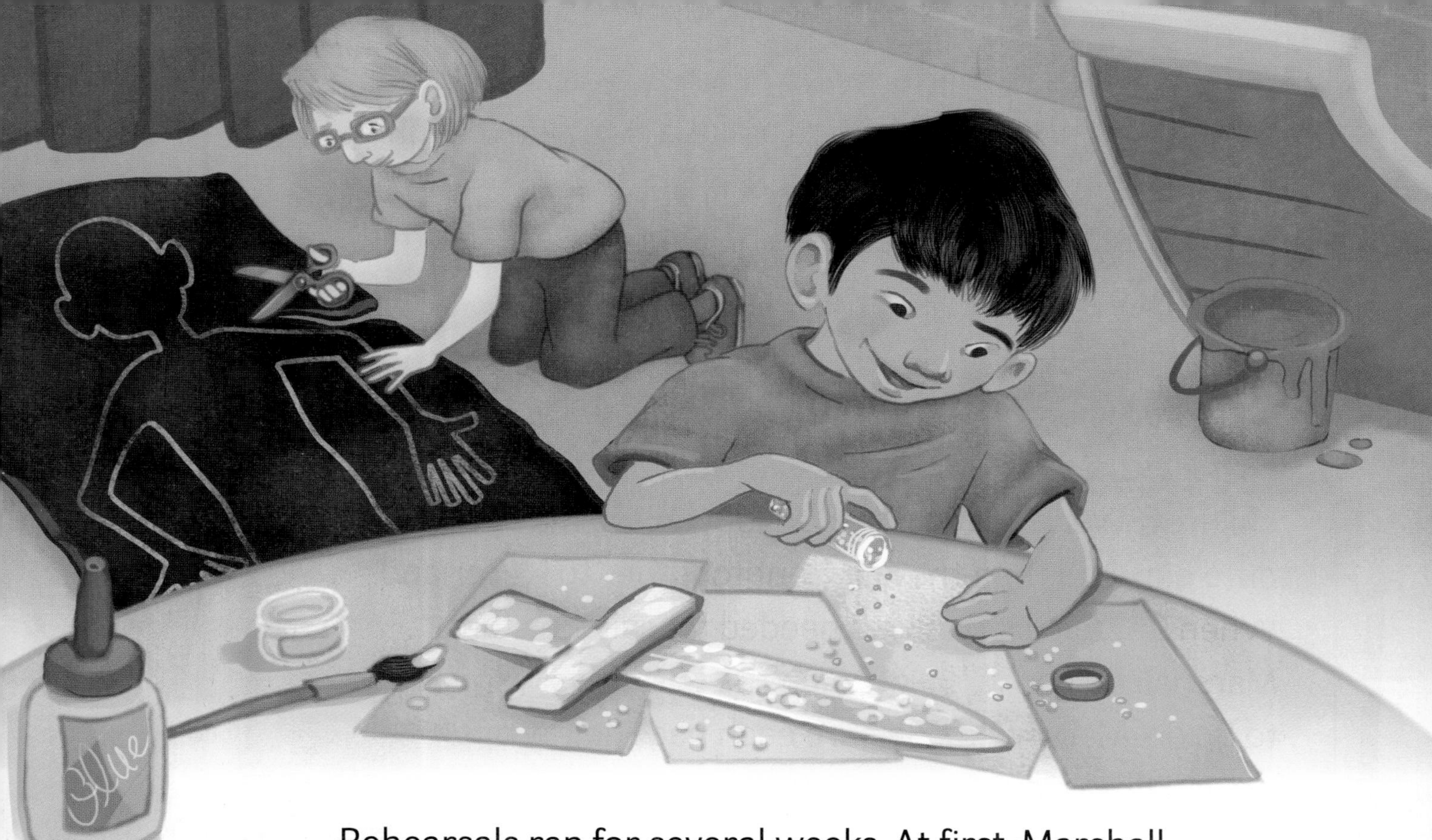

Rehearsals ran for several weeks. At first, Marshall barely focused on his work backstage. He was too busy watching the actors practicing their lines and moves onstage. But as the days passed, he became more and more interested in creating the sets and props.

He and Elise painted Captain Hook's ship. It was mostly made of cardboard, but they designed it to look like solid wood. Even the actors were fooled. Elise cut black felt to be Peter Pan's shadow. Marshall fashioned swords out of sturdy cardboard and glued silver glitter on the blades. He painted the handles gold. *They look sharp!* he thought.

Marshall watched intently as Mr. Baca himself worked on the harness and wires that would make Peter Pan fly through the air. Nothing could go wrong with them, or Luke would tumble to the ground.

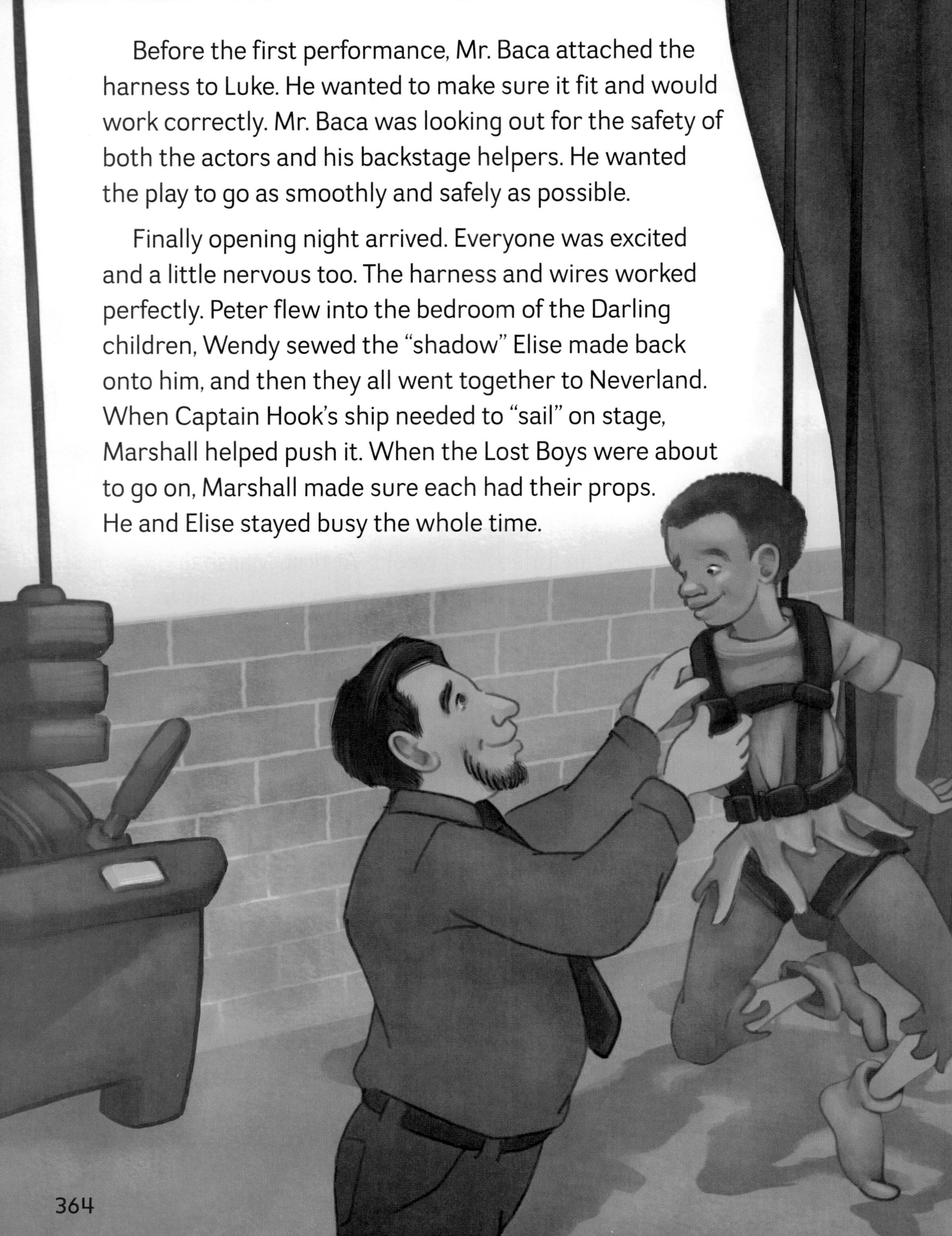

Before the first performance, Mr. Baca attached the harness to Luke. He wanted to make sure it fit and would work correctly. Mr. Baca was looking out for the safety of both the actors and his backstage helpers. He wanted the play to go as smoothly and safely as possible.

Finally opening night arrived. Everyone was excited and a little nervous too. The harness and wires worked perfectly. Peter flew into the bedroom of the Darling children, Wendy sewed the "shadow" Elise made back onto him, and then they all went together to Neverland. When Captain Hook's ship needed to "sail" on stage, Marshall helped push it. When the Lost Boys were about to go on, Marshall made sure each had their props. He and Elise stayed busy the whole time.

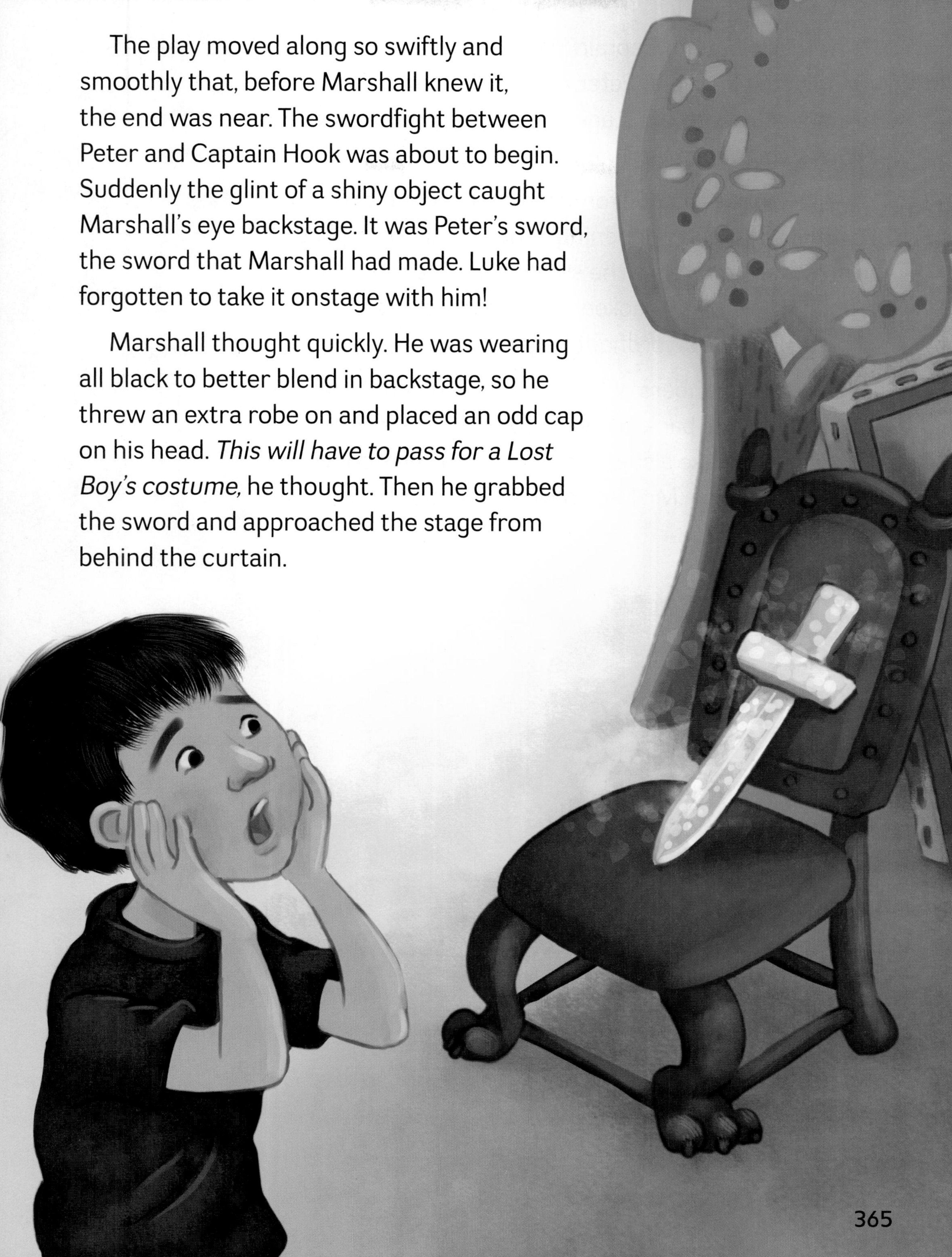

The play moved along so swiftly and smoothly that, before Marshall knew it, the end was near. The swordfight between Peter and Captain Hook was about to begin. Suddenly the glint of a shiny object caught Marshall's eye backstage. It was Peter's sword, the sword that Marshall had made. Luke had forgotten to take it onstage with him!

Marshall thought quickly. He was wearing all black to better blend in backstage, so he threw an extra robe on and placed an odd cap on his head. *This will have to pass for a Lost Boy's costume,* he thought. Then he grabbed the sword and approached the stage from behind the curtain.

At that moment, Captain Hook flashed his magnificent sword at Peter. Marshall raced dramatically onto the stage and loudly proclaimed, "Your sword, Peter!"

Luke looked startled for just a split second before he realized what was happening. "Thank you!" he replied just as loudly and took the sword from Marshall with a flourish. Marshall backed off the stage as Peter spun around, and the swordfight began.

Offstage members of the crew smiled and thumped Marshall on the back, but very quietly, because they knew not to make a sound while the play was going on. Elise hugged him. Mr. Baca gave him a thumbs up.

When the play ended, the audience gave a standing ovation and cheered loudly. Luke and the other actors took three long bows. Then the curtain was lowered.

Luke walked offstage and went straight to Marshall. "I can't thank you enough!" he exclaimed. "You saved me! Maybe they'll let you act onstage every night as one of the Lost Boys."

"Thanks," Marshall said. "But that's okay. I really enjoy it back here with the sets and props. Besides, as far as I'm concerned, a backstage role is just as important as an onstage role."

Essential Question

What does it feel like to perform in front of others?

The Play

by Margaret Shannon
illustrated by Stephen Costanza

Today's the day! I'm going to act
with all my classmates in the play.
I practiced every afternoon
to be ready for this day.

When they raise the curtain high,
it's time for me to play my part.
I take a breath and step on stage
to say the lines I know by heart.

I see the set, I see the lights,
I see the faces in the crowd.
But I am brave. I'm not afraid.
Today my voice is clear and loud.

When I act, I make-believe.
In my costume, I pretend
to be a character onstage.
I wish the play would never end.

But when the curtain falls, I know
my make-believe is done for now.
All the people clap their hands.
It's time to smile and take a bow.

You will answer the comprehension questions on these pages as a class.

Text Connections

1. What jobs do the tech crew perform in *Peter Pan*?
2. What do you think would happen if Marshall did not hand Luke his sword?
3. In this selection you read about a play. What are some other kinds of stage performances you have read about in this unit? What kinds of responsibilities might tech crews have for these performances?
4. The phrase "behind the scenes" originally described the work that tech crews do during stage performances. However, now this phrase also describes other kinds of creative work that is unseen by the public. How can you use the phrase "behind the scenes" to describe work that happens at your school?

Did You Know?

Sources say that the first actor to appear on stage was Thespis, in 534 B.C. It is from his name that we got the term *thespian,* meaning "a theatrical performer."

Look Closer

Keys to Comprehension

1. What motivates Marshall to become a member of the *Peter Pan* tech crew?
2. How does Marshall feel about being on the tech crew at the beginning of the story? Do his feelings ever change? Explain your answer.
3. Reread page 367. What sentence on this page contains the central message for the whole story? How is the central message supported by the story's events?

Write

Describe a time when you worked "behind the scenes." What were your responsibilities?

Writer's Craft

4. Reread the first sentence of the second paragraph on page 366. The phrase "a split second" is an example of an idiom. What do you think the phrase means? What clues in the phrase's context help you clarify its meaning?

Concept Development

5. Reread page 365. How does the illustration help you understand what is happening in this part of the story?

Read the article. Then discuss it with your class.

Vocabulary Words

- **audition**
- **flourish**
- **glint**
- **harness**
- **opening night**
- **props**

Stage Management

Some people think that auditioning or performing in a play is stressful. However, being a stage manager is much more so! A stage manager is involved in all aspects of a play. The stage manager oversees set, costume, and lighting design. He or she also schedules rehearsals and hosts meetings for the cast and crew.

The stage manager's job starts before rehearsals even begin. He or she meets with the director to discuss a vision for the play. Is special scenery needed, with moving parts or glinting lights? Is special equipment needed, such as harnesses or smoke machines? The stage manager asks questions such as these and then helps bring the director's vision to life.

During rehearsals, the stage manager writes a plan for making the play run smoothly. It includes notes about how the actors move across the stage. It names each prop and tells when the prop is used. It even includes lighting cues, or signals, that the stage lights needs to change.

From opening night to closing night, the plan is executed. And the stage manager helps ensure it happens perfectly! This, of course, is an impossible job—something always goes wrong. Then the stage manager finds a quick solution.

After the actors' final flourishes and bows, the stage manager is still hard at work. There are sets to break down and a cast party to throw. The stage manager makes sure these important things happen. Then he or she locks the theater doors before leaving the building.

Concept Vocabulary

Think about the word *spotlight.* When is a spotlight used? How does a spotlight improve a performance?

Extend Vocabulary

Many words contain Greek or Latin roots. These roots carry the main meaning for the words in which they are found. For example, consider the word *auditorium.* It contains the root *aud,* which means "hear." Copy the word *auditorium* into your Writer's Notebook, along with the root *aud* and its meaning. Then write a sentence or two about how the meaning of *aud* connects to the meaning of *auditorium.* Finally, use a dictionary to find and write two more words with *aud.* Explain how the meanings of these words relate to the meaning of *auditorium.*

Read this Science Connection. You will answer the questions as a class.

Text Feature

A **caption** tells about a picture and adds information to an article or story.

Predicting Motion

In "Marshall's Role," Mr. Baca sets up a harness with wires for Luke. With this apparatus, he creates the illusion that Luke can fly! Here is how the harness works:

- Luke wears the harness around his body.
- Wires suspend the harness from a scaffold above the stage.
- In his flight harness, Luke can swing and swoop across the stage. However, he needs help. A trained technician steers Luke's careens and dives.

Controlling movement is not always an easy thing to do! In order to control movement, we must first be able to predict it. In order to make a prediction, we must experiment. During the experiments, we must observe where and how quickly an object moves. We must also measure the distance an object moves when a certain amount of force is applied. Then we must record our observations and measurements and study them until we find patterns. A pattern is an event that always repeats itself. By finding patterns in motion, we can predict future motion.

When a baseball player hits a ball with his bat, he uses the bat to control the motion of the ball.

1. How is the caption helpful?
2. Recall what you know about force and motion. How can the baseball player make the ball travel faster? Should he hit the ball lightly or forcefully? How can the baseball player make the ball travel a longer distance? Should he hit the ball lightly or forcefully?
3. Do you think the ball player can control the direction the ball goes? Explain your answer.

Go Digital

What are examples of conditions that affect an object's motion?

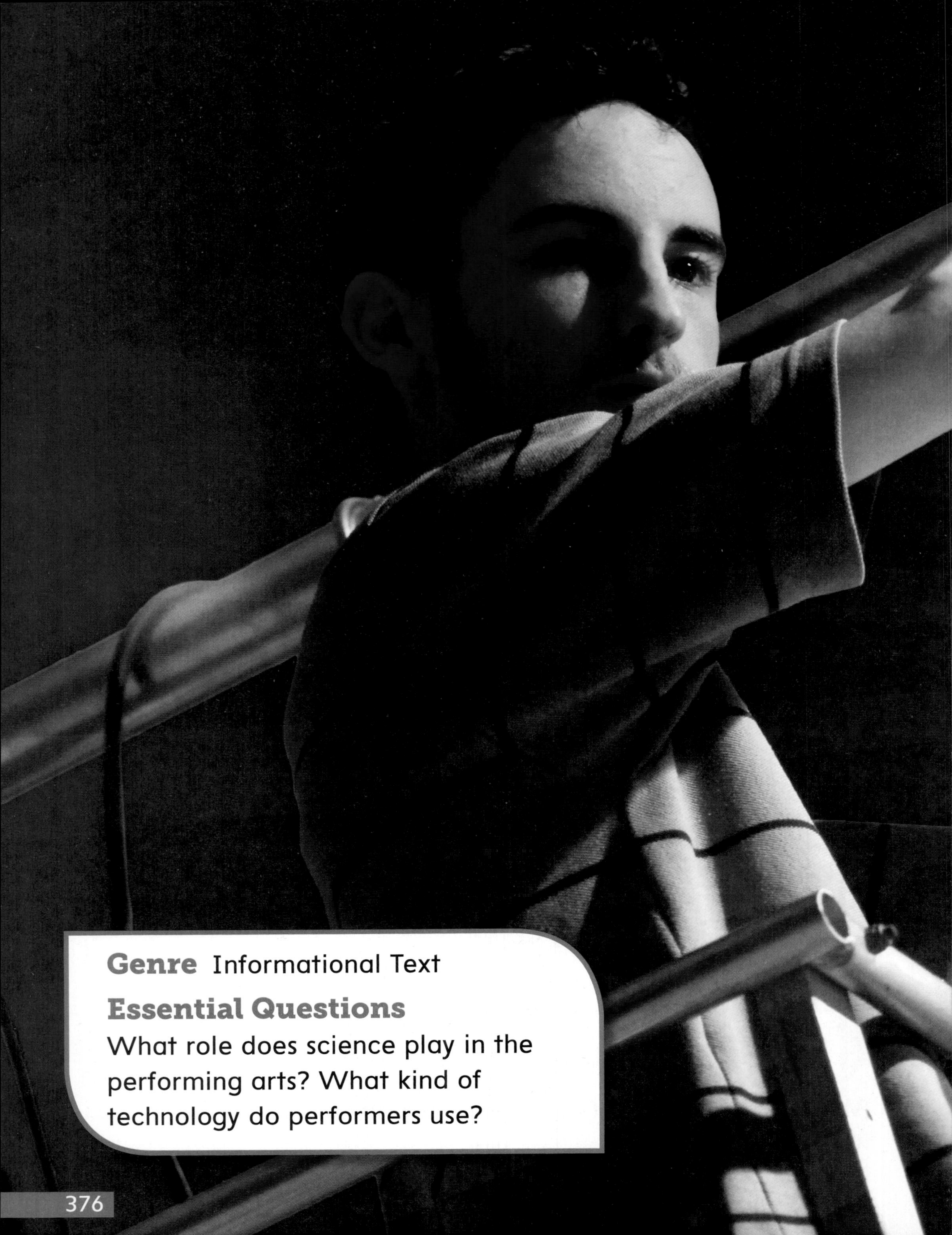

Genre Informational Text

Essential Questions

What role does science play in the performing arts? What kind of technology do performers use?

Behind the Scenes

by Tina Messerly

Opening Night

The lights dim. The curtains open. Get ready to enjoy the magic of theater! In a play, the action may appear to be only on the stage. But behind the scenes, people are hard at work. They change the set, or the background scenery that shows different locations. They control the music and lights that add excitement to the show. Perhaps they work to make actors or scenery fly through the air. To make all this happen, the people who put on plays use the laws of physics.

Physics is the study of how matter and energy work together. Matter is the stuff we see around us every day. Rocks, water, cars, your pet, and even you are all forms of matter. Energy is the force, or power, that makes matter move and change. In a play, a lot of matter moves and changes. A lot of energy is used.

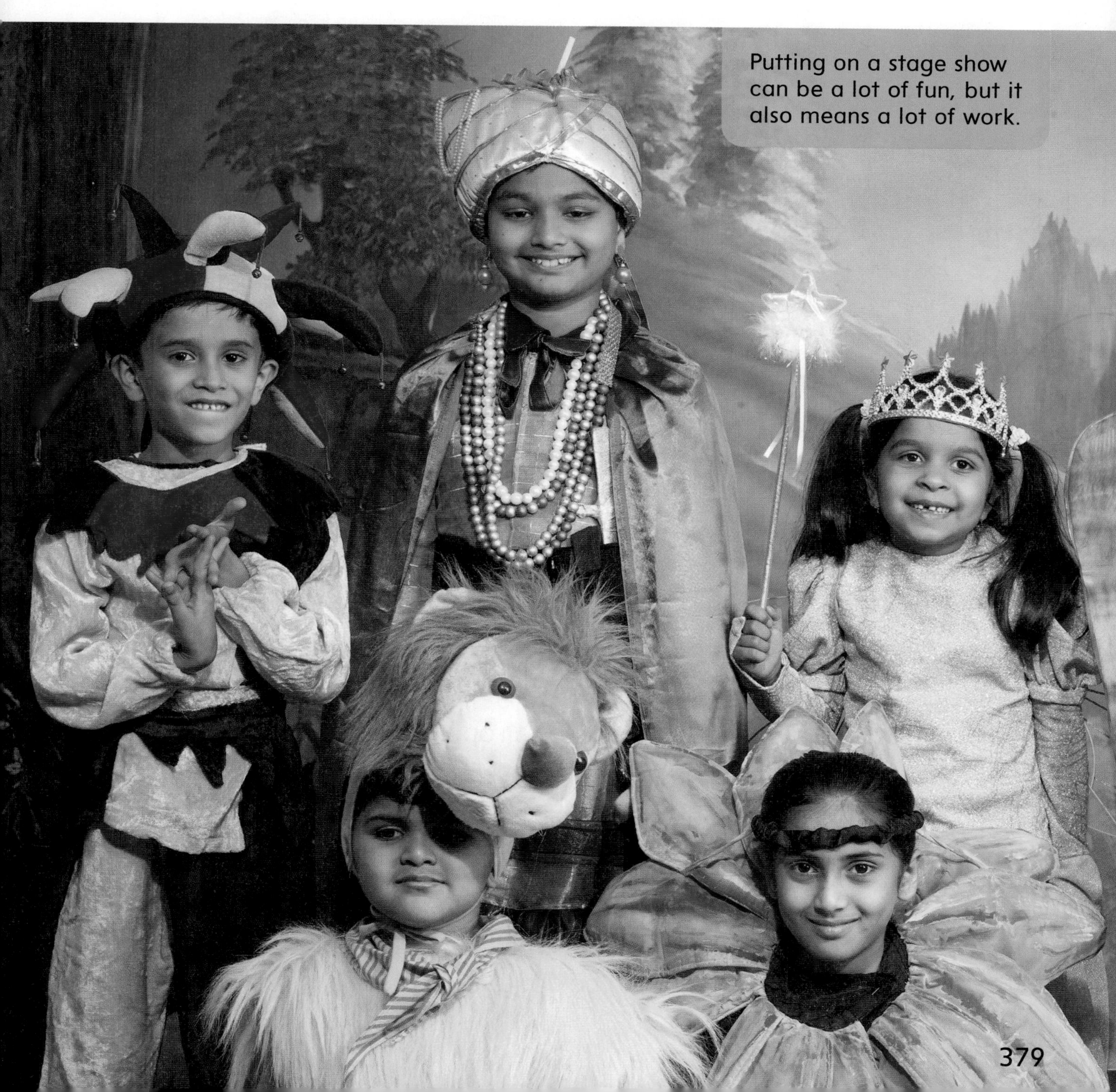

Putting on a stage show can be a lot of fun, but it also means a lot of work.

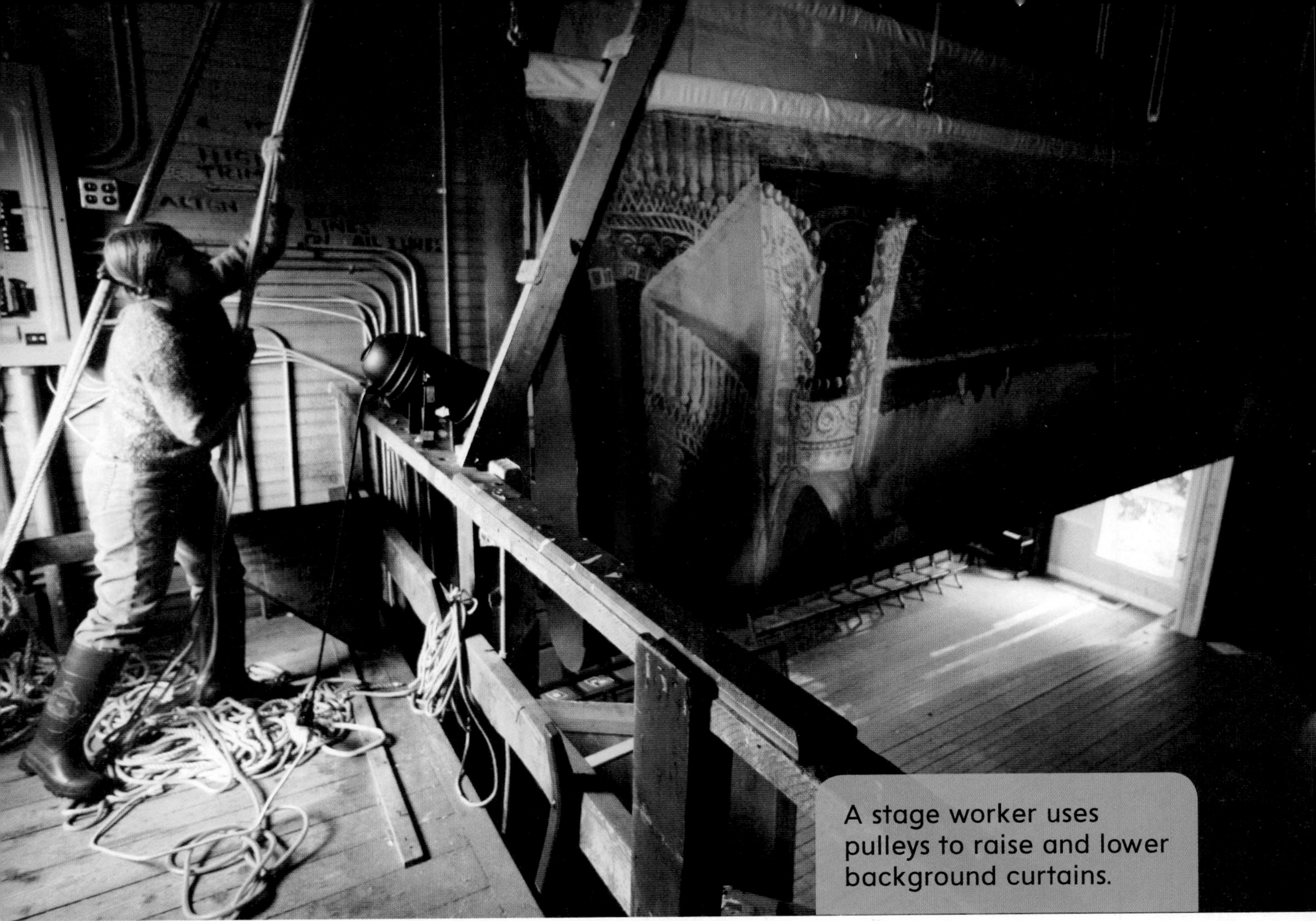

A stage worker uses pulleys to raise and lower background curtains.

Moving Heavy Loads

The curtains, lights, and sets in large theaters are heavy. They need to be raised, lowered, and moved from side to side. One of the ways to move heavy things is to use a pulley, or a grooved wheel with a rope passed over it. Pulleys change the direction of force. A stage worker attaches a rope to a load and then passes it through a pulley overhead. A person can pull down on the other end of the rope to raise the load. That is how the set, curtains, and lights are often raised. Most of these loads are often too heavy for one person to move with a simple pulley, but with the help of counterweights, it can be done.

Counterweights make it easier to raise and lower heavy curtains, lights, and sets in a theater.

Think about trying to pull a huge load off the ground with just your strength. You could not do it. But what if you have a lot of extra weight helping you pull? This extra weight is called *counterweight*. Counterweights are heavy steel plates. Stage workers place enough counterweights to match the weight of whatever they need to move. When the weights on each side are equal, the set or the curtains stay put. They do not move unless somebody pulls the cable. Whenever somebody needs to move them it is not too difficult. Thanks to the counterweights, the stage workers do not need to pull the cables hard to raise or lower items that can be very heavy.

These actors seem to fly through the air with the help of pulleys and counterweights.

Flying on Stage

Sometimes actors and performers appear to be flying. On-stage flight also uses counterweights and pulleys. Flying on stage may be simple or it may be complicated. In simple flying, a pulley and a counterweight lift and lower the actor. The flying gets more complicated when the actor does twists, turns, and tumbles in the air.

One stage play famous for its flying stunts is *Peter Pan.* Peter, Wendy, Tinker Bell, and a few other characters in this play fly. Peter and Tinker Bell tumble in the air as well. Each actor wears a special harness that allows these movements.

Actors appear to be flying when they swing like pendulums.

A simple machine called a pendulum creates the illusion of flying. A pendulum is a weight that swings from a cable. In the case of stage flying, the weight is the actor. The cable attaches to a point on the ceiling. The actor may swing from side to side or in a circle. But the actor's anchor point on the ceiling does not move. When the flight ends, the actor is lowered down, at or near the takeoff spot. He or she does not move too far from that spot.

We use a law of physics to determine the time it takes for a pendulum to swing back and forth once. It depends on the length of the cable. With the cable a certain length, stage workers can time an actor's takeoffs and landings. Stage hands know just how far an actor can swing from the starting point. The actor may swing all around the anchor point. But he or she always lands in a point somewhere in a circle. The length of the cable determines the size of the circle. This helps the stage workers design the set so the flying actor does not crash into other actors or things on stage.

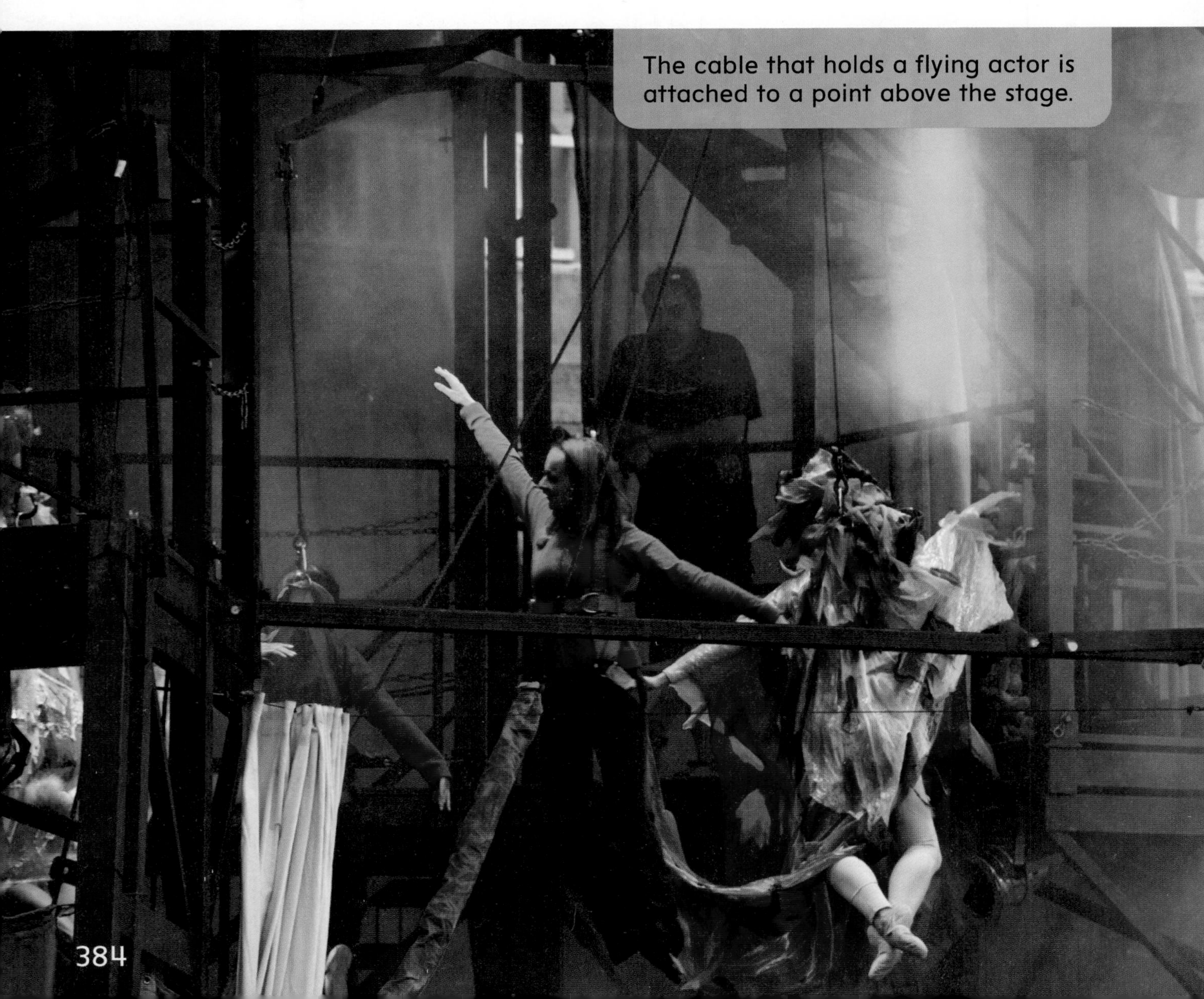

The cable that holds a flying actor is attached to a point above the stage.

Making Sounds Louder

Physics also plays a part in what you hear at the theater. Many theaters are very large. People in the seats far from the stage cannot hear the actors without help. Microphones and speakers help amplify, or increase, the volume of the actors' voices. These devices change sound into electricity and back again. Electricity, a form of energy, can easily travel through wires.

Sound is also a form of energy, but it moves in waves through the air. As sound waves travel, they push on the air. When they reach your ears, they vibrate your eardrum. The changes make your eardrum send signals to the brain. The brain then makes sense of the signals.

Speakers make sounds from the stage louder so the audience can hear.

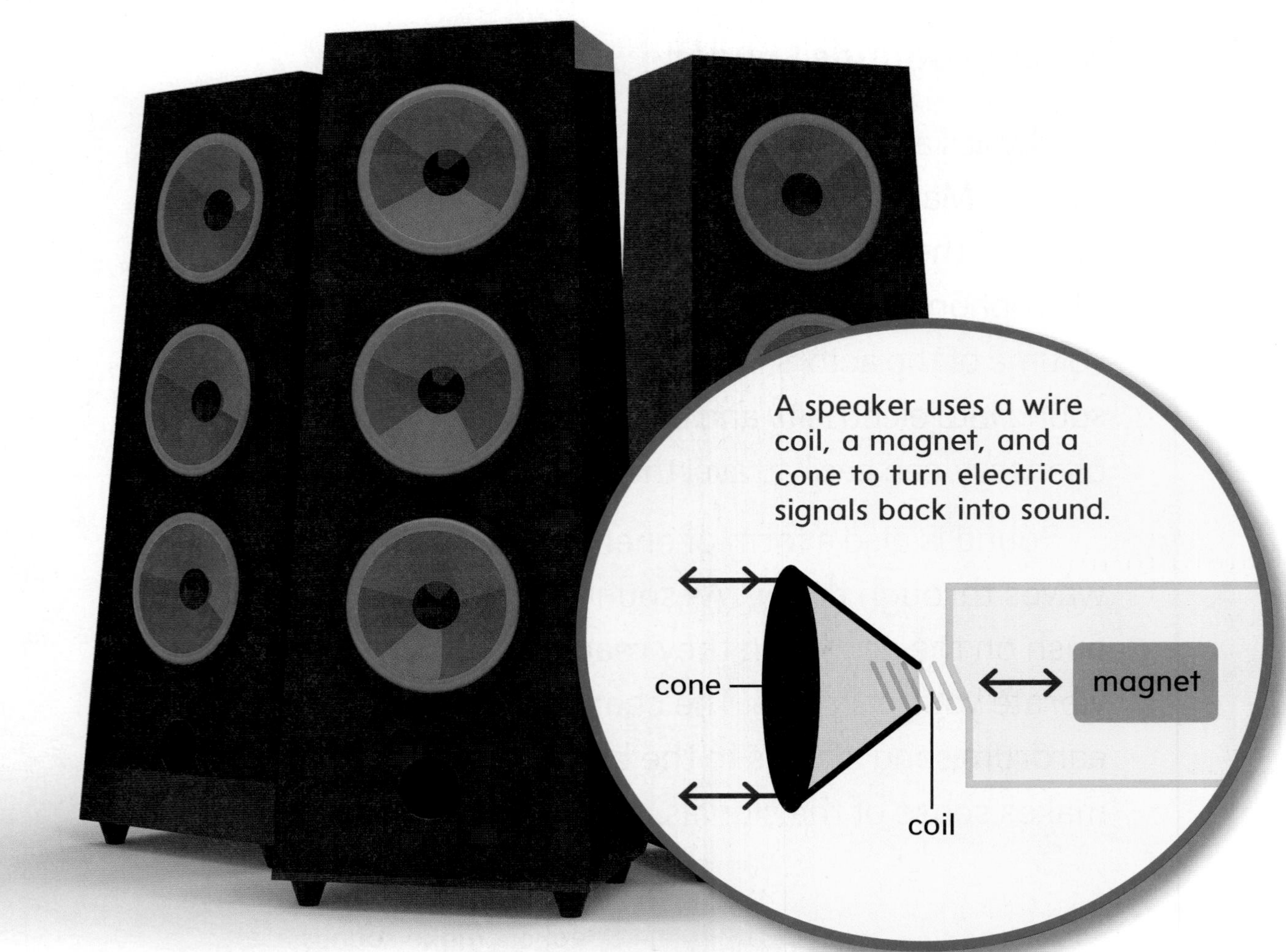

A speaker uses a wire coil, a magnet, and a cone to turn electrical signals back into sound.
cone
magnet
coil

In a large theater, those sound waves reach your ears through the use of speakers. Speakers change an electrical signal into sound waves. The electrical signal enters the speaker and flows into a coil of wire. The coil is near a permanent magnet (similar to a refrigerator magnet, but much stronger). When the electric current flows in, it magnetizes the coil. That causes the coil to be attracted to, or pulled toward, the magnet. When the current flow is reversed, the coil is pushed away from the magnet. By rapidly switching the direction of the current, the coil can be made to move in and out very quickly. The coil is also attached to a cone. The movement of the coil causes the cone to move as well, which creates sound waves.

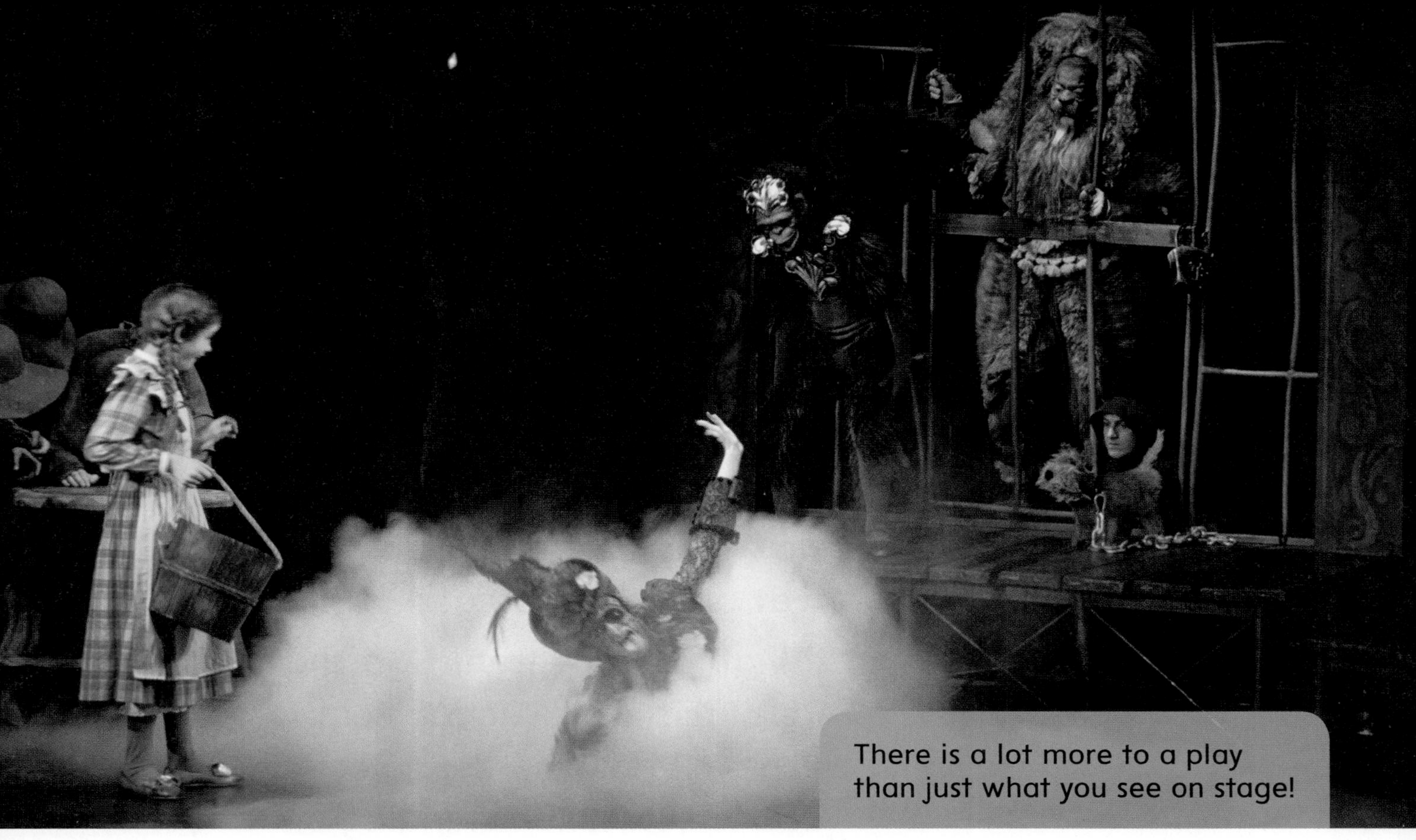
There is a lot more to a play than just what you see on stage!

The electrical signal the speakers receive often comes from a microphone. One kind of microphone works just like a loudspeaker, but in reverse! It uses a magnet to change sound into electricity. Sound waves strike a thin piece of material called a diaphragm. The diaphragm is attached to a coil of wire. The sound waves make the diaphragm move back and forth very quickly. This makes the coil move, too. Near the coil is a magnet. When the wire coil moves close to the magnet, the magnet gives it an electric current. The current then travels through the wire and to the speakers.

Microphones and speakers help make a play sound great. Weights and pulleys keep heavy things moving smoothly, even when the actors fly through the air! Stagecraft could not exist without physics.

Respond

Comprehension

You will answer the comprehension questions on these pages as a class.

Text Connections

1. What are some examples of heavy loads that must be moved during theatrical productions?
2. At one time, there were no such things as microphones and speakers. How do you think this affected the way plays were staged?
3. What machine from "Marshall's Role" did this selection help to explain? How did this selection add to your understanding of the machine?
4. Pulleys, counterweights, and pendulums are not used only in theaters. Where are some other places you have seen one or more of these machines used?

Did You Know?

Galileo Galilei is an important scientist who lived nearly 400 years ago. He discovered that a pendulum's motion is very predictable. This discovery led to the invention of the first clock.

Look Closer

Keys to Comprehension

1. What is the main idea of this selection? What details support this main idea?
2. How does the length of a cable affect the time it takes for a pendulum to swing back and forth? Why are pendulums used in the theater?
3. What does a microphone do to sound waves? Why does a microphone need speakers to work? Why are microphones and speakers used in theaters?

Writer's Craft

4. The word *matter* has multiple meanings. Within the context of this selection, does it mean "a problem" or "something that has mass and occupies space"? How do you know?

Concept Development

5. Reread page 381. How does the photograph help you understand the text?

Write

Describe a time when one of the machines from this selection would have helped you.

Read the article. Then discuss it with your class.

Vocabulary Words

- **coil**
- **current**
- **devices**
- **dim**
- **loads**
- **physics**

The Lightbulb

Today in physics class I learned about the lightbulb. The lightbulb is a device that turns electrical energy into light. My teacher explained how it works: Each lightbulb has a metal base, a filament, and a glass bulb. The metal base carries an electric current to the lightbulb's filament. The filament is a thin wire made of tungsten. The tungsten carries currents, but not easily—it resists them. This causes the filament to get so hot that it glows and makes light! As the filament glows, it is important to keep air away from it. Air could cause the filament to catch fire. This is why there is a glass bulb around the filament—the glass bulb protects it.

The more tungsten a lightbulb's filament has, the brighter the lightbulb glows. However, brighter bulbs also need more electricity to work. This is a problem because it takes loads of natural resources to make electricity. It is important to conserve natural resources, so people need to consider using dimmer lightbulbs. That is, they did until compact fluorescent lights (CFLs) were invented. These CFLs look and work differently from incandescent lightbulbs.

A CFL has a coiled glass tube. Inside the tube is a gas and chemical mix. This mix glows when it carries electricity, just like the filament of an incandescent lightbulb does. However, the mix does not resist the flow of electricity as much as a filament. This means a CFL needs less electricity to work.

Concept Vocabulary

Think about the word *engineer.* What kinds of things do engineers make? Where does an engineer get new ideas for inventions?

Extend Vocabulary

Physics is an example of a word formed from a Latin root. Its root is *phys-,* which means "nature." Copy the word *physics* into your Writer's Notebook, along with the root *phys-* and its meaning. Then write a sentence or two about how the meaning of *phys-* connects to the meaning of *physics.* Finally, use a dictionary to find and write two more words with *phys-.* Explain how the meanings of these words relate to the meaning of *physics.*

Read this Science Connection. You will answer the questions as a class.

Text Feature

A **numbered list** is a way of organizing information that needs to happen in a specific order.

Designing to Solve Problems

Think about the machines you read about in "Behind the Scenes." Why were these machines invented? Each was invented to solve a problem! For example, the stage had heavy set pieces, so someone engineered a way to move those set pieces around more easily.

You, too, can be an engineer! Here is an activity for you to try:

1. Think about how pulleys, counterweights, and magnets help people perform work.
2. Find a partner. Brainstorm a list of problems that could be solved using a pulley, counterweights, magnets, or a combination of these things.
3. Work with your partner to define one of the problems.
4. Brainstorm different ways to use pulleys, counterweights, or magnets to solve the problem.
5. Work with your partner to choose the best design.
6. Draw your design, and write an explanation of how it works. Tell about the scientific ideas it applies.
7. Present your design to an audience.

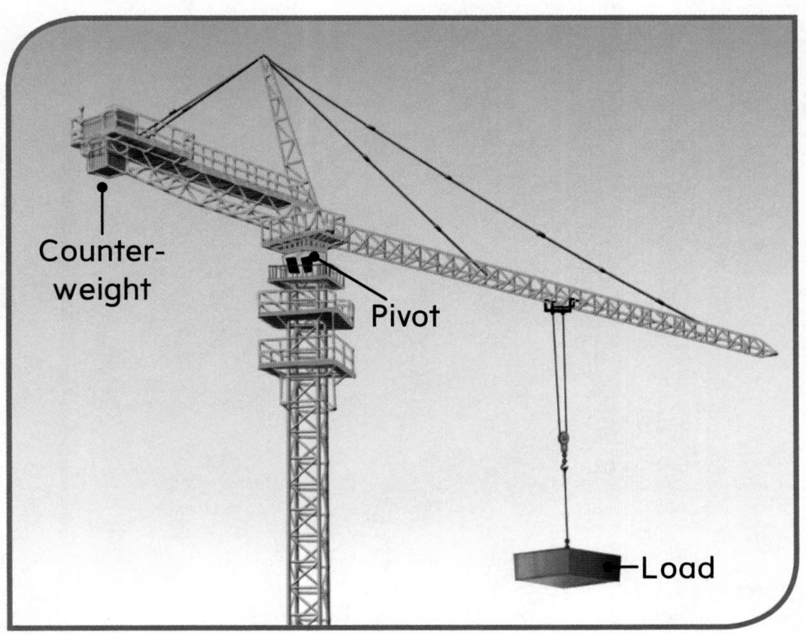

Counterweights can balance a heavy load.

Pulleys can make it easier to lift heavy objects.

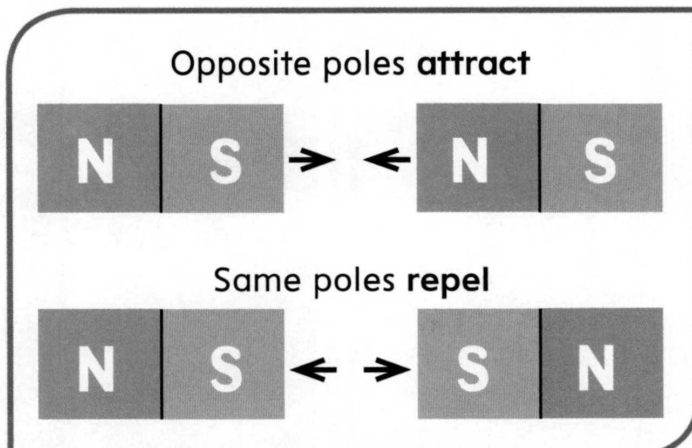

Magnets can pull toward each other or push away from each other.

1. How is having the activity in a numbered list helpful?
2. Which tools can help with lifting loads?
3. Which tools can help with holding a load in place?

Go Digital

What are some machines that combine pulleys, counterweights, and magnets in the same device? How are these machines used?

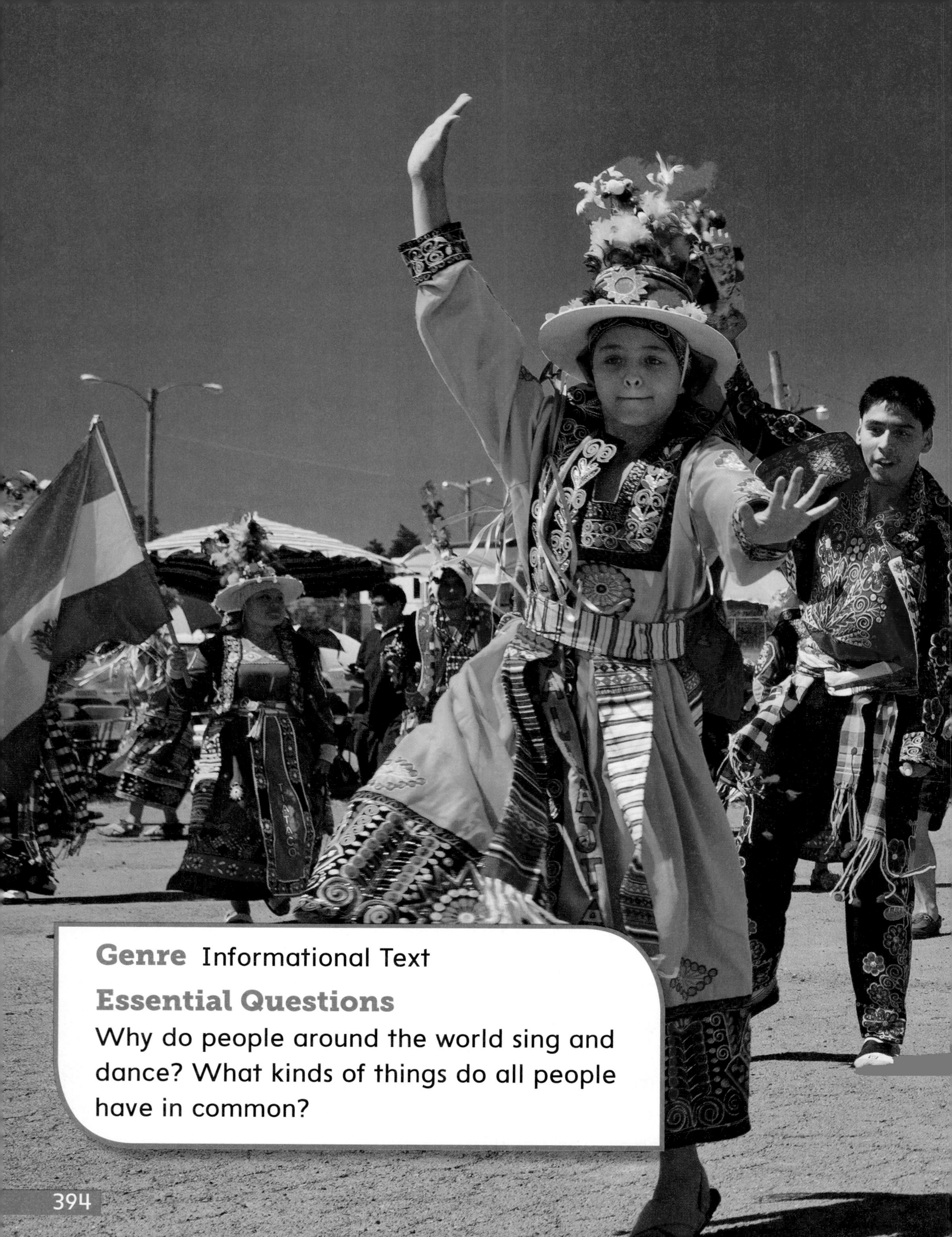

Genre Informational Text

Essential Questions

Why do people around the world sing and dance? What kinds of things do all people have in common?

A World Tour in Song and Dance

by Jack Stearns

pan flute

hollow gourd

All over the world, people go through similar stages in life. Music is often used to mark these stages. Musicians give soldiers courage to go into battle. Singers ease some of the pain when a loved one dies. Dancers celebrate a birthday or a wedding. Music and dance help people celebrate, mourn, or just show friendship.

Music and dance differ from place to place and from culture to culture. Some instruments are cultural and are used only in certain regions. Types of music can be very different, with sounds and rhythms that vary widely. What seems normal to one group often may be unfamiliar to another.

It does not matter what specific melodies we sing or what dance steps we use. It does not matter what instruments we play or where we come from. All people make and enjoy music!

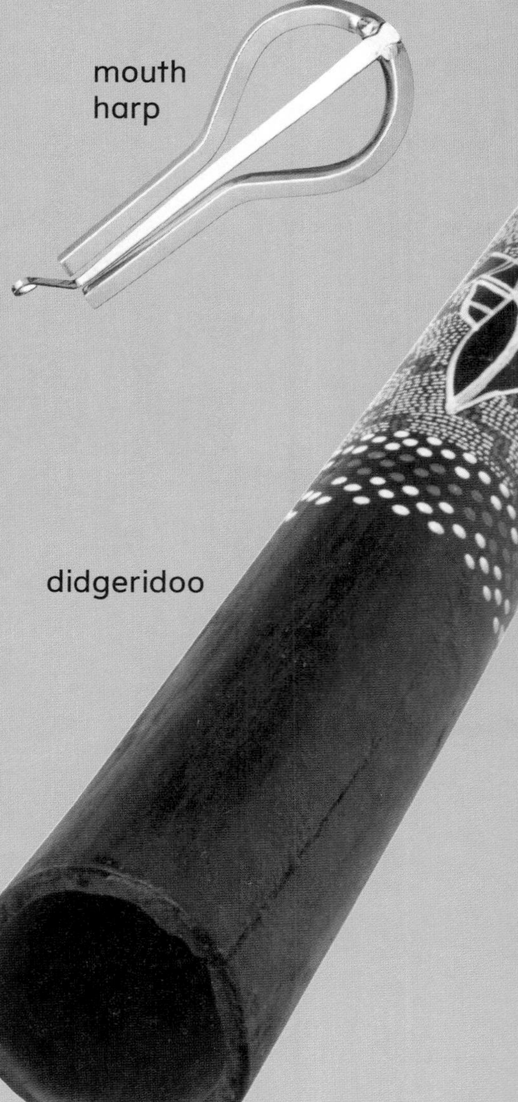

mouth harp

didgeridoo

kobza

Music Old and New

Some songs and dances are rather old. They have been handed down from generation to generation. These songs and dances are traditional and are often used to tell stories.

For instance, imagine a woman who lived in India 2,000 years ago. She would probably recognize some Indian songs and dances today. Not only do Indian dancers use facial expressions to act out a story, but they also use body movements and hand gestures. They have done this over many generations.

Some of the Indian dancers' motions are simple to understand. To show anger, dancers stomp firmly with their feet as they jump. To show great delight, they grin broadly.

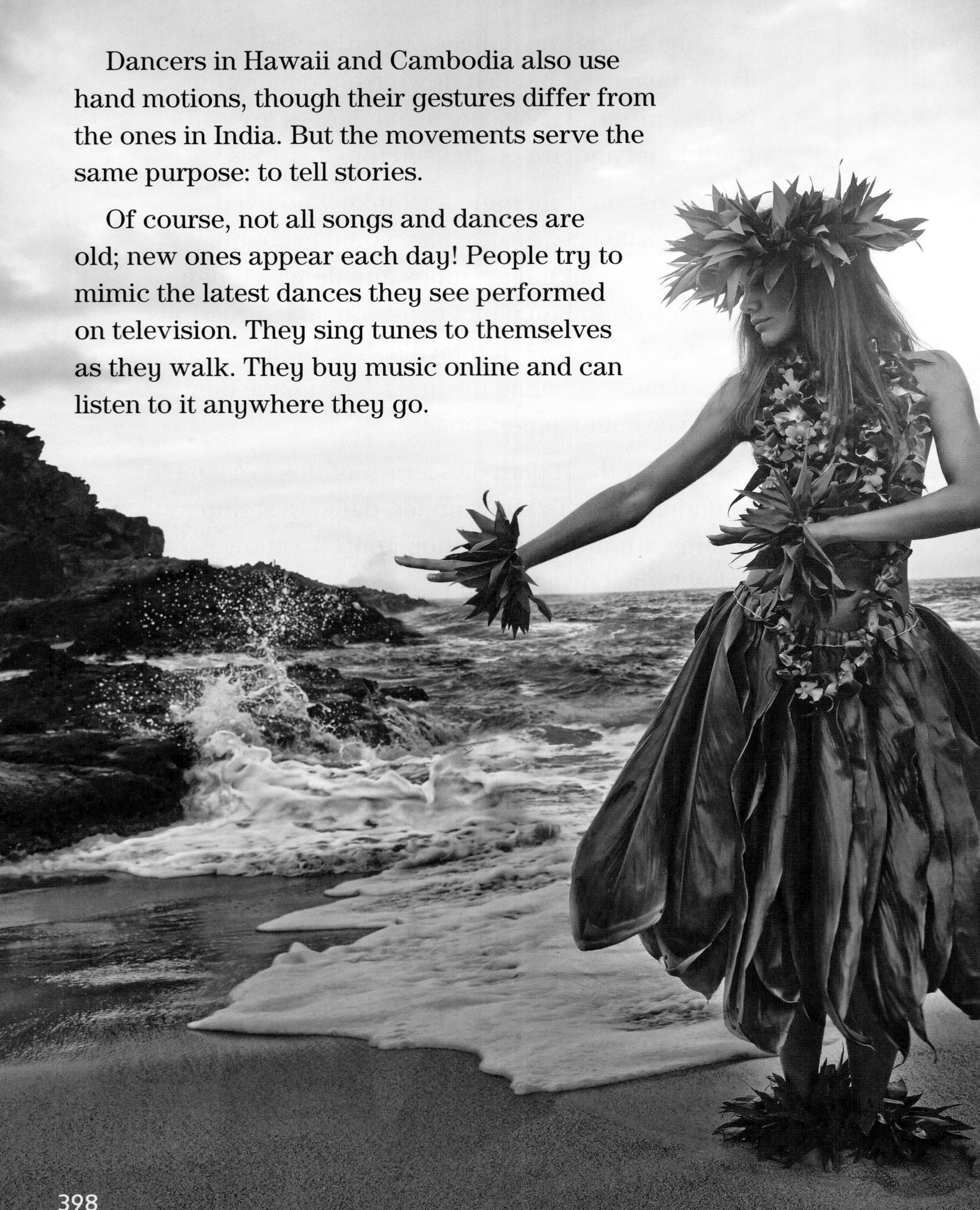

Dancers in Hawaii and Cambodia also use hand motions, though their gestures differ from the ones in India. But the movements serve the same purpose: to tell stories.

Of course, not all songs and dances are old; new ones appear each day! People try to mimic the latest dances they see performed on television. They sing tunes to themselves as they walk. They buy music online and can listen to it anywhere they go.

When people sing and dance with one another, they bring different generations together. Older relatives often teach younger people the songs and dances of their cultures. By knowing these songs and dances, family members can take part in cultural celebrations.

Songs and dances reveal what each culture thinks is important. By learning traditional songs and dances, people discover who they are and where they come from.

Celebrating a wedding might seem like a good reason to use music. But what about mourning the dead at a funeral?

In New Orleans, Louisiana, jazz funerals are famous. The tradition comes from a mix of African, European, and American cultures. A jazz funeral commences with a march to the cemetery. A brass band plays somber music while family and friends walk slowly.

After the burial the music becomes more upbeat. The band plays popular jazz songs and marches faster. The people who trail the band as it marches are called the second line. They sometimes twirl umbrellas or wave handkerchiefs in the air. Others may dance to celebrate the life of the person who has died.

The Tujia people of China also dance at funerals. When a person dies, the community gathers together. The people, dressed in colorful clothes, gather around the coffin. Many Tujia think of death as natural, like the change of seasons. Some people beat out rhythms on drums; others sing. Everyone else dances to the music.

In Ireland a tradition of keening over a dead body was once common. A "keen" was part sad song and part wild cry. The keeners honored the dead person by singing questions and answers about his or her life. Women usually keened, but sometimes men joined in with their deeper voices. Other people swayed or clapped along to honor the life of the deceased.

Khattak dancers sometimes use handkerchiefs instead of swords.

People also sing and dance in stressful times, such as war. Many cultures have used songs or dances to prepare soldiers for battle. Armies all over the world have played drums to inspire fighters.

Khattak is the name of a warlike dance performed by a cultural group in Pakistan. Khattak is danced to a rapid beat. The dancers have to be very well trained to perform it. Musicians beat their drums with sticks. Groups of men dance together to the sound. The dancers carry swords and perform acrobatic movements.

Capoeira has become so popular that there are special schools that teach it all over the world.

Capoeira is a very popular art form in Brazil. It was brought there in the 1600s by enslaved people from Angola, a country in Africa. They recalled the warrior music of their culture with capoeira. It is part dancing and part fighting, with many leaps and spins.

For capoeira, musicians play drums and tambourines. They also play an instrument called a berimbau. The dancers form a circle and sing and clap in rhythm with the instruments. A pair goes to the center and pretends to fight. Although it began as a martial art, many people now consider capoeira a type of performance.

Everyday Music

Do people require special occasions to make music? Do they have to wait for a funeral or battle? Of course not!

People all over the world sing and dance for the sheer fun of it. They sing or hum in the shower, while going somewhere, or just to make a task seem easier. They dance at parties and clubs, and even in schoolyards.

Some people sing and dance wherever they can.

A Japanese drummer named Daisuke Inoue realized that almost everyone loves to sing. In 1971 he invented a machine for karaoke. The name means “empty orchestra” in Japanese. The machine plays the instrumental music of a song, and a person sings along. Karaoke quickly spread throughout Asia. Eventually it reached the rest of the world and became very popular.

But people do not always want to perform with a machine. Some of them want to create their own music. They may form a band and practice wherever they can. These groups sometimes hold rehearsal in a family's garage, so they are called "garage bands." Most garage bands do not strive to become famous. The musicians just enjoy making music together.

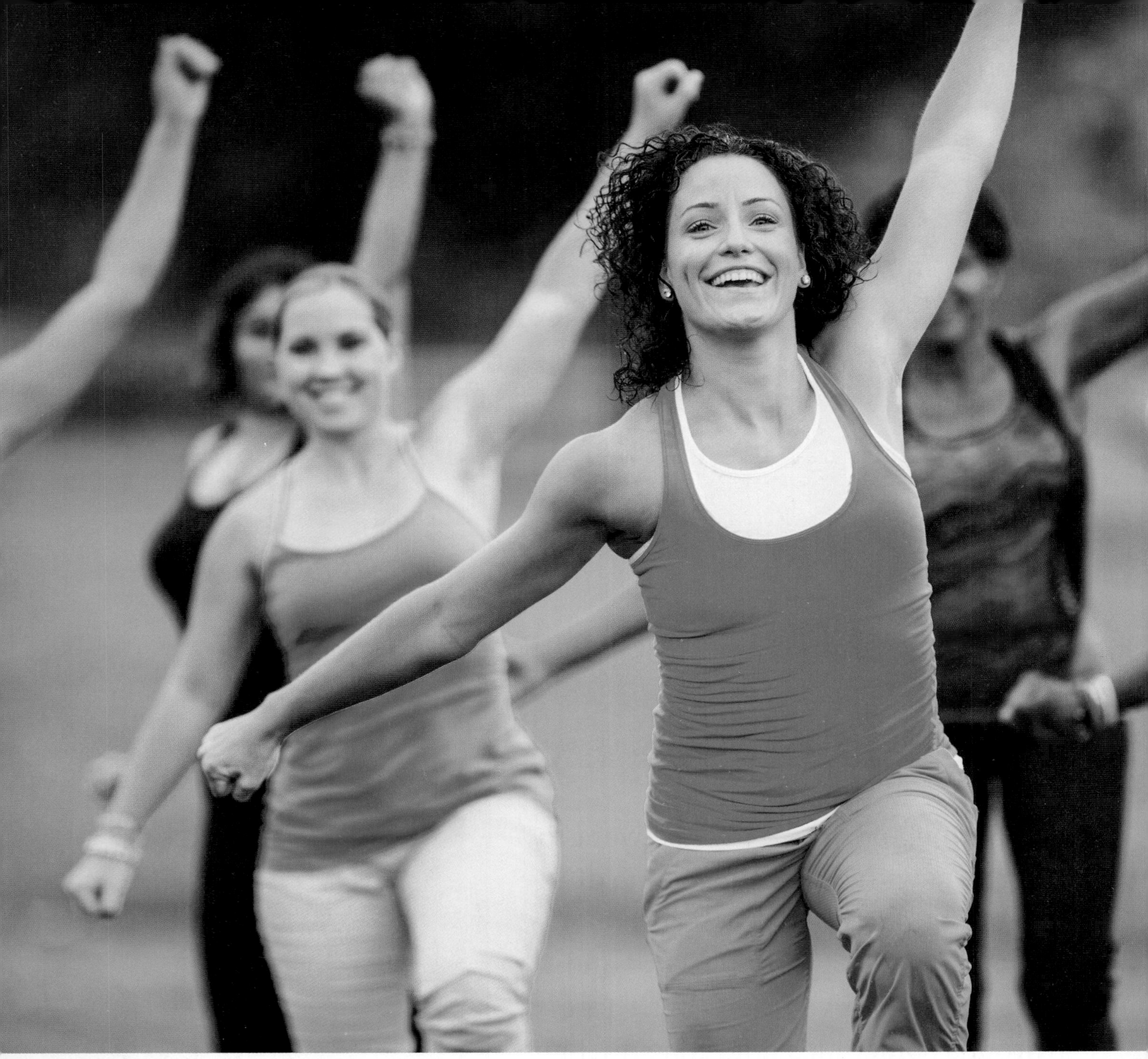

Everyone needs exercise, but sometimes it can be boring. To make working out more interesting, many people keep their bodies fit by dancing. Some may take classes with a group. Others just dance by themselves at home to a video. Anyone can dance!

Music and You

So far, you have traveled to Brazil and Pakistan. You have been to a funeral in New Orleans, you have danced in China, and you have sung in Ireland. Everywhere you have traveled, you have heard music and have seen dancing.

Next time you create or listen to music, stop and think: millions of other people all over Earth are also singing, dancing, and listening to music at the very same time!

You will answer the comprehension questions on these pages as a class.

Text Connections

1. The word *universal* describes something that happens nearly everywhere on Earth. What are some universal life stages that people experience?
2. Why do you think music and dance are often used to mark universal life stages?
3. Think about what you read in "Little Melba and Her Big Trombone." How was Melba's trombone playing part of a musical tradition, or music handed down through generations?
4. Why do you think that people around the world like to sing along with karaoke machines?

Did You Know?

Dancing has been important to humans for thousands of years. Some of the oldest paintings of dancers were found in Indian and Egyptian tombs from 3300 B.C.

Look Closer

Keys to Comprehension

1. One main idea in this selection is that some music is traditional. What are some ways that music and dance connect people across generations?
2. Another main idea in this selection is that people do not always require special occasions to dance. What are some ways that people dance and make music just for fun?
3. Recall what you learned about music from this selection. What questions do you have after reading this information? Where could you look to find their answers?

Writer's Craft

4. The word *keen* can mean "very good," "having a very sharp edge," or "a funeral lament." Which meaning is used in this selection?

Concept Development

5. Reread page 400. How does the photo on this page help you understand what is described in the text?

Write

Describe a time when music or dancing helped you feel connected to the people around you.

Read the story. Then discuss it with your class.

Vocabulary Words

- beat
- commences
- gestures
- inspire
- mimic
- mourning
- rehearsal
- require
- somber
- specific
- stressful
- vary

A Musical Revelation

Jake and I never disputed the goodness of our grandmother. She always helped us in any way she could. But thinking of her as *fun* required some imagination—at least it did for us. Being around Grandmother could be stressful. It seemed she was always after us to be respectful and mind our manners.

Sometimes Jake and I could be mournful about visiting her, but Mom always told us to stop being dramatic. She also encouraged us to enjoy the time that we spent with Grandmother.

Then Uncle Cliff came for a visit. Uncle Cliff was a piano player who performed across the country. He was passing through town on the way to a new gig.

When he came to the door, there was no somberness in the way he greeted Grandmother. He and Grandmother instantly commenced laughing together while remembering stories from the past. This was quite a surprise to Jake and me! But the real stunner came when Uncle Cliff sat at our piano and started beating out a rowdy tune. He gestured wildly for Grandmother to come join him. "Come on, Mom, you know this one!" he said.

The rest of what happened has become legend to Jake and me—the specifics of the story vary, depending on who tells it. But we agree that when Grandmother jumped up and belted out that tune, it was nothing short of inspirational! She knocked our socks off, without even so much as a rehearsal. She even danced, mimicking the moves of great, and much younger, Broadway performers.

Since then, Jake and I have come to see Grandmother a little bit differently. And we agree that we've both witnessed the power of music!

Concept Vocabulary

Think of the word *expression.* What are some different forms of expression? Why is expression an important way to communicate?

Extend Vocabulary

Synonyms are words with similar meanings. For example, think about these words: *serious, solemn, depressed, grave.* All are synonyms for *somber.* However, each word describes a slightly different state of mind. Copy these words into your Writer's Notebook. Then write a sentence for each word that uses the word in the correct context. If you need help, use a dictionary to clarify the precise meaning of each word.

Read this Science Connection. You will answer the questions as a class.

Text Feature

A **caption** tells about a picture and adds information to an article or story

Traits and Survival

You have learned that people living around the globe have many of the same kinds of feelings. Therefore, you may not be surprised to learn that many share a love of dogs! Dogs have been companions and helpers to people for thousands of years. For as long as dogs have been kept as pets, people have been breeding them.

The goal when breeding animals is to produce baby animals that are like their parents. The breeder chooses parents with specific characteristics that enable them to survive easily, find mates, and have healthy children. The breeder hopes these characteristics will be passed down to the animals' offspring.

The traits that enable an animal to survive depend on the animal's environment. That environment may be warm or cold. It may also have unique food sources. Think again of dogs. Some are tiny, while others are enormous. Some have long hair, while others have short hair. Humans have bred dogs to have certain traits that help them thrive in a particular place.

Irish Wolfhound

Alaskan Malamute

Brazilian Mastiff

Each of these dogs is from a different place in the world. How are the dogs similar? How are they different?

1. How are the captions helpful?
2. Which breed of dog is found in Alaska? Which breed of dog is found in Ireland? Which breed of dog is found in Brazil?
3. Which of the dog breeds look like they could thrive in cold weather? What characteristics do they share?

Go Digital

Where do small dogs thrive? How is being small an advantage to them?

Genre Informational Text

Essential Questions

Why do people create music? What are different kinds of musical performances?

Ah, Music!

by Aliki

What is Music?

Music is Sound

If you hum a tune,

play an instrument,

or clap out a rhythm,

you are making music.
You are listening to it, too.

Music is Rhythm

That is the beat I can clap.

BOOM! BOOM! biddyboom BOOM!

Rhythm is a marching-band beat, a puffing-train beat,

CHUGGA
chugga
CHUGGA
chugga

a beating-the-eggs beat, a heart beat.
Some rhythm beats are stronger than others.
You can count the accents.

A two-beat pattern is ONE two, ONE two.
A four-beat pattern is ONE two three four, ONE two three four.
A three-beat pattern is ...
... ONE two three, ONE two three.

A person who cannot hear
can feel the vibration of the beat.

Music is Melody

That is the tune I can hum.

or the song that is sung
if words are set to music.
Often the words are poetry.

Twinkle, twinkle,
little star,
How I wonder
what you are.
Up above the world
so high,
Like a diamond
in the sky . . .

I didn't know
you could sing.

Music is Pitch and Tone

Pitch is the highs and the lows of the sound.
Tone is the color—the brightness or darkness of the sound.
Some instruments have a high, bright pitch.

High, sharp pings can sound like piercing light.

Some instruments have a deep, low pitch.
They can sound dark, shadowy, and mysterious.

Music is Volume

That is the loudness or the softness of the sound.

Shhhh.

Music is Feeling

It sets a mood.

Music speaks not with words, as in a song.
It speaks with expression.
It is a universal language that unites people.
Everyone can understand music,
because everyone has feelings.
Music can make you feel happy or sad or scared.
It can make you want to dance, to march, to sing,
or to be quiet, to listen, and to dream.

Ah, music!

*Here will we sit
and let the sounds of music
creep in our ears.*

Shakespeare said that.

I listen to music,
and I can see pictures in my head.

I imagine I hear
twittering birds.

I hear a cool waterfall.

I see a brilliant sunrise.

I see a scary dark forest.

I hear a noisy city.

Music is a Creative Art

Just as a writer uses words,

Words, words

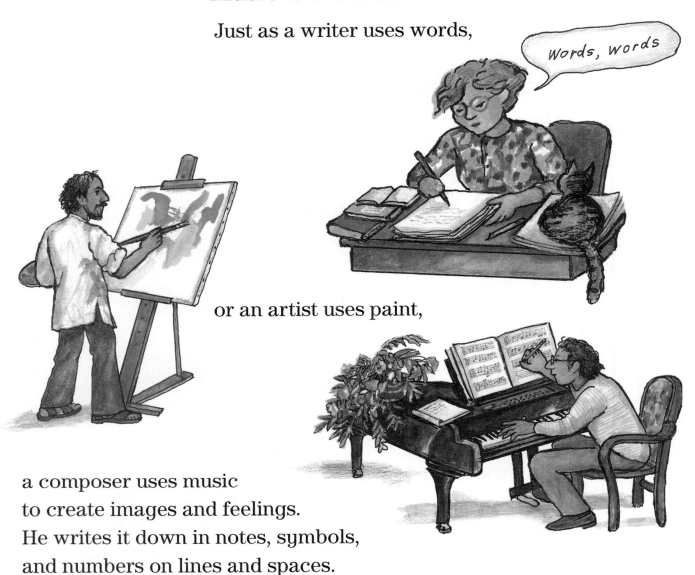

or an artist uses paint,

a composer uses music
to create images and feelings.
He writes it down in notes, symbols,
and numbers on lines and spaces.
The notations describe the rhythm, tone, pitch,
feeling, and even the silences of the piece.

The Written Music

Every note shows its time value.
Some notes are long. Some are short.
Every note's placement on the staff
shows a pitch value.
Symbols show pauses, and how loud, soft, fast,
or slow the notes are played.

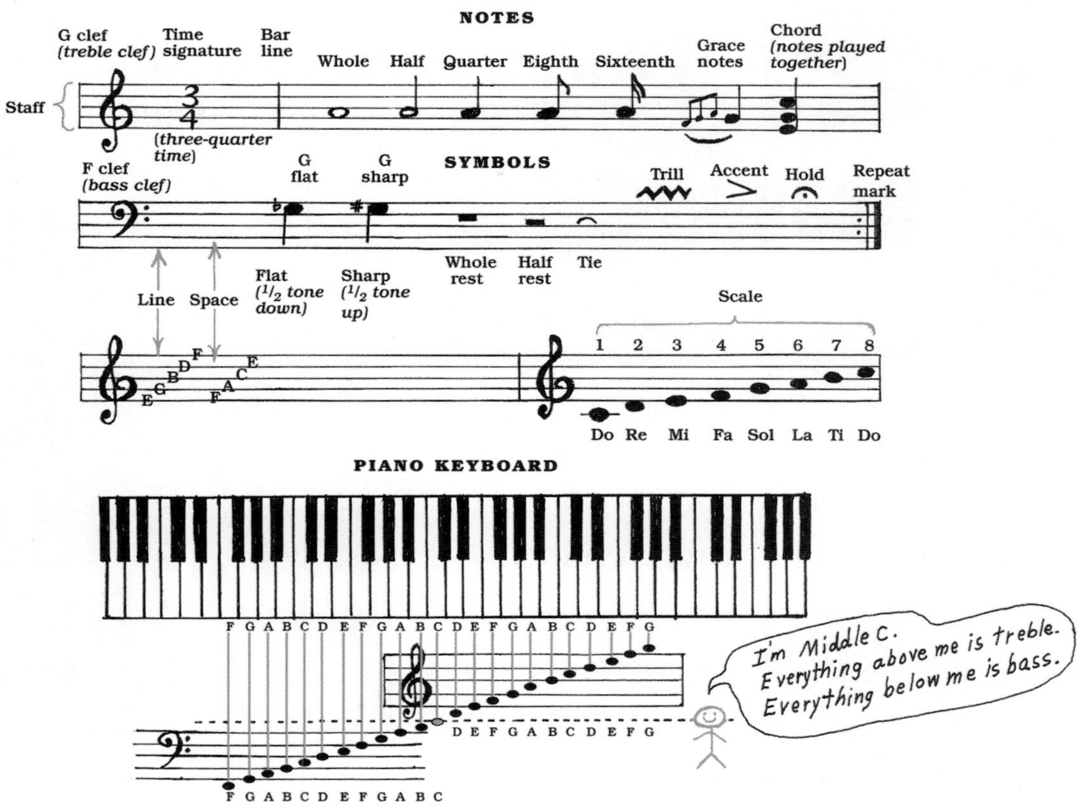

Reading the written music is like
reading a composer's handwriting.

Bach　　Mozart　　Bartók

The Creation Comes to Life

A musician will perform the composition.
She will bring to life the composer's written work.

She reads the music and studies it.

She practices the piece on her instrument, the cello.

The instrument makes the sound, and gives the music color. The musician puts her own feeling into the music too. At last, she is ready to perform the piece for others to enjoy.

Music is composed
for one instrument,

for a group of instruments,

Chamber music is played by two to ten musicians in a room or small, intimate hall.

or for a whole orchestra.

An orchestra plays in a large auditorium. Some music has been written for over one hundred instruments, and even a chorus—all playing and singing together as a team. It is a thrilling sound.

Some Instruments of the Orchestra

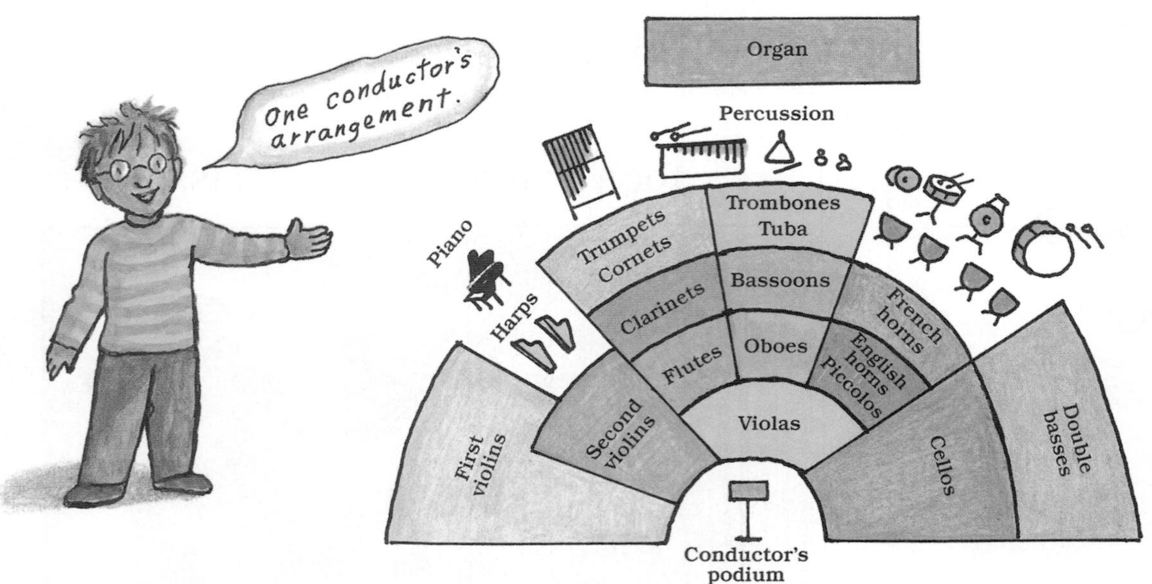

STRINGED INSTRUMENTS

Played with a bow, or plucked or strummed.
The strings vibrate to make the sound.

Violin Viola

Cello

Double Bass

Bow

Piano
Keys hit the strings inside

Harp

Harpsichord
Quills pluck the strings inside.

Plectrum
to pluck with

Guitar

Lute

Mandolin

WIND INSTRUMENTS

Woodwinds and brass are blown to make the sound. Sound vibrates inside a hollow tube.

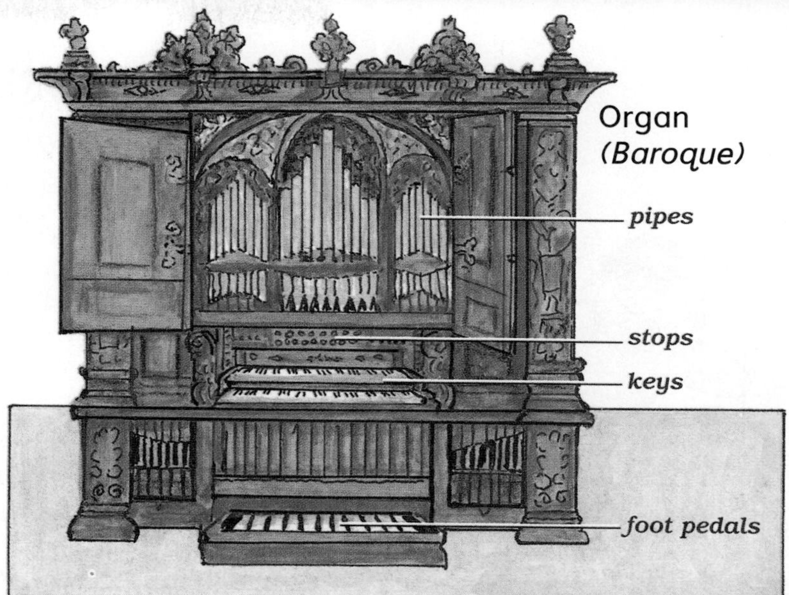

Hands and feet pump air into organ pipes to change the sounds. A large organ may be built directly into an auditorium, cathedral, church, or synagogue.

WOODWINDS

Reed Instruments
Air blown through reed mouthpiece.

BRASS

Air blown into metal mouthpiece.

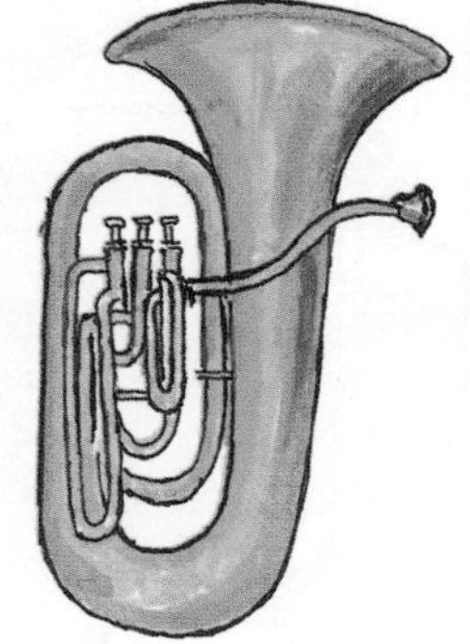

PERCUSSION INSTRUMENTS

Hit or shaken to make the sound.

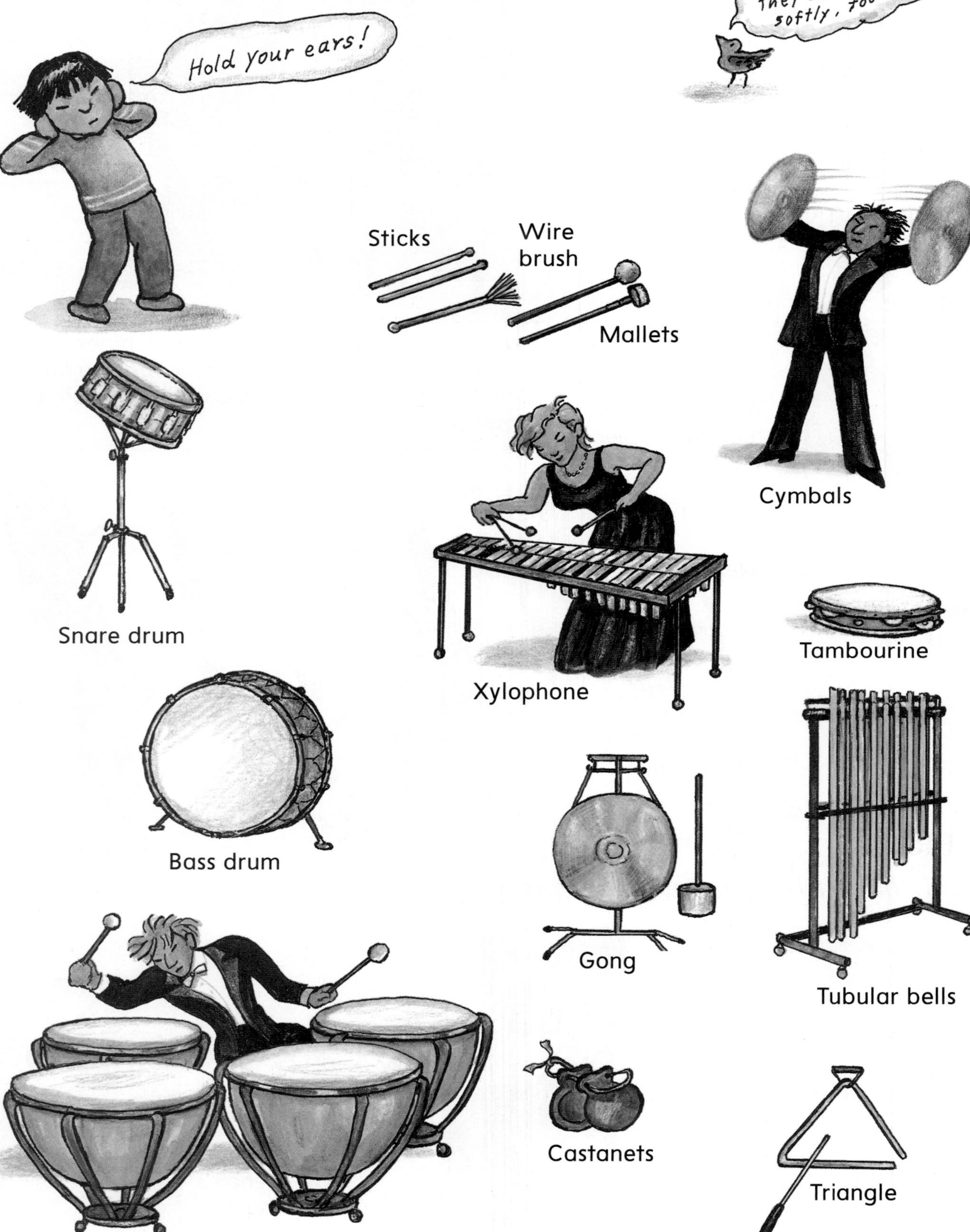

The Conductor

A conductor, or maestro, leads the orchestra. Some conductors hold a baton.

He follows the score, which shows all the instrumental and vocal parts of the piece.
The maestro signals the musicians when to start, stop, to play louder, softer, faster, or slower.
He directs them with feeling.
Each instrument is unique and important, whether it is played alone or with others.
It is the musicians who make the instruments come alive, and they do their very best.

The Voice is an Instrument Too

All kinds of music have been composed for one or more voices.

Popular songs, spirituals, jazz, Lieder, opera, musicals, and choral music tell stories in both words and music.

Popular songs, Ballads

Jazz, Blues, Spirituals

Lieder (German songs)

Opera

Musicals, Operettas

Chorus, Choir, Glee club

Children's choir

Singers' voices have different pitches.
Women's voices can reach higher.
Men's voices can reach lower.

Soprano is very high.
Alto is lower.
Tenor is lower.
Bass is way down lowest.

And some voices are even higher and in between.
Mezzo soprano
Counter tenor
Bass baritone
Or lower. CROAK!

Music is Harmony

Harmony is the sound of different notes that blend together.

We sing in harmony.

We play in harmony.

plink plink

Plink plink is not harmony.

We're a chorus.

We sing a cappella, without accompaniment.

We'll sing you a round.

Some people call it a canon.

We start and end at different times.

You have to concentrate.

Ha Ha

LET'S GO!

Row, row, row your boat
Gently down the stream,
Merrily, merrily, merrily, merrily~
Life is but a dream.

Row, row, row your boat.
Gently down the stream,
Merrily, merrily, merrily, merrily~
Life is but a dream.

NOW LET'S COUNT!

ONE is a solo.

TWO, a duet.

THREE is a trio.

FOUR, a quartet.

BARBER SHOPPE

FIVE is a quintet.

SIX, a sextet.

SEVEN is a septet.

HA HA

But we don't fit!

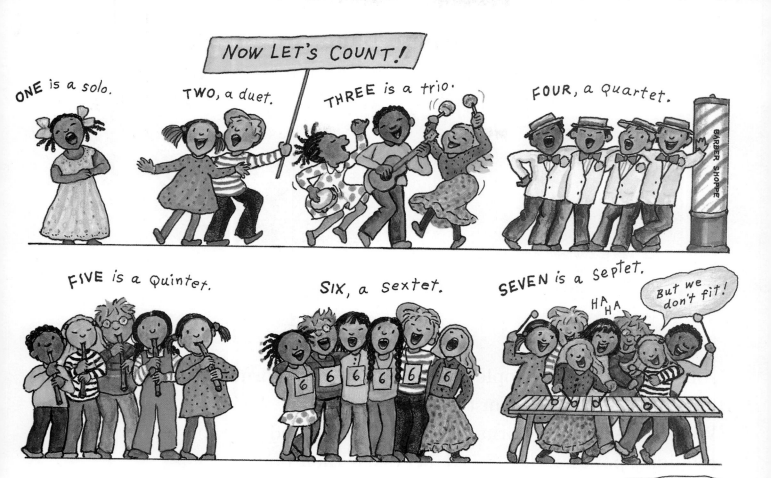

Dynamics, Tempo, and Italian

Dynamics is the softness or loudness of the music.

PP pianissimo (very soft)	*P* piano (soft)	*mp* mezzopiano (medium soft)	*mf* mezzoforte (medium loud)	*f* forte (loud)	*ff* fortissimo (very loud)

Tempo is the slowness or quickness of the music.

Largo (very slow)	*Adagio* (slow)	*Andante* (walking)	*Moderato* (medium)	*Allegro* (fast)	*Vivace* (fast and lively)	*Presto* (very fast)

Music is to Dance to

GOTTA DANCE!
When I hear the beat,
I can't control my feet.
I tap, I stamp, I whirl, I fly.
I'm free as a leaf. That's why!

All over the world, people dance for fun, in performance, to express themselves, or to tell a story. Whatever the dance form—classical ballet, modern, tap, religious, popular, or folk—dancers use their bodies to express the music.

Modern dance

Ballet

Tap

Square dance

Ballroom dance

Jazz
(The Charleston)

Ice dance

Stomp

Flamenco
(Spain)

Cossack dance
(Russia)
Maypole dance
Bharath Natyam
(India)
Break dancing
is twisting
like a pretzel!
Without
breaking.
Get it?
HA
HA
Cancan
(France)

OPPA!
Syrtos
(Greece)
Eagle dance
(Native American)
Kabuki
(Japan)
Lion dance
(China)
Drum dance
(East Africa)
I feel the music with my whole body.
It carries me away!

And now for some History.

Earliest Music

Prehistoric

Conch shell horn

Music making began thousands of years ago. When people celebrated a hunt, signaled dangers, worshiped, or told stories, they danced, clapped, banged on hollow logs, shook pebbles, and chanted. Later, they made primitive instruments from stone, bone, shells, and metal that archaeologists would discover. Variations of some are used even today.

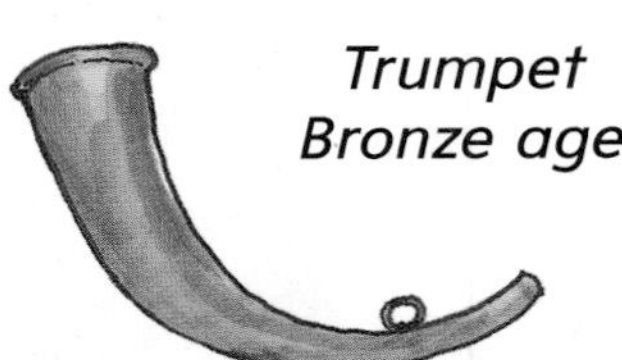

Trumpet Bronze age

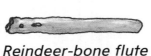

Reindeer-bone flute 30,000 B.C. (Czechoslovakia)

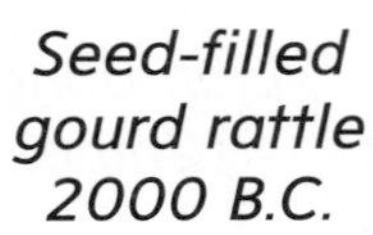

Seed-filled gourd rattle 2000 B.C.

Skin-covered drum

Bone signal whistle 40,000 B.C. (Moravia)

Earthenware rattle (Mexico)

Someday I'm going to be an archaeologist and dig things up!

They find buried history.

I can do that, too!

Ancient Music

2600 – 400 B.C.

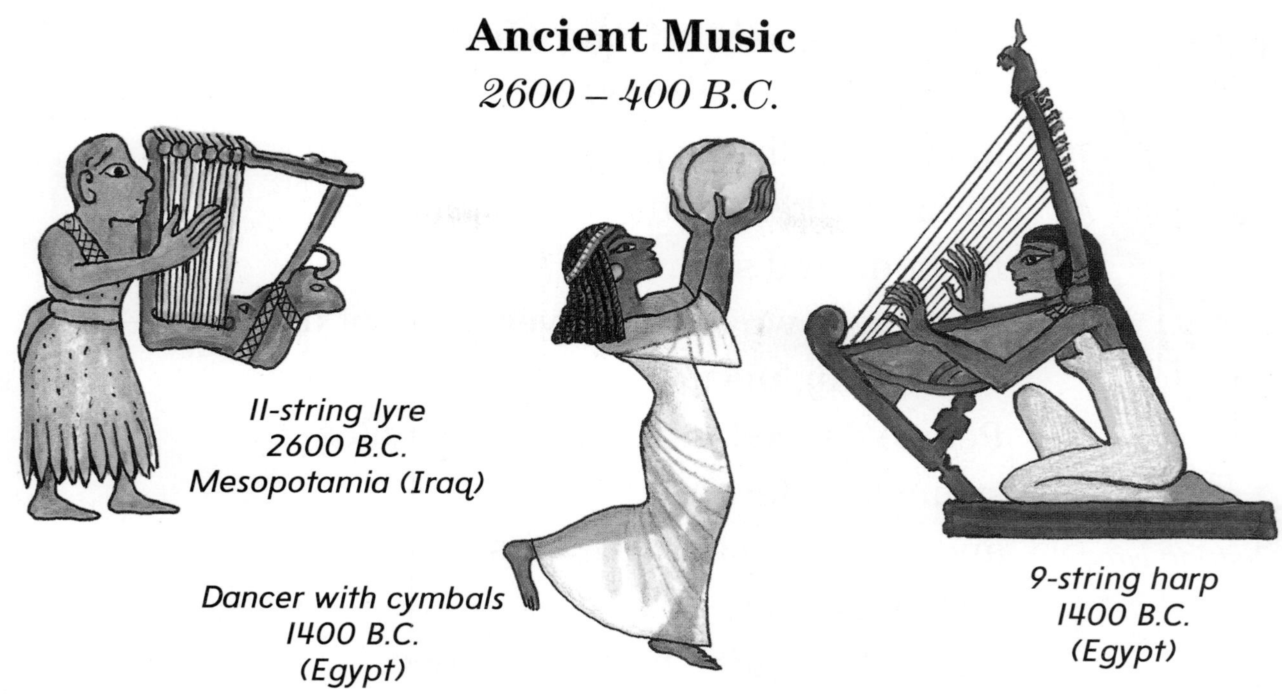

11-string lyre
2600 B.C.
Mesopotamia (Iraq)

Dancer with cymbals
1400 B.C.
(Egypt)

9-string harp
1400 B.C.
(Egypt)

Throughout the ancient world, music became part of religious rituals and military ceremonies, festivals and entertainment.
Egyptians danced to harps and cymbals.
Since biblical times Jews have blown the shofar—one of the oldest instruments in continuous use.
The Chinese had orchestras of bells, gongs, drums, and zithers, and invented a form of written music.

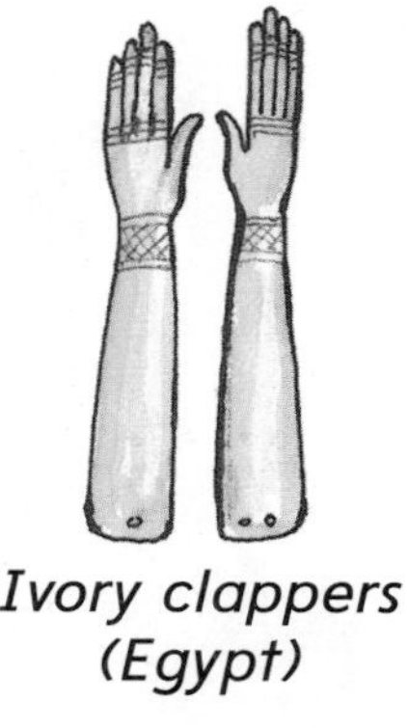

Ivory clappers
(Egypt)

Mayan trumpeter
(Mexico)

Cornu
(bronze horn)
(Rome)

Shofar (ram's horn)

Po-chung bell
(China)

7-string lyre

Music of the Gods

500 – 400 B.C.

In ancient Greece people loved music.
Great thinkers said it was important
for body and soul.
Music was woven into every part of daily life—
work, play, theater, sports, and religion.
People danced, sang, piped the aulos,
strummed the lyre,
and chanted magical myths about their
gods and goddesses.
We have to guess how it sounded,
as there is no record of the written music.

Dancer

Double aulos
(reed flute)

The shorter the string, the higher the pitch.

In 500 B.C., Pythagoras proved through mathematics that vibrations cause the pitch and tone of sound.

Panpipes
(named for Pan,
the god of nature)

Apollo was the god of Music.
His brother Hermes invented the lute when he was one day old.
What took him so long?

"Music" comes from "muse," a spirit who inspired beautiful music and song.
Greek Myths

Music through the Ages

1st – 15th Centuries A.D.

In 1030 an Italian monk, Guido d'Arezzo, devised the basis of the music notation system we still use—with staffs, lines, spaces, and notes.

Music grew from one century to the next.
In the early and middle ages,
new forms of music developed.
Christianity inspired church music.
Music became polyphonic—played
and sung in two or more melodic parts.
Notations were invented. Music was
no longer a one-time performance.
Now it would be written and preserved
for other musicians and generations.

Minstrels in England wandered the streets singing and strumming.

Masked musicians, singers, and dancers acted out plays.

Troubadours in France traveled from palace to palace to entertain the courts with romantic ballads.

Musicians played assorted instruments in groups.

Diversity of Music

Every country has its own sounds, rhythms, instruments, songs, and dance.
The music reflects the culture and the people.
The diverse sounds have influenced both classical and popular music.

A Scottish bagpiper makes music by squeezing a bag of air.

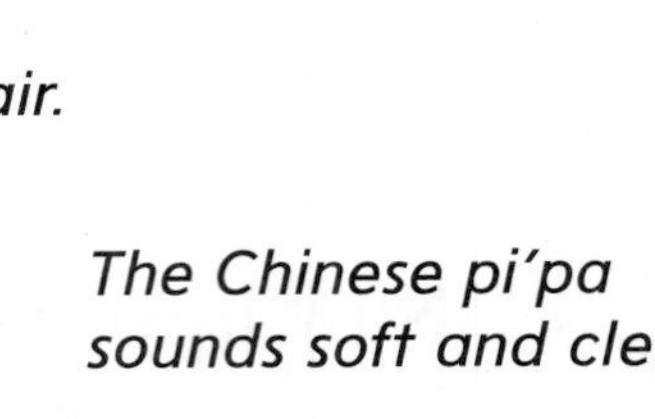

The Chinese pi'pa sounds soft and clear.

Bands of primitive pipes and drums play in the streets of Bolivia.

Long Indian ragas are improvised on the sitar and tabla.

Steel drum bands play calypso folk songs on used, tuned oil drums in the West Indies.

The didgeridoo, a tree branch hollowed out by ants and termites, has been played by Aboriginal Australians for 3,000 years.

Bells, gongs, xylophones, and drums make up a gamelan in Indonesia.

The expressive koto is a kind of zither played in Japan.

The African sansa has metal strips plucked with the thumbs.

The alphorn and accordion are favorite folk instruments in Switzerland.

Music is Therapy

Everyone has a favorite kind of music
that brings comfort and pleasure.
Music makes work easier in factories,
in offices, or at home.
It inspires all kinds of artists
who listen to music as they create.
Music is good for everyone.

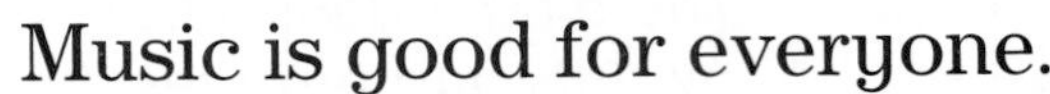

Music helps tense people relax.

It helps babies fall asleep.

It helps sick people feel better.

It helps calm angry people.

Music cheers sad people.

Music helps people create.

It feels good to make music with friends.

Some people like listening to different kinds of
music while doing different things.

In the kitchen

In the workroom

In the bathroom

Music is Good for Animals, Too

I like Bach best.
It helps cows give more milk.
It helps hens lay bigger eggs.
It helps shy elephants perform.

Songbirds, whales, wolves, and other animals make their own kind of music. Their song sounds inspire composers and others.

whale dolphin seal wolf

Don't mind Boomer. He likes to sing along.

BARTOK

Even plants grow happy with a song!

Practice Makes Perfect

We make music.
Making music is hard fun.
It takes lots of practice to learn
to play an instrument.

But when you do, it is forever.

That's the hard part.

Here's the fun part.

As you practice and learn,
you begin to make
beautiful sounds.
Practice becomes fun.

You learn new pieces to play.
You feel proud.
Your music teacher says
you will play in a recital.
You will play for an audience.

A metronome helps keep time.

The Performance

At your recital it is your turn to play.
Everyone is looking at you.

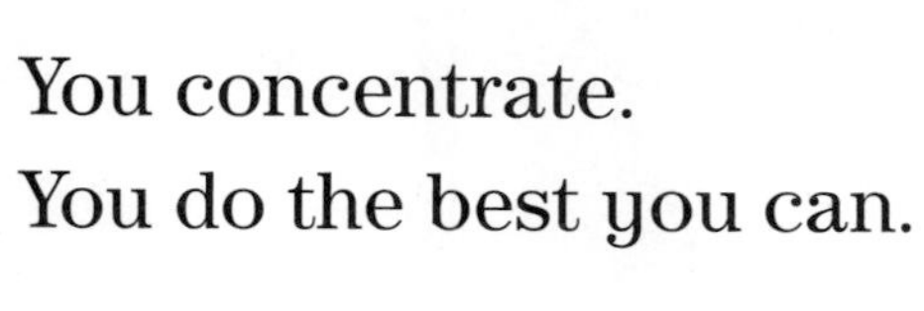

You concentrate.
You do the best you can.

When you finish, everyone claps.
It sounds like waves breaking.
It feels good. You take a bow.
You feel relieved and very proud.

You celebrate.
Everyone says you did well.
Next time it will be even
better, because you are
learning more every day.
Practice makes perfect.

What is Music?
♫?
WILD!
COOL.
DRAMATIC.
Patriotic.
Passionate.
Spiritual.
Fresh!
PROFOUND.
Nostalgic.
Sublime.

Music is for Everybody

You will answer the comprehension questions on these pages as a class.

Text Connections

1. What are the essential parts of music?
2. The author says music helps people create pictures in their heads. How might music sound when it represents a dark, scary forest? How might its sounds be different when it represents a cool waterfall?
3. Think about what you read in "A World Tour in Song and Dance." How was music used to set a mood in that selection?
4. Why might a piece of music sound a little different each time it is played, even if it is always played on the same instrument?

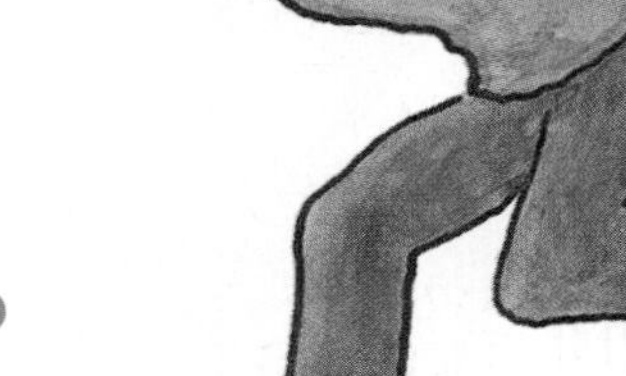

Did You Know?

Music distracts the mind at the same time that it focuses the mind.

Look Closer

Keys to Comprehension

1. What do the written symbols in a piece of music communicate?
2. How are string instruments played? How are wind and brass instruments played? How are percussion instruments played?
3. One of the main ideas in this selection is that music helps people. What details does the selection include about how music is used as therapy?

Writer's Craft

4. Reread page 428. What do you think the author means when she says that when an instrument makes a sound, it "gives the music color." What do you think *color* means in this context?

Concept Development

5. Reread page 425. How do the illustrations on this page add to your understanding of the text?

Write

Describe a time when music made you visualize a scene in your head. What qualities did the music have? What was the scene?

Read the story. Then discuss it with your class.

Vocabulary Words

- **accents**
- **brilliant**
- **composition**
- **diverse**
- **metronome**
- **mood**
- **primitive**
- **recital**
- **record**
- **rituals**
- **universal**
- **variations**

Melodic Reminders

Some people keep journals to remember the events of their lives. I, on the other hand, compose music. For me, this is the best way to record the feelings I have about my experiences.

Composing is something I do ritually, as part of my daily piano practice. First I warm up by playing scales. Next I learn technique by playing pieces by other musicians. Then I wrap up by putting away the metronome and playing just for me. The music I play varies, depending on how I feel. Often it is not the kind of music you hear at recitals—I don't worry about playing brilliantly! Notes meander and change tempo along with my thoughts. I create a diversity of sounds by striking the piano keys in different ways. Often this produces very primitive sounding music! But experimentation leads me to little discoveries—a moody progression of chords or an unusual way of accenting notes. These little discoveries often become the building blocks for new songs. I use them to construct melodies that are more universally appealing. In this way, my torrents of feeling become stories with beginnings, middles, and ends.

Once I have finished composing a piece, I write all its notes as sheet music. This allows me to share my songs, if I want to. However, there are many songs that I just keep for myself. They serve as reminders of who I was at particular times in my life.

Concept Vocabulary

Think about the word *fundamental.* What kinds of skills are described as being fundamental?

Extend Vocabulary

Copy the word web in your Writer's Notebook. Then fill it in with four words that name universal feelings.

Read this Science Connection. You will answer the questions as a class.

Text Feature

A **bulleted list** is a way to set off information from the main text that has a specific connection to one part of the text.

Designing Fair Tests

Think of all the inventions you use in a day, from pencils and lightbulbs to computers and stereo systems. Each started as an idea. An inventor built its prototype, using whatever materials were at hand. It is likely that the prototype looked pretty different from the device you use today.

It is common for an invention to take many different forms over the span of its life. Each form addresses a problem with the form that came before it.

As inventors consider ways to improve their inventions, they plan and carry out tests. These tests help with identifying what to improve.

- It is important to make the tests fair. Inventors try to think of variables that could affect the test's results. (Variables are conditions that can change. For example, the user could change or the weather could change.)
- It is important to try to predict what the test will show about the invention's success and failure points. Inventors hope the test will give them good data. Then they can move forward with designing brilliant improvements.

1940s record player

1980s boombox

2000s compact disc player with headphones

Today's MP3 player with speakers

1. Why do you think the writer set the last two paragraphs in bullets?
2. How have stereos changed over the years?
3. Think about ways each version of the stereo might have been tested. What are some variables inventors needed to consider?

Go Digital

How can you design your own prototypes or models? Where can you find more information about planning and carrying out fair tests of your inventions?

Glossary

Pronunciation Key

a	as in **a**t	**ô**	as in br**ou**ght and r**aw**	**ə**	as in **a**bout, chick**e**n, penc**i**l, cann**o**n, circ**u**s
ā	as in l**a**te	**oi**	as in c**oi**n	**ch**	as in **ch**air
â	as in c**a**re	**o͝o**	as in b**oo**k	**ng**	as in ri**ng**
ä	as in f**a**ther	**o͞o**	as in t**oo**	**sh**	as in **sh**op
e	as in s**e**t	**or**	as in f**or**m	**th**	as in **th**in
ē	as in m**e**	**ou**	as in **ou**t	**t̸h**	as in **th**ere
i	as in **i**t	**u**	as in **u**p	**zh**	as in trea**s**ure
ī	as in k**i**te	**ū**	as in **u**se		
o	as in **o**x	**ûr**	as in t**ur**n, g**er**m, l**ear**n, f**ir**m, w**or**k		
ō	as in r**o**se				

The mark (´) is placed after a syllable with a heavy accent, as in **chicken** (chik´ ən).
The mark (´) after a syllable shows a lighter accent, as in **disappear** (dis´ ə pēr´).

abundance (ə bun´ dəns) *n.* a quantity that is more than enough; plentiful or overflowing supply

accents (ak´sents) *n.* plural form of **accent:** an emphasis given to certain chords or notes

advantage (ad van´ tij) *n.* something that helps to make someone or something more likely to succeed than others

adversaries (ad´vûr sâr´ ēz) *n.* plural form of **adversary:** a person or group that is hostile toward or competing with another; opponent or enemy

amateur (am´ ə chûr) *adj.* being a person who does something for pleasure, rather than as a profession or for money

ambassadors (am ba´ sə dûrz) *n.* plural form of **ambassador:** an official of a government who is sent to represent his or her country in another country

anniversary (an´ə vûr´ sə rē) *n.* the yearly return of the date on which some important event occurred in an earlier year

appropriate (ə prō´prē it) *adj.* suitable for an occasion; proper

archaeologists (ar´ kē ol´ə jists) *n.* plural form of **archaeologist:** a student or expert who studies the way people lived in the past

architecture (ar´ ki tek´ chûr) *n.* buildings or structures planned by an architect, a person who has studied design and engineering

ashamed (ə shāmd´) *adj.* feeling upset or guilty over doing something wrong or silly

audition (ô dish´ ən) *n.* a short performance that tests the abilities of a performer

B

banquets (bang´ kwits) *n.* plural form of **banquet:** a large, elaborate meal

basis (bā´ sis) *n.* a fundamental part on which a thing rests or depends; foundation

beamed (bēmd) *v.* a form of the verb **beam:** to smile happily

beamed

beat (bēt) *v.* to hit again and again in order to make rhythms

belong (bi long´) *v.* to have a special or right place

blessing (bles´ ing) *n.* a wish for happiness or success

bold (bōld) *adj.* having courage; fearless

brilliant (bril´yənt) *adj.* shining or sparkling with light

Pronunciation Key: **a**t; l**ā**te; c**â**re; f**ä**ther; s**e**t; m**ē**; **i**t; k**ī**te; **o**x; r**ō**se; **ô** in b**ou**ght; c**oi**n; b**o͝o**k; t**o͞o**; f**or**m; **ou**t; **u**p; **ū**se; t**û**rn; **ə** sound in **a**bout, chick**e**n, penc**i**l cann**o**n, circ**u**s; **ch**air; ri**ng**; **sh**op; **th**in; **th**ere; **zh** in trea**s**ure.

C

campaign (kam pān´) *n.* an organized series of actions carried on for a particular purpose

candidate (kan´di dāt´) *n.* a person who seeks to be chosen for an office

carry (kâr´ē) *v.* to send or transmit

challenge (chal´ ənj) *v.* to invite or call to take part in a struggle or contest

chamber (chām´bûr) *n.* a hall where the legislature meets

chemical (kem´i kəl) *adj.* produced by the way a substance changes and reacts with other substances

cling (kling) *v.* to stick together

coil (koil) *n.* a spiral of wire for conducting electricity

coil

collapsed (kə lapst´) *v.* a form of the verb **collapse:** to fail or break down completely or suddenly

colonists (kol´ə nists) *n.* plural form of **colonist:** a person who helped found one of the thirteen British colonies that became the first states

commences (kə mens´ ez) *v.* a form of the verb **commence:** to begin; start

company (kum´pə nē) *n.* companionship

composed (kəm pōzd´) *v.* a form of the verb **compose:** to put together; create

composition (kom´pə zi´shən) *n.* a work of art, especially music, created by a composer

compost (kom´ pōst) *n.* a mixture of decayed plants, manure, and the like, used to fertilize soil

cooperate (kō op´ ə rāt´) *v.* to work with others for a common purpose

corporation (kor´ pə rā´ shən) *n.* an organization of a group of people who have been given the legal power to act as one person

craggy (krag´ ē) *adj.* having a rough and uneven surface

craggy

crisis (krī´ sis) *n.* a condition or period of difficulty or danger

current (kûr´ ənt) *adj.* happening or occurring now; belonging to the present time

current (kûr´ ənt) *n.* the flow of electricity

daydreamed (dā drēmd) *v.* a form of the verb **daydream:** to think about pleasant things as if dreaming

debate (di bāt´) *v.* to discuss the merits of something at a meeting

decisions (di si´zhənz) *n.* plural form of **decision:** the act or result of making up one's mind about an issue

defenses (di fens´ ez) *n.* plural form of **defense:** something that is used to protect yourself

devices (di vīs´ ez) *n.* plural form of **device:** a piece of equipment made or invented to serve a special purpose or perform a particular function

devour (di vour´) *v.* to eat up with great greed or vigor

dim (dim) *v.* to reduce in brightness

discouraged (dis kûr´ ijd) *adj.* having lost courage, hope, or confidence

Pronunciation Key: **a**t; l**ā**te; c**â**re; f**ä**ther; s**e**t; m**ē**; **i**t; k**ī**te; **o**x; r**ō**se; **ô** in b**ou**ght; c**oi**n; b**o͝o**k; t**o͞o**; f**or**m; **ou**t; **u**p; **ū**se; t**û**rn; **ə** sound in **a**bout, chick**e**n, penc**i**l cann**o**n, circ**u**s; **ch**air; ri**ng**; **sh**op; **th**in; **th**ere; **zh** in trea**s**ure.

diverse (di vûrs´) *adj.* different; unlike

documents (dok´ yə mənts) *n.* plural form of **document:** an important paper that gives official proof or information about something

economy (i kon´ ə mē) *n.* a system, method, or result of managing the production, distribution, and use of money, goods, natural resources, and services

effect (i fekt´) *n.* the power or ability to influence

election (i lek´ shən) *n.* the act of electing, or choosing something by voting

election

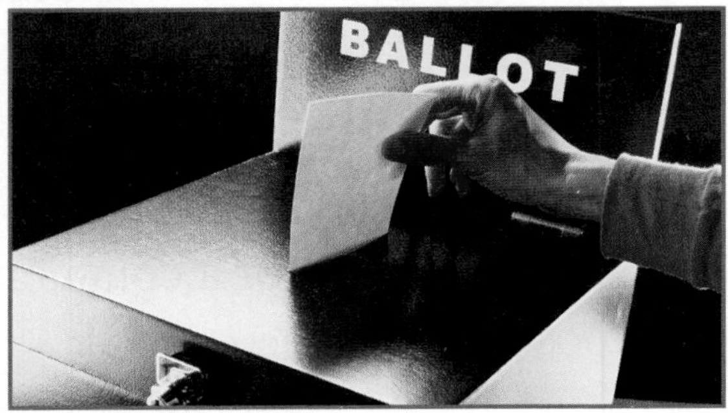

elements (el´ ə mənts) *n.* the elements; the forces of the atmosphere, such as rain, wind, or snow

empire (em´ pīr) *n.* a group of countries, lands, or peoples under one government or ruler

endured (en dûrd´) *v.* a form of the verb **endure:** to put up with; to tolerate

entreated (en trēt´ id) *v.* a form of the verb **entreat:** to ask earnestly; beg

Eurasian (yûr´ ā zhən) *adj.* relating to or from both Europe and Asia

execute (ek´ si kūt´) *v.* to carry out; fulfill

exoskeletons (ek´ sō ske´ lə tənz) *n.* plural form of **exoskeleton:** an external hard covering, such as the shell of a lobster or the scales and plates of a fish

factory (fak´ tə rē) *n.* a building or group of buildings where things are manufactured

fairly (fâr´ lē) *adv.* honestly; justly

flex (fleks) *v.* to tighten or contract a muscle

flourish (flûr´ ish) *n.* a bold or sweeping gesture

foundation (foun dā´ shən) *n.* the basic idea or principle upon which something stands or is supported

fragrant (frā´ grənt) *adj.* sweet smelling

frantic (fran´ tik) *adj.* wildly excited by worry, grief, fear, or anger

G

gestures (jes´ chûrz) *n.* plural form of **gesture:** a movement showing what a person is thinking or feeling

glint (glint) *n.* a bright, quick flash

government (guv´ ûr mənt) *n.* the group of people in charge of ruling a country, state, city, or other place

harness (har´ nis) *v.* to control and make use of

harness (har´ nis) *n.* a combination of straps and bands that attach a person to another object

harness

humankind (hū´ mən kīnd) *n.* all human beings as a group

immediately (i mē´ dē it lē) *adv.* right away; now

Pronunciation Key: **a**t; l**ā**te; c**â**re; f**ä**ther; s**e**t; m**ē**; **i**t; k**ī**te; **o**x; r**ō**se; **ô** in b**ou**ght; c**oi**n; b**o͝o**k; t**o͞o**; f**or**m; **ou**t; **u**p; **ū**se; t**û**rn; **ə** sound in **a**bout, chick**e**n, penc**i**l cann**o**n, circ**u**s; **ch**air; ri**ng**; **sh**op; **th**in; **th**ere; **zh** in trea**s**ure.

inadequate (in ad´ i kwit) *adj.* less than required; not adequate

inspire (in spīr´) *v.* to fill with a strong, encouraging feeling

interpret (in tûr´ prit) *v.* to explain the meaning of

interview (in´ tûr vū´) *n.* a meeting between a reporter and a person from whom information is wanted

landed (land´ id) *v.* a form of the verb **land:** to arrive at a destination by air

level (lev´ əl) *n.* a position in a process, series, or order

liberty (lib´ ûr tē) *n.* freedom from tyranny or foreign domination; political independence

lively (līv´ lē) *adj.* full of life or energy; cheerful

loads (lōdz) *n.* plural form of **load:** something that is carried

lure (lo͞or) *v.* to tempt or attract strongly

luxury (luk´ shə rē) *n.* a way of life that gives great comfort or pleasure

lyre (līr) *n.* a stringed musical instrument, used by the ancient Greeks to accompany singing

lyre

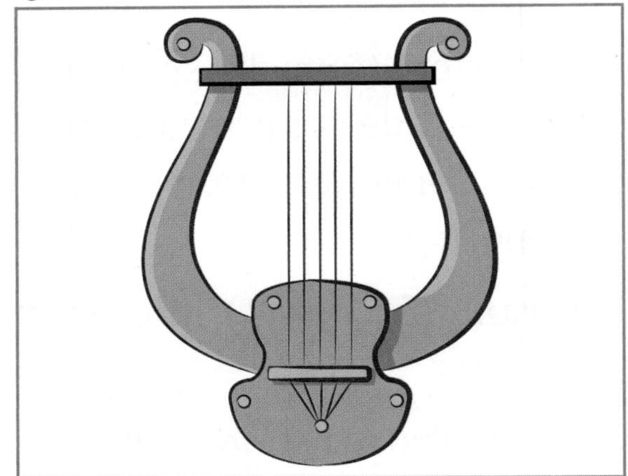

marched (marcht) *v.* a form of the verb **march:** to walk with regular, measured steps, especially in an orderly group or formation

melodic (me´ lô´ dik) *adj.* having the form of a pleasant series of notes from a song

metronome (met′ rə nōm′) *n.* a mechanical device used for indicating an exact tempo to be used in music

metronome

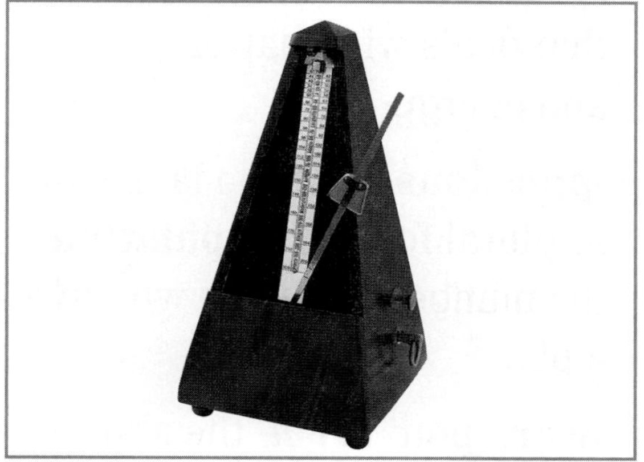

mimic (mim′ ik) *v.* to imitate

mood (mo͞od) *n.* a state of mind or feeling at a particular time

moral (mor′ əl) *n.* a lesson about right and wrong that is taught in a story or fable

mount (mount) *v.* to get on top of

mourning (mor′ ning) *v.* a form of the verb **mourn:** to feel or show sadness or grief

Muses (mūz′ ez) *n.* plural form of **Muse:** any of the nine goddesses of the arts and science from Greek mythology

mussel (mus′ əl) *n.* an animal that looks like a clam; a shellfish

musty (mus′ tē) *adj.* having a stale or moldy odor or taste

N

nation (nā′ shən) *n.* a group of people living under one government and usually sharing the same history, culture, and language

nourish (nûr′ ish) *v.* to furnish with food or other substances necessary for life and growth

numerous (no͞o′ mûr əs) *adj.* consisting of a great number; many

ominous (om′ ə nəs) *adj.* telling of trouble or bad luck to come

opening night (ō′ pə ning nīt) *n.* the first night of a performance

orchestras (or′ kə strəs) *n.* plural form of **orchestra:** a group of musicians playing together on various instruments

orchestra

Pronunciation Key: **a**t; l**ā**te; c**â**re; f**ä**ther; s**e**t; m**ē**; **i**t; k**ī**te; **o**x; r**ō**se; **ô** in b**ou**ght; c**oi**n; b**o͝o**k; t**o͞o**; f**or**m; **ou**t; **u**p; **ū**se; t**û**rn; **ə** sound in **a**bout, chick**e**n, penc**i**l cann**o**n, circ**u**s; **ch**air; ri**ng**; **sh**op; **th**in; **th**ere; **zh** in trea**s**ure.

organ (or´ gən) *n.* a part of the body that has a particular function

ornamental (or´ nə ment´ əl) *adj.* used for decoration

pace (pās) *n.* the rate of speed while walking, running, or moving

palaces (pal´ is es) *n.* plural form of **palace:** the official residence of a ruler or other high-ranking person

participate (par tis´ ə pāt´) *v.* to join with others and take part in something

peaceful (pēs´ fəl) *adj.* free from war or disorder; quiet and calm

persevere (pûr´ sə vēr´) *v.* to continue in a course of action or purpose despite difficulties

pesky (pes´ kē) *adj.* troublesome; annoying

philosophy (fə los´ ə fē) *n.* the study of the basic nature and purpose of humanity, the universe, and life itself

physics (fiz´ iks) *n.* the science that deals with matter and energy

populations (pop´ yə lā´ shənz) *n.* plural form of **population:** the number of people who live in a place

power (pou´ ûr) *n.* the ability to do, act, or bring about a particular result or effect

preferred (pri fûrd´) *v.* a form of the verb **prefer:** to like better; choose above others

primitive (prim´ i tiv) *adj.* characteristic of an early original stage

primitive

priority (prī or´ə tē) *n.* the condition of coming before another or others, as in order of importance

probe (prōb) *v.* to investigate or explore thoroughly

process (pros´ es) *n.* a series of actions performed in order to make or do something

prominent (prom´ ə nənt) *adj.* well-known or important

proposed (prə pōzd) *adj.* suggested for consideration

props (props) *n.* plural form of **prop:** an object used in a play

R

rally (ral´ ē) *n.* a meeting for a common purpose

ratify (rat´ ə fī´) *v.* to consent or officially approve

recital (ri sī´ təl) *n.* a performance of music or dance

record (rek´ ûrd) *n.* an account in writing or in another permanent form

region (rē´ jən) *n.* any large area or territory

rehearsal (ri hûr´ səl) *n.* a time to practice or train for a performance

remains (ri mānz´) *n.* something that is left

reproduce (rē´ prə dōōs´) *v.* to have offspring

require (ri kwīr´) *v.* to have a need of

resided (ri zīd´ id) *v.* a form of the verb **reside:** to make one's home permanently or for a time

revolution (rev´ ə lōō´ shən) *n.* the overthrow of a system of government in order to set up a new or different system of government; revolutions are often carried out through the use of force

revolution

rhythms (rith´ əmz) *n.* plural form of **rhythm:** a regular or orderly repeating of sounds or movements

rituals (rich´ ōō əlz) *n.* plural form of **ritual:** a system of special ceremonies

Pronunciation Key: **a**t; l**ā**te; c**â**re; f**ä**ther; s**e**t; m**ē**; **i**t; k**ī**te; **o**x; r**ō**se; **ô** in b**ou**ght; c**oi**n; b**o͝o**k; t**o͞o**; f**or**m; **ou**t; **u**p; **ū**se; t**û**rn; **ə** sound in **a**bout, chick**e**n, penc**i**l cann**o**n, circ**u**s; **ch**air; ri**ng**; **sh**op; **th**in; **th**ere; **zh** in trea**s**ure.

root (ro͞ot) *v.* to dig around for something

routes (ro͞ots) *n.* plural form of **route:** a road or other course used for traveling

ruins (ro͞o´ inz) *n.* the remains of something destroyed or decayed

S

saliva (sə lī´ və) *n.* a colorless liquid that comes from the mouth. Saliva keeps the mouth moist, moistens food, and starts digestion of starches

scarce (skârs) *adj.* difficult to get or find

schemes (skēmz) *n.* plural form of **scheme:** an underhanded or secret plan; plot

scoop (sco͞op) *v.* to pick up, make hollow, or dig out

scrumptious (skrump´ shəs) *adj.* very pleasing or delightful, especially to the taste

scrutinized (skro͞o´ tə nīzd) *v.* a form of the verb **scrutinize:** to look at or examine closely; inspect carefully

simple (sim´ pəl) *adj.* easily done, used, or understood

slogan (slō´ gən) *n.* a phrase, statement, or motto used by a group, such as a club or political party

solo (sō´ lō) *n.* music that only one person sings or plays on an instrument

somber (som´ bûr) *adj.* dark or gloomy

specific (spi si´ fik) *adj.* exact; particular

spectators (spek´ tā tûrz) *n.* plural form of **spectator:** a person who watches but does not take part

spectators

stage (stāj) *n.* a step or period in a process, progression, or development

steady (sted´ ē) *adj.* at an even rate

strange (strānj) *adj.* unusual; odd

strenuous (stren´ yə wəs) *adj.* requiring great effort or exertion

stressful (stres´ fəl) *adj.* full of harmful pressure caused by worry or too much work

suffrage (suf´ rij) *n.* the right or privilege of voting

support (sə port´) *v.* to provide for

T

tame (tām) *adj.* gentle or obedient; not fearful or shy

technology (tek no´ lə jē) *n.* the use of scientific knowledge for practical purposes, especially in industry

terrain (tə rān´) *n.* the physical features of a specific place

thrill (thril) *n.* something that gives a sudden feeling of pleasure or excitement

tilt (tilt) *v.* to raise one end or side of; tip

tolerate (tol´ ə rāt) *v.* to experience without being harmed

tone (tōn) *n.* a particular style or manner of speaking

tranquility (tran kwi´ lə tē) *n.* the state or quality of being free from disturbance; calm; peace

tranquility

trend (trend) *n.* a growing style or preference; a direction or tendency that seems to be followed

U

undercoat (un´ dûr cōt) *n.* a growth of short fur or feathers concealed by longer ones above

unity (ū´ ni tē) *n.* the state of being in full agreement and in harmony

universal (ū´ nə vûr´ səl) *adj.* shared by all; affecting everything or everybody

Pronunciation Key: **a**t; l**ā**te; c**â**re; f**ä**ther; s**e**t; m**ē**; **i**t; k**ī**te; **o**x; r**ō**se; **ô** in b**ou**ght; c**oi**n; b**o͝o**k; t**o͞o**; f**or**m; **ou**t; **u**p; **ū**se; t**û**rn; **ə** sound in **a**bout, chick**e**n, penc**i**l cann**o**n, circ**u**s; **ch**air; ri**ng**; **sh**op; **th**in; **th**ere; **zh** in trea**s**ure.

vain (vān) *adj.* overly concerned with or proud of one's appearance, abilities, or accomplishments

variations (vâr ē ā´ shənz) *n.* plural form of **variation:** something that is based on but differs from another thing

vary (vâr´ ē) *v.* to be different

vast (vast) *adj.* very large

volunteers (vol´ ən tērz´) *n.* plural form of **volunteer:** a person who offers to help by choice and without pay

vote (vōt) *n.* a formal expression of a wish or choice; a vote can be taken by ballot, by voice, or by a show of hands

ward off (word ôf) *v.* to keep or force away

wing (wing) *n.* a structure attached to the side of a building

zeal (zēl) *n.* an intense desire or devotion

Reading Resources

Reading Comprehension

Comprehension Strategies will help you understand what you are reading.

Asking and Answering Questions

As you read, ask yourself the following questions:

1. What do I already know about this topic?
2. What else would I like to know about this topic?
3. What questions do I think the author will answer as I read this selection?
4. How does this information connect to what I already know about the topic?
5. How does this information connect to the unit theme?
6. What is not making sense in this selection?
7. What is interfering with my understanding?
8. How does this information answer my question?
9. Does this information completely answer my question?
10. Do I have more questions after finding some of my answers?
11. Can I skim the text in order to find an answer to my question?

Clarifying

As you read, ask yourself the following questions:

1. What does not make sense? If it is a word, how can I figure it out? Do I use context clues, word analysis, or apposition, or do I need to ask someone or look it up in the dictionary or glossary?
2. If a sentence is complicated, have I reread it as well as the sentences around it to see if the meaning is clarified? Have I read the sentence part by part to see exactly what is confusing? Have I tried to restate the sentence in my own words?

3. The paragraph is long and full of details. What can I do to understand it? How much will I need to slow down to make sure I understand the text? Do I need to back up and reread part of the text to understand it?
4. Do I need to take notes or discuss what I have just read in order to understand it?
5. What is the main idea of what I just read?
6. Can I put what I just read into my own words?

Making Connections

As you read, ask yourself the following questions:

1. What does this remind me of? What else have I read like this?
2. How does this connect with something in my own life?
3. How does this connect with other selections I have read?
4. How does this connect with what is going on in the world today?
5. How does this relate to other events or topics I have studied in social studies or science?

Predicting

As you read, ask yourself the following questions:

1. What clues in the text can help me predict what will happen next?
2. What clues in the text tell me what probably will not happen next?

Revising/Confirming Predictions

As you read, ask yourself the following questions:

1. How was my prediction confirmed?
2. Why was my prediction *not* confirmed?
3. What clues did I miss that would have helped me make a better prediction?

Summarizing

As you read, ask yourself the following questions:

1. What is this selection about?
2. What are the big ideas the writer is trying to get at?
3. Have I said the same thing more than once in my summary?

4. What can I delete from my summary? What is not important?
5. How can I put what I have just read into my own words?

Visualizing

As you read, ask yourself the following questions:

1. What picture do the words create in my mind? What specific words help create feelings, actions, and settings in my mind?
2. What can I see, hear, smell, taste, and/or feel in my mind?
3. How does this picture help me understand what I am reading?
4. How does my mental picture extend beyond the words in the text?

Accessing Complex Text Skills will help you understand the purpose and organization of a selection.

Cause and Effect

Cause-and-effect relationships help you understand connections between the events in a story. The cause is why something happens. The effect is what happens as a result. A cause produces an effect.

Classify and Categorize

An author often includes many details in a story. Putting the like things together, or classifying those like things into categories, helps you see how actions, events, and characters from a story are related.

Compare and Contrast

To compare means to tell how things, events, or characters are alike. To contrast means to tell how things, events, or characters are different. Writers compare and contrast to make an idea clearer or to make a story more interesting.

Fact and Opinion

Writers often use facts and opinions in their writing to make their writing more believable, to explain things, or to persuade readers. A fact is a statement that can be proven true. An opinion is something a person or a group feels or believes is true, though others may disagree. Opinions are not necessarily true.

Main Idea and Details

The main idea is what the story or paragraph is mostly about. Writers use details to tell more about or explain the main idea.

Making Inferences

You make inferences when you take information in the selection about a character or an event and add this information to what you already know. You can then use this combination of information to make a statement or conclusion about that character or event.

Sequence

Sequence is the order in which things happen in a story. The more you know about the sequence of events in a story, the better you will understand the story. Writers use time and order words such as *first, then, finally, tonight,* and *yesterday* to tell the order of events.

Writer's Craft

Author's Purpose

Everything is written for a purpose. That purpose may be to entertain, to persuade, or to inform. Knowing why a piece is written—what purpose the author had for writing the piece—gives the reader an idea of what to expect and perhaps some prior idea of what the author is going to say. It is possible for an author to have more than one purpose.

Character

A character is a person or creature that interacts with others within a story. There are different kinds of characters in stories, and different ways to describe them. Readers learn to identify the different characteristics of the characters (physical features, character types such as heroes or villains, personality types, feelings, and motivations), and the ways the author describes the characters, such as with descriptive details, dialogue, and illustrations.

Genre Knowledge

Readers learn to recognize the differences between fiction and nonfiction. Subgenres of fiction include realistic fiction, fantasy, fairy tales, folktales, plays, and poems. Subgenres of nonfiction include informational texts, biographies, and reference books. Readers determine which features are used for these different subgenres.

Language Use

Readers learn to recognize the ways authors communicate important details and events in a story. Language use may include rhyme, repetition, sentence structures (simple, compound, declarative, interrogative, imperative, and exclamatory), alliteration, simile, metaphor, exaggeration, onomatopoeia, personification, sensory details, descriptive words, effective adjectives and adverbs, dialogue, and formal vs. informal language.

Plot

Readers learn to recognize the overall structure, or plot, of a story. A plot usually includes a beginning, a problem that must be solved, the climax or highest point of the story, a resolution of the problem, and an ending. Authors may use sequence, cause and effect, details, and dialogue to build the plot.

Point of View (Narrative/Fiction)

Point of view in a narrative involves identifying who is telling the story. If a character in a narrative is telling the story, that character uses his or her point of view to describe the action in the story and tell about the other characters. This is called first-person point of view. If the narrative is told in third-person point of view, someone outside the story who is aware of all the characters' thoughts, feelings, and actions is relating them to the reader.

Point of View (Informational or Persuasive Text)

The author's point of view in an informational text is the position or perspective the author takes on the subject he or she is writing about. The author may arrange topics in a certain sequence, or the author might present facts in such a way as to inform or to persuade his or her audience.

Setting

The setting of a story is composed of three pieces: the place where the story occurs, the timeframe or when the story takes place, and the amount of time that passes within the story from the beginning to the end.

Text Features

Text features are usually used in informational texts, and they help readers make sense of what they are reading. Text features may include headings, illustrations, photos, captions, diagrams, charts, maps, punctuation, font size or color, and numbered or bulleted lists.

Vocabulary Strategies

Apposition

Sometimes the word is defined within the text. In apposition, the word is followed by the definition, which is set off by commas.

Context Clues

When you come to an unfamiliar word in your reading, look for clues in the sentence or in the surrounding sentences. These clues might help you understand the meaning of the word.

Word Analysis

Examining the parts of a word can help you figure out the word's meaning. For example, the word *unfriendly* can be broken down into word parts: the prefix *un-*, the base word *friend*, and the suffix *-ly*. Knowing the meaning of each part will help you come up with the definition "not friendly."

Comprehension Discussion Strategies

Asking and Answering Questions

1. What if . . .
2. How do we know . . .
3. I wonder what would happen if . . .
4. What do we know about . . .
5. I wonder why the author chose to . . .
6. I found I could skim the material because . . .

Clarifying

1. I have a question about . . .
2. I am still confused about . . .
3. Does anyone know . . .
4. Could we clarify . . .
5. I figured out that . . .
6. I had difficulty understanding __________ because . . .
7. I still do not understand . . .
8. What did the author mean when he or she wrote __________?
9. Who can help me clarify __________ ?
10. Why did the author __________?
11. I decided to read this more slowly because . . .

Making Connections

1. This made me think . . .
2. I was reminded of . . .
3. This selection reminds me of what we read in __________ because . . .
4. This selection connects to the unit theme because . . .
5. I would like to make a connection to . . .
6. I found __________ interesting because . . .

7. This author's writing reminds me of . . .

Predicting

1. I expect . . .
2. I predict . . .
3. Based on ________, I predict . . .
4. I can support my prediction by/with . . .
5. I would like to change my prediction because . . .
6. My prediction was confirmed when/by . . .
7. My prediction was not confirmed because . . .

Summarizing

1. I think the main idea is . . .
2. I think an important supporting detail is . . .
3. I think the best evidence to support the main idea is . . .
4. To summarize . . .
5. I learned . . .
6. I can conclude . . .

Visualizing

1. When I read ________, I visualized . . .
2. The author's words ________ helped me visualize . . .
3. Visualizing helped me understand . . .
4. The author made the story really come alive by . . .

Collaborative Conversation Starters

Personal Response

1. I did not know that . . . .
2. I liked the part where . . . .
3. I agree with ________ because . . . .
4. I disagree with ________ because . . . .
5. The reason I think ________ is . . .
6. I was surprised to find out . . .
7. I like the way the author developed the character by . . .

Agreeing with a Response

1. I agree because . . .
2. I see what you mean because . . .

Disagreeing with a Response

1. I disagree because . . .
2. I think we can agree that __________, but . . .

Rules for Collaborative Conversation

Speaking Rules

☐ Speak clearly.

☐ Speak at an appropriate pace.

☐ Stay on topic.

☐ Use appropriate language for the setting.

☐ Make eye contact with the audience.

Listening Rules

☐ Look at the person who is speaking.

☐ Respect speakers by listening attentively.

☐ Keep your hands still and in your lap when someone is speaking.

☐ Do not talk when someone else is speaking.

☐ When you want to say something, raise your hand and wait to be called on.

☐ Ask a question if you do not understand something you heard.

Discussion Rules

☐ Listen carefully as others speak.

☐ Do not interrupt a speaker.

☐ Raise your hand when you want to speak.

☐ Ask questions to get more information from a speaker.

☐ Keep quiet as others speak.

☐ Take turns speaking.

☐ Respond to questions that others have asked you.

☐ Keep your questions and responses focused on the item being discussed.

Photo Credits

Front Cover: Stocktrek Images / Getty Images, Emrah Turudu / E+ / Getty Images, LEONELLO CALVETTI / Science Photo Library / Getty Images, goktugg / E+ / Getty Images. **10–11** TomazKunst/iStock/Getty Images Plus; **11** NPS Photo by Willis Peterson, Jonathan Heger/Getty Images, Design Pics/John Pitcher; **29** Chris Lishman/Getty Images, Juniors/SuperStock, NHPA/George Bernard, Justus de Cuveland/Getty Images, ansonsaw/Getty Images, ASO FUJITA/age fotostock; **51** ©DLILLC/Corbis,tbkmedia.de/Alamy, Ingram Publishing; **64–65** Christian Musat/Alamy; **72–73** Christian Heinrich/imageBROKER/age fotostock; **74** Comstock Images/Getty Images; **74–75** ©Theo Allofs/Corbis; **75** David Cox/McGraw-Hill Education, Gallo Images-Anthony Bannister/Getty Images, iStockphoto.com/VisualCommunications; **76–77** ©Martin Strmiska/Alamy; **77** ©David Shale/Nature Picture Library/Corbis; **78** Hashim Pudiyapura/Getty Images; **79** Yishai Eliason/Alamy, Charlie Varley/Sipa Press/Newscom; **80** NHPA/SuperStock; **81** NSP-RF/Alamy; **82–83** JohnCarnemolla/Getty Images; **85** ©David Shale/Nature Picture Library/Corbis; **90–91** iStockphoto.com/JohnCarnemolla; **92** iStockphoto.com/lucafabbian; **93** ©JK Enright/Alamy, NHPA/Robert Thompson, Malcolm Schuyl/Alamy, iStockphoto.com/Justinreznick; **94** ©moodboard/Corbis, Pat Canova/Alamy, NOAA/OAR/Great Lakes Environmental Research Laboratory, iStockphoto.com/moniaphoto; **95** ©Stock Up Images/Alamy; **97** NOAA MESA Project; **98–99** Zoonar GmbH/Alamy; **100** U.S. Fish and Wildlife Service/Ryan Hagerty; **102–103** U.S. Fish and Wildlife Service; **104** iStockphoto.com/Dean_Fikar; **105** ©Photo by Peggy Greb/USDA; **106** Jerry Whaley/Getty Images; **107** Cliff Keeler/Alamy; **109** iStockphoto.com/Justinreznick; **113** Purestock/SuperStock, Purestock/SuperStock, Fuse/Getty Images; **158** ilbusca/E+/Getty Images; **159** ROCHE AMANDINE/SIPA/Newscom, ©Hill Street Studios/Blend Images LLC/Glow Images, Image Source/Photodisc/Getty, ©Image Source Plus/Alamy, McGraw-Hill Education, Ingram Publishing. **160–161** North Wind Picture Archives; **162** Digital Vision/Getty Images, McGraw-Hill Education; **162–163** ©Hill Street Studios/Blend Images LLC/Glow Images; **163** Blend Images/Alamy, CDC/Cade Martin; **164–165** Glow Images, National Archives and Records Administration; **166** Ivy Close Images/Alamy; **167** ©National Geographic Society/Corbis; **169** ©Stapleton Collection/Corbis; **171** Bloomberg/Contributor/Getty Images; **172** DIPTENDU DUTTA/AFP/Getty Images; **173** Mohammed Abed/AFP/GettyImages, Hill Street Studios/Getty Images; **174** Glow Images; **184** Dennis MacDonald/Alamy; **185** Ariel Skelley/Getty Images; **186** Architect of the Capitol; **187** ©Odilon Dimier/PhotoAlto/Corbis, ©Hill Street Studios/Blend Images LLC/Glow Images, iStockphotos.com/kizilkayaphotos; **189** iStockphoto.com/alexeys; **191** ©Ocean/Corbis; **192** ©Hill Street Studios/Blend Images LLC/Glow Images; **196** ©iStockphoto.com/alexeys; **202–203** Jeff Malet Photography/Newscom; **204–205** ©Image Source, all rights reserved; **205** Jill Braaten /McGraw-Hill Education; **206–207** Architect of the Capitol, Courtesy of the United States Senate; **208** Exactostock/SuperStock; **208–209** Blend Images - Dave and Les Jacobs/Getty Images; **210–211** Glow Images/Alamy; **211** Hill Street Studios/age fotostock; **213** National Archives and Records Administration; **214** Jeff Malet Photography/Newscom; **219** McGraw-Hill Education; **220–221** Photographs in the Carol M. Highsmith Archive, Library of Congress, Prints and Photographs Division, Jonathan Larsen/Getty Images; **223** Drawings (Documentary), Library of Congress, LC-DIG-ppmsca-22593; **224–225** ©Library of Congress Prints & Photographs Division [LC-DIG-ppmsca-02160]; **226** Library of Congress Prints and Photographs Division, LC-USZ62-86281, Library of Congress Prints and Photographs Division, HABS DC,WASH,1--1, Prints & Photographs Division, Library of Congress, LC-USZC4-4583; **227** National Geographic Image Collection/Alamy, Photographs in the Carol M. Highsmith Archive, Library of Congress, Prints and Photographs Division; **228** Yale University Art Gallery, Photographs in the Carol M. Highsmith Archive, Library of Congress, Prints and Photographs Division; **229** YAY Media AS/Alamy; **230** Library of Congress Prints and Photographs Division, LC-DIG-highsm-03194; **230–231** Photographs in the Carol M. Highsmith Archive, Library of Congress, Prints and Photographs Division.; **232** Photographs in the Carol M. Highsmith Archive, Library of Congress, Prints and Photographs Division; **237** ©Pixtal/age fotostock; **258** PhotoSpin, Inc/Alamy, Library of Congress, Prints and Photographs Division (LC-B2-2684-2); **258–259** Library of Congress, Prints and Photographs Division (LC-B201-3643-12); **260** PhotoSpin, Inc/Alamy; **313** Leland Bobbe/Digital Vision/Getty Images; **314–315** bobbidog/iStock/Getty Images Plus; **315** KidStock/Getty Images, Fuse/Getty Images, Thinkstock images/Stockbyte/Getty images; **316–317** ©Rick Barrentine/Corbis; **322** Alan King Cyprus/Alamy; **322–323** Glow Images; **324** Digital image courtesy of the Getty's Open Content Program, Digital image courtesy of the Getty's Open Content Program.; **324–325** Highsmith, Carol M., 1946- Carol M. Highsmith Archive, Library of Congress Prints and Photographs Division, LC-DIG-highsm-06583; **326–327** Ron Chapple/Getty Images; **328** ©Alan King Cyprus/Alamy; **333** IAISI/Getty Images, Image Source/Alamy; **350–351** Comstock Images/SuperStock; **375** moodboard/age fotostock; **376–377** Ingram Publishing; **378** iStockphoto.com/MadCircles; **379** SCPhotos/Alamy; **380** Toby Talbot/AP Images; **381** iStockphoto.com/lacatr; **382** epa european pressphoto agency b.v./Alamy; **383** ZUMA Press, Inc/Alamy; **384** Richard Wayman/Alamy; **385** iStockphoto.com/phoopanotpics; **386** iStockphoto.com/Talaj; **387** GREG RYAN/Alamy; **388** ZUMA Press, Inc/Alamy; **394–395** Rob Crandall/Alamy; **396** C Squared Studios/Getty Images, iStockphoto.com/KateLeigh, C Squared Studios/Getty Images, iStockphoto.com/Topaz777, music Alan King/Alamy; **397** Dinodia/age fotostock; **398–399** Blend Images - Colin Anderson/Getty Images; **399** Buzz Pictures/Alamy; **400** RSBPhoto/Alamy; **401** TAO Images Limited/Alamy; **402** Tom O Hare/IMAGES/Getty Images; **403** Pakistan Press International Photo/Newscom; **404** Losevsky Pavel/Alamy; **405** ©Heide Benser/Corbis, iStockphoto.com/Rawpixel; **406** ©Paul Bradbury/age fotostock; **407** ©Juice Images/Corbis,

©moodboard/Corbis; **408** iStockphoto.com/CEFutcher; **410** ©iStockphoto.com/Topaz777; **415** Juniors Bildarchiv GmbH/ Alamy, ranker666/Getty Images, Liliya Kulianionak/Getty Images; **459** ©Comstock Images/Alamy, trekandshoot/ Alamy, ©Comstock Images/Alamy, McGraw-Hill Education; **461** ©Christina Kennedy/Alamy; **462** Marek Uszynski/Alamy; **463** ©Brand X Pictures/Superstock; **464** Digital Vision Ltd./ SuperStock; **465** Image Source/Javier Perini CM; **467** Stockbyte/SuperStock; **467** ©Cultura Creative (RF)/Alamy; **468** Ingram Publishing/age fotostock; **469** Yale University Art Gallery; **470** Chris Whitehead/Getty Images; **471** Sara Winter/Getty Images; **ix** Ingram Publishing, Rob Crandall/ Alamy; **v** Yishai Eliason/Alamy, Jerry Whaley/Getty Images; **vi** National Archives and Records Administration, Architect of the Capitol, Courtesy of the United States Senate; **vii** Jonathan Larsen/Getty Images; **viii** Highsmith, Carol M., 1946- Carol M. Highsmith Archive, Library of Congress Prints and Photographs Division, LC-DIG-highsm-06583. **Back Cover:** Stocktrek Images / Getty Images, goktugg / E+ / Getty Images.